D1041038

Rocky Mountain Trees

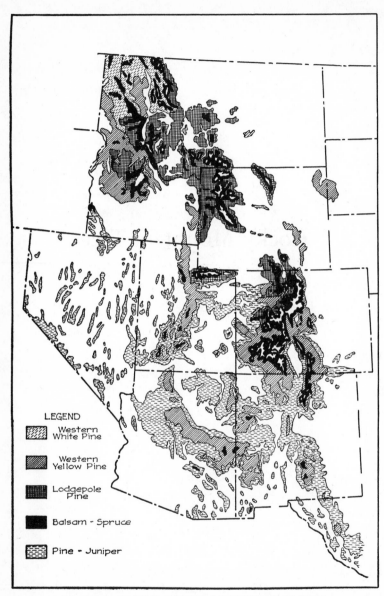

LEGEND

Western
White Pine

Western
Yellow Pine

Lodgepole
Pine

Balsam - Spruce

Pine - Juniper

FORESTS OF THE ROCKY MOUNTAIN REGION

Rocky Mountain Trees

A HANDBOOK OF THE NATIVE SPECIES

WITH PLATES & DISTRIBUTION MAPS

by Richard J. Preston, Jr., Ph. D.

School of Forestry, North Carolina State University at Raleigh

THIRD REVISED EDITION

DOVER PUBLICATIONS, INC., NEW YORK

Published in Canada by General Publishing Company, Ltd., 30 Lesmill Road, Don Mills, Toronto, Ontario.
Published in the United Kingdom by Constable and Company, Ltd., 10 Orange Street, London WC 2.

This Dover edition, first published in 1968, is a revised and corrected republication of the work as published by the Iowa State College Press in 1947. This edition contains a new Preface and a revised index prepared by the author.

International Standard Book Number: 0-486-21898-8
Library of Congress Catalog Card Number: 68-20408

Manufactured in the United States of America
Dover Publications, Inc.
180 Varick Street
New York, N. Y. 10014

TO MY PARENTS
Who so generously and wisely
made possible the experiences
and opportunities that have
enriched my life

PREFACE TO THE DOVER EDITION

Since the second edition appeared in 1947, there have been several changes in nomenclature. In this third edition, the scientific and common names have been revised to conform with the United States Department of Agriculture Handbook No. 41, *Check List of Native and Naturalized Trees of the United States,* 1953, with the exception that *Pseudotsuga taxifolia* has been retained for the Douglas-fir. Some of the maps showing distribution of pines have been modified. In addition, the text and illustrations have been photographically enlarged by 7 per cent to take advantage of the new, larger format.

1968

PREFACE TO THE SECOND EDITION

The one major change in this edition has been to bring the nomenclature up to date. The 1944 *Check List of the Native and Naturalized Trees of the United States, Including Alaska,* differed from the preceding 1927 edition in adopting the latest International Rules of Nomenclature in accordance with conservative usage. The author has carefully checked these changes in nomenclature and incorporated them into the present edition. In a few cases trees formerly treated as distinct species have been relegated to varieties or synonyms.

1947

PREFACE TO THE FIRST EDITION

Public interest in trees and forests has increased greatly in recent years. As a result of this awakening interest, numerous manuals of native trees have appeared in different sections of the country, making available to the people the technical knowledge necessary for the identification and understanding of the trees which they find around them. To date, no such manual has appeared for the Rocky Mountain region, and therefore this book has been written. It has been planned to meet the needs of trained foresters, students, and others interested in knowing the trees. Plates showing descriptive characters, distribution and zone maps, concise descriptions of botanical and silvical characters, check lists of species by states, and extensive keys have been included. Care has been taken to insure the inclusion of all native or naturalized trees within this region, and 252 species representing 85 genera and 40 families have been treated, as well as numerous varieties. Of the 129 full-page plates used in this manual, 77 are original, the work of Bruce Eastman, who graduated from the Division of Forestry of Colorado A & M College in 1938. These plates were prepared from herbarium material available either in the college herbarium or borrowed from the University of Wyoming. Care was taken to include the characters which would be most valuable in identification. The plates of the conifers, except those on pages 4, 20 60, and 90, were made wholly or in part from drawings used in Sudworth's bulletins on the trees of the Rocky Mountains, with the permission of the United States Forest Service. The plates on pages 4 and 64 were used with the permission of the Oregon State Board of Forestry. The plates opposite pages 101, 107, 123, 151, 155, 157, 161, 173, 189, 191, 195, 207, 233,

263, and 277 were made from those in Otis' *Trees of Michigan,* with the permission of the University of Michigan. The frontispiece and the plate on page 284 were used with the permission of the United States Department of Agriculture.

The descriptions of genera and species are based largely on material secured from the sources listed under the selected bibliography. Several references were used for each species and the characters carefully checked to insure that no errors were carried into the descriptions. Additional material, not available in these references, was gathered through study of herbarium material and through correspondence or conversation with the following men who generously cooperated in giving needed characters or opinions for numerous species:

Dr. F. A. Barkley, Montana State University; W. A. Dayton, Senior Forest Ecologist, United States Forest Service; L. N. Goodding, Soil Conservation Service, Albuquerque, N. M.; Dr. I. T. Haig and staff, Division of Silvics, United States Forest Service; Dr. R. E. McArdle and staff, Rocky Mountain Forest and Range Experiment Station; Dr. Aven Nelson, University of Wyoming; F. C. W. Pooler, Regional Forester, Albuquerque, N. M.; Professor E. C. Smith, Colorado State College; Dr. J. J. Thornber, University of Arizona; Dr. Ivar Tidestrom, Catholic University; A. Upson and staff, Southwestern Forest and Range Experiment Station; S. N. Wyckoff and staff, Northern Rocky Mountain Forest and Range Experiment Station.

The descriptions include not only the botanical characters of the species, but also silvical characters such as habitat, tolerance, roots, enemies, reproduction, and associates.

Extreme care was taken to make the maps showing distribution as accurate as possible in the light of our present information. All of the references in the selected bibliography were used in drawing up the original maps. These were then photostated and separate sets sent to each of the following individuals who kindly made such corrections or additions as he saw fit and returned them: W. A. Dayton, Senior Forest Ecologist, United States Forest Service; L. N. Goodding, Soil Conservation Service, Albuquerque, N. M.; Dr. I. T. Haig and staff, Division of Silvics, United States Forest Service; Dr. R. E. McArdle and staff, Rocky Mountain Forest and Range Experiment Station; Dr. Aven Nelson, University of Wyoming; Dr. F. Shreve, Desert Laboratory, Tucson, Arizona; Dr. J. J. Thornber, University of Arizona; A. Upson and staff, Southwestern Forest and Range Experiment Station; S. N. Wyckoff and staff, Northern Rocky Mountain Forest and Range Experiment Station.

The maps were then carefully drawn into their final form on the basis of these corrections and additions.

The author also wishes to acknowledge excellent assistance in editing and preparing the manuscript from J. R. Miller, I. G. Kinghorn, R. Randall, R. C. Hall, and D. Devet.

1940

TABLE OF CONTENTS

INTRODUCTION

THE ROCKY MOUNTAIN REGION

EXTENT. In this manual the Rocky Mountain region has been broadly defined as the area lying between the Great Plains and the Pacific Coast states. Montana, Idaho, Wyoming, Colorado, Utah, Nevada, Arizona, New Mexico, extreme western Texas, and the Black Hills of South Dakota are included, as well as the Canadian territory lying north of these states. Mexican species were included only when their range extended into the southwestern states.

CHARACTER. This region, while greatly diversified as to topography and climate, is, on the whole, an arid one. Tree growth is largely restricted to high elevations or to water courses at lower altitudes. The flora varies all the way from subtropical to alpine, and from that found on the humid upper mountains to true desert types. Moisture, temperature, and topography are important factors limiting the distribution of species. The aspect and steepness of the slope are major factors in determining the altitude to which a species will grow, which in itself is important in determining the range of a species. Wherever helpful, the altitudinal range has been given to supplement the distribution maps. In a region extending in latitude from Mexico into Canada, altitude alone is strictly limited in usefulness, and therefore a more important factor is discussed in some detail, i. e., the life zones into which the trees tend to group themselves.

LIFE ZONES. The work of Dr. C. Hart Merriam and others disclosed the fact that both plants and animals tend to group themselves into definite life zones or belts, and that the same or very similar forms of life usually will be found in regions having similar climatic conditions. These zones tend to increase in altitude as they become

[xv]

more remote from the polar regions, so that typical arctic plants growing near sea level in polar regions might be found at elevations of 10,000 feet in Montana, 12,000 feet in Colorado, and 13,500 feet in Arizona. It has been stated that a change of 300 feet in elevation is approximately the equivalent of 100 miles in latitude. As an example, Dr. Merriam states that nine species of plants growing on the bleak summit of San Francisco Mountain, Arizona, were brought back from Lady Franklin Bay above the arctic circle by Lt. A. W. Greely. As a rule these life zones can be readily identified, and are a very convenient aid in determining the local distributions of species.

Six life zones or belts are recognized in the Rocky Mountain region; the three higher zones belonging to the Boreal or cooler region, and the three lower to the Austral or subtropical region. Although the tropical region enters this area in the valley of the lower Colorado River in Arizona, it is arid in nature and here classed with the Lower Sonoran. On the whole these zones become progressively warmer and dryer from the Alpine to the Lower Sonoran.

1. *Alpine or Arctic-Alpine Zone*

This area corresponds to the arctic barren grounds and lies above timber line. It is a bleak region, covered with snow during the greater part of the year, and one in which the variety of life has been reduced to a minimum. Much of the vegetation consists of mosses, lichens, and dwarf willows, although flowers bloom in profusion during the short summers.

2. *Hudsonian Zone*

In the Rocky Mountains this is a region of dwarfed, stunted conifers located just below timber line and corresponding to the northern part of the great transcontinental coniferous forest. This region, while sharply defined

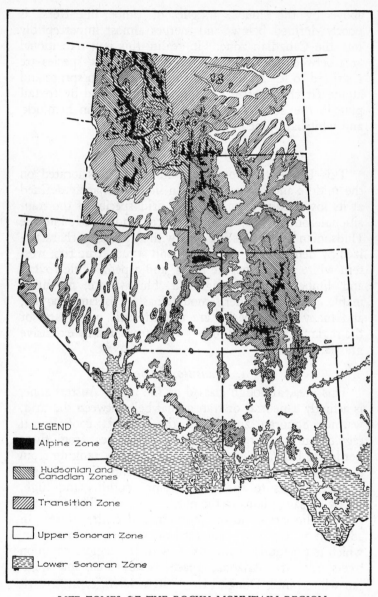

Alpine Zone

Hudsonian and
Canadian Zones

Transition Zone

Upper Sonoran Zone

Lower Sonoran Zone

LIFE ZONES OF THE ROCKY MOUNTAIN REGION

above by the sinuous tongues of timber-line trees, is poorly defined below, and merges almost imperceptibly into the Canadian zone. In reality this is a transitional area between the zones bordering it, and few species are restricted to it. Small, malformed Engelmann spruce and alpine fir characterize the zone, supplemented by foxtail pine in the south and alpine larch, mountain hemlock, and whitebark pine in the north.

3. *Canadian Zone*

This last of the Boreal and humid belts is located on the middle and higher mountain slopes. Sharply defined at its lower edge from the more arid species of the transitional zone, its upper border merges indistinctly into the Hudsonian zone. This is a zone with a rich flora characterized by dense stands of Engelmann spruce, true firs, western white and lodgepole pines, and aspen; while foxtail and limber pines, Douglas-fir, blue spruce, mountain maple, thinleaf alder, mountainash, balsam, poplar, and many other species are characteristic over parts of the region. Often the forests are interrupted by extensive grassland parks.

4. *Transition Zone*

This area, although classed as the upper Austral zone, is actually a neutral or transitional belt between the arid, warmer Sonoran zones and the humid, cool Boreal region, and is largely made up of species from these bordering belts. The zone is a variable one, ranging from the grassy or forested middle mountain slopes in the southern states to the yellow pine foothills and high, grassy or sage plains in the northern states. The forested portions lie largely in the southern and central states. In addition to the very characteristic western yellow pine, which is practically coextensive with the region, common tree species are: Arizona, Apache, Chihuahua, and Mexican white pines, Douglas-fir, western larch, cypress, vari-

ous oaks, narrowleaf cottonwood, water birch, big-
toothed maple, southwestern locust, wild plum, chokecherry, hawthorns, serviceberry, mountain-mahogany,
hophornbeam, and buckthorn. From Wyoming north,
this belt for the most part becomes open and treeless and
so is less conspicuously characterized than in the south-
central regions. Vast plains of gray sage, rabbit brush,
and other dry-land species occupy the arid sections, and
tree growth is restricted to stream borders. On the moister sites are high grassy plains or, occasionally, yellow pine
foothill stands. Where treeless, only the upper border
of this belt is clearly defined at that point where the sage
gives way to the aspens and conifers of the Canadian
zone.

5. *Upper Sonoran Zone*

This arid division of the upper Austral zone is semi-
tropical in nature and ranges from the high plains and
foothills of the southern states to the low plains and valleys in the north. The zone is typified by the pinyon-
juniper forests or the broad-leaved cottonwoods along
the streams in grassy or barren plains. Ash, elm, plum,
sand cherry, black sage, boxelder, saltbrush, walnut,
Mexican alder, sycamore, Cowania, hackberry, mulberry,
and hoptree are also found in this zone.

6. *Lower Sonoran Zone*

This lower or southern desert belt, the arid division of
the lower Austral zone, is typically Mexican, extending
into the United States over the low plains and along the
river valleys of the southwestern states. While uniform
both as to climate and species, this is a region of most
extreme conditions for plant growth, rainfall being very
scanty and the temperature often exceeding 120 degrees
Fahrenheit. Few plants reach tree size, and these, growing along stream bottoms, are for the most part unlike
those of any of the other zones. Mesquite and creosote

bush characterize this belt, although other small tree forms are found, such as Koeberlinia, Parkinsonia, Acacia, Leucaena, Cercidium, Sophora, Eysenhardtia, desert-willow, Parosela, walnut, soapberry, Wizlizenius poplar, and cactus.

The vertical boundaries of these life zones are highly variable and for a large region can only be given as approximations. These boundaries depend upon various governing factors such as steepness of slope, exposure, wind, moisture, and deforestation, which either allow the species to grow above normal limits, or force them to levels below normal. It must be remembered too, that on the border of each zone is a belt of varying vertical width (usually between 400-800 feet) in which the species of the two bordering zones mingle. The following table indicates the approximate elevations of the life zones in three sections of the region:

Zone	New Mexico	Central Colorado	Montana
Alpine	12,500-13,300 ft.	11,500-14,400 ft.	9,000-12,000 ft.
Hudsonian	11,500-12,500 ft.	10,500-11,500 ft.	8,000- 9,000 ft.
Canadian	9,000-11,500 ft.	8,000-10,500 ft.	6,000- 8,000 ft.
Transition	7,500- 9,000 ft.	6,000- 8,000 ft.	5,000- 6,000 ft.
Upper Sonoran	4,200- 7,500 ft.	3,000- 6,000 ft.	2,000- 5,000 ft.
Lower Sonoran	2,800 4,200 ft.		

TREE CHARACTERS

A brief discussion of the structural and silvical characters which are necessary in identifying trees is presented here to aid students without previous botanical training.

DEFINITION OF A TREE. There is no clear-cut line of demarcation between a tree and a shrub, and it is often impossible to place a plant definitely in one group or the other. Frequently a species treelike under favorable environmental conditions will be shrublike over most of its range. In general, height, form and diameter must be taken into account in determining the classification of a doubtful form. In this manual, Sudworth's definition of a tree as a woody plant having one well-defined stem, a more or less definitely formed crown, and attaining a minimum height of eight feet and a diameter of not less than two inches, has been followed.

TERMINOLOGY. While appearing cumbersome to the beginner, the use of technical terms in describing characters is often necessary for a concise, accurate description. These technical terms have been avoided wherever their omission did not impair the meaning of the passage, and a glossary explaining all technical terms used has been included. The student should familiarize himself with the more commonly used terms early in his study of the trees.

NAME. Most species of trees have been given one or many common names which usually describe some character of the tree and are easily learned by students. Unfortunately, these common names have many limitations; some are merely local, others apply to two or more entirely different species, and some apply to trees belonging to different genera. Because of this, while common names may be useful and convenient, it is essential that each species of tree have a definite, individual name that can be accepted throughout the world and which cannot be applied to any other species. Botanists and scientists as a whole have agreed that these scientific names should be in Latin, as this is a dead language and not subject to change. Botanists have further agreed that the name of a tree should consist of three parts: a generic name referring the species to the group to which it belongs and which is capitalized; a specific name referring to the single species and beginning with a small letter; and the full or abbreviated name of the authority or person first describing the plant. Thus, the scientific name of western yellow pine is *Pinus ponderosa* Laws. When a variety of a species is recognized, the varietal name follows the specific name, so in the case of Nogal, a larger variety of the Southwestern little walnut, the scientific name is *Juglans rupestris* var. *major* Torrey. When the names of two authorities are given, one appearing in parentheses, it indicates that the species was first described by the authority indicated in the parentheses, but placed in the wrong genus, and that this error was rectified by the second authority. This is the case with the western hemlock, *Tsuga heterophylla* (Raf.) Sarg. In this work the nomenclature accepted by the United States Forest Service (as amended to Jan. 23, 1940) has been followed, as it was felt that this would be of most service to foresters.

HABIT. This refers to the general appearance of a tree, usually as seen from a distance. The size; appearance and form of the trunk; shape, density and size of crown; the number, size, and direction of growth of the branches, are all factors helpful in distinguishing trees. In the conifers there is typically a trunk that extends to the tip of the tree without dividing (*excurrent*), while most of the hardwoods have the trunk breaking up into several large branches (*deliquescent*). Both the crown and branches may vary greatly in the same species depending upon whether the tree is growing in the open or in a dense stand where it is shaded on the sides by its neighbors.

LEAVES. Since leaves display characteristic patterns, they are probably the most useful organs in identifying trees. Leaves consist of an expanded portion or *blade,* a supporting stalk or *petiole,* and small leaflike or scaly structures (*stipules*) attached in pairs at the base of the petiole. Leaves having no stipules are termed *exstipulate,* and those without petioles are called *sessile.* Those species which are evergreen can be identified by their leaves throughout the year, while species which shed their leaves annually (*deciduous*) must be identified by other characters during the winter months. Leaves may be arranged *alternately* (with one leaf attached to the

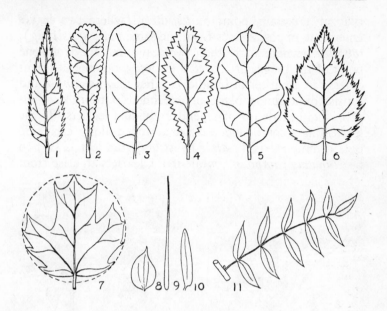

LEAF PATTERNS

Leaf Shapes

1-Lanceolate.   2-Oblanceolate.   3-Oblong.   4-Elliptical.   5-Oval.
6-Ovate.   7-Orbicular.   8-Subulate.   9-Acicular.   10-Linear.

Leaf Margins

1-Serrate.   2-Crenate   3-Entire.   4-Dentate.   5-Sinuate.   6-Doubly
serrate.   7-Lobed.

Leaf Apices

1-Acuminate.   2-Rounded.   3-Emarginate.   4-Obtuse.   5-Mucronate.
6-Acute.

Leaf Bases

1-Obtuse.   2-Cuneate.   3-Rounded.   4-Acute.   5-Rounded.   6-Cor-
date.   7-Truncate.

Leaf Types

1 to 10-Simple leaves.   11-Pinnately compound leaf.

twig at a certain point), *oppositely* (where two leaves emerge at opposite sides from the same place on a twig), *whorled* (where more than two leaves emerge from one point of the twig), or *fascicled* (where a number of leaves emerge in a cluster or bundle.) They may be *simple* and consist of a single blade or expanded portion, or *compound* and made up of several individual leaflets. If the leaflets in a compound leaf are arranged along each side of a common axis (*petiole* or *rachis*), the leaf is said to be *pinnately compound,* while if the leaflets all arise from

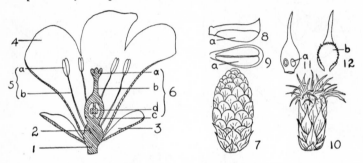

FLOWER STRUCTURE

Perfect Flower   Flowers of Pine

1-Peduncle.   2-Receptacle.   3-Sepal (Calyx).   4-Petal (Corolla). 5-Stamen;   a-Anther,   b-Filament.   6-Pistil;   a-Stigma,   b-Style, c-Ovary, d-Ovule.   7-Staminate conelet.   8 and 9-Stamen, or pollen-bearing scale, showing side and lower surfaces.   10-Pistillate conelet. 11 and 12-Pistillate scale showing inner and outer surfaces respectively; a-Ovule, b-Bract.

the apex of the petiole, the leaf is termed *palmately compound.* Other characters used in identification are the shapes and types of margin, apex, and base (p. xxiii). Texture, color, and the surface, whether smooth or hairy, are also useful characters.

FLOWERS. All trees have flowers, although frequently they are small and inconspicuous. These are the reproductive organs by means of which the species is perpetuated. Floral characters are the most accurate means of identifying many trees, although they are little used in the field because they bloom for so short a period. Flowers vary greatly in form, structure, and size. A *complete* flower (p. xxiv) is made up usually of leaflike *sepals* (*calyx*), often brightly colored *petals* (*corolla*), *stamens* (the male organs which bear the *pollen* in saclike *anthers*), and a *pistil* (the female organ consisting of a terminal *stigma* which catches the pollen, a *style,* and an *ovary.*) The ovary may consist of one or more compartments (*cells*) and contain one to many *ovules* which later

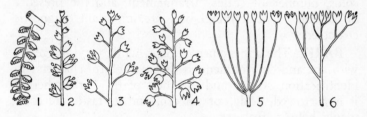

TYPES OF INFLORESCENCES

1-Ament. 2-Spike. 3-Raceme. 4-Panicle. 5-Umbel. 6-Corymb.

mature into seeds. In Gymnosperms the pistil is replaced by a seed-bearing scale which does not enclose the seed. If the ovary is inserted on top of the other flower parts it is *superior,* while if it appears enclosed within the calyx it is *inferior.* Flowers may be *perfect* (contain both stamens and pistil) or *imperfect* (contain one sex but not the other.) Plants having imperfect flowers are termed either *monoecious* (both sexes present in different flowers on the same plant) or *dioecious* (each sex borne on a different plant.) When the only functioning sex organs in an imperfect flower are stamens the flower is termed *staminate,* while one in which the pistil is the active organ is *pistillate.* Plants which bear some perfect and some imperfect flowers are termed *polygamous.* Flowers may appear singly or in clusters (*inflorescences,* above).

FRUIT. While varying greatly in type and appearance, fruits are very useful in identification. The seeds included in the fruit contain the embryo plant. To the layman these are generally of secondary utility in identification.

TWIGS. The color, stoutness, central pith, or surface coverings and markings may be very useful in identifying trees, especially during the winter months. As buds, stipules, and leaves fall off they leave scars on the twig which are frequently characteristic. Buds are conspicuous on most twigs and helpful in identification. The shape, size, color, number of scales, arrangement, and the presence or absence of a terminal bud are important diagnostic characters.

BARK. The appearance of bark, while varying greatly with age and environment, is often a helpful character in identification. Color and thickness of the bark, whether it is furrowed, scaly, or smooth, and its taste, are commonly helpful features.

WOOD. The characters of the wood of trees form a separate means of identification which is more technical and difficult than the use of external characters. In this manual only the outstanding wood characters are given, such as the weight, color, and arrangement of large pores (whether *ring-porous* in a definite ringlike zone, or *diffuse-porous* and scattered throughout the wood). A statement as to importance and the uses of the woods is also included.

SILVICAL CHARACTERS. The tolerance, sites, associates, reproduction, enemies, roots, life zones, and altitudinal distributions of species are often helpful in identification, and have been included wherever possible.

In identifying trees it must be remembered that characters are variable and often overlap with those of closely related trees. Wherever possible, identification should not be based on a single character, but on as many as are available.

CHECK LIST OF THE TREES FOUND WITHIN EACH STATE

BY SCIENTIFIC AND COMMON NAMES

ARIZONA

Conifers (21 species)

		PAGE
Abies concolor	White Fir	63
Abies lasiocarpa	Subalpine Fir	59
Cupressus arizonica	Arizona Cypress	71
Juniperus deppeana	Alligator Juniper	87
Juniperus gymnocarpa	Openseed Juniper	81
Juniperus monosperma	One-seed Juniper	81
Juniperus osteosperma	Utah Juniper	85
Juniperus pinchotii	Pinchot Juniper	91
Juniperus scopulorum	Rocky Mountain Juniper	79
Pinus engelmannii	Apache Pine	21
Picea pungens	Blue Spruce	45
Pinus aristata	Bristlecone Pine	17
Pinus cembroides	Mexican Pinyon	13
Pinus edulis	Pinyon Pine	15
Pinus engelmannii	Apache Pine	21
Pinus flexilis	Limber Pine	11
Pinus leiophylla	Chihuahua Pine	23
Pinus monophylla	Singleleaf Pinyon	15
Pinus ponderosa	Ponderosa Pine	19
Pinus ponderosa arizonica	Arizona Pine	21
Pseudotsuga taxifolia	Douglas-fir	53

Broadleaf Species (118)

COLORADO
Conifers (14 species)

IDAHO
Conifers (21 Species)

Broadleaf Species (39)

Broadleaf Species (46)

NEW MEXICO
Conifers (19 Species)

PAGE

UTAH
Conifers (17 Species)

KEY TO THE GENERA

a. Leaves needle-shaped, linear, or scalelike, mostly 1-nerved.......
................................*CONIFERS* and *TAMARIX.*
  b. Leaves deciduous.
    c. Leaves single, scalelike, feathery; showy flowers; fruit a capsule; south and central...............TAMARIX, p. 247.
    c. Leaves in clusters on dwarf branches, linear; fruit a cone; Northern ....LARIX, p. 28.
  b. Leaves persistent; fruit a woody cone or berry-like.
    c. Leaves fascicled, in clusters of.1-5, enclosed at base by sheath, needle-shaped ....PINUS, p. 2.
    c. Leaves single, without basal sheath.
      d. Leaves scattered, alternate, linear.
        e. Fruit a woody cone with numerous scales and separate bracts; needles not decurrent.
          f. Cones erect, their scales deciduous from axis, leaves sessile without sterigmata............ABIES, p. 54.
          f. Cones pendulous, their scales persistent on axis.
            g. Bracts of cone exserted, leaves petioled, without sterigmata...............PSEUDOTSUGA, p. 53.
            g. Bracts of cone inserted; twigs roughened by sterigmata.
              h. Leaves sessile, harsh to touch....PICEA, p. 36.
              h. Leaves stalked, soft to touch....TSUGA, p. 46.
        e. Fruit a single seed surrounded by scarlet, aril-like disk; needles decurrent...................TAXUS, p. 93.
      d. Leaves ternate or decussate, usually scalelike.
        e. Fruit a woody cone; leaves scalelike, decussate.
          f. Cone oblong, 2 seeds under each scale.
            g. Cone with 6 scales.......LIBOCEDRUS, p. 67.
            g. Cone with 8-12 scales............THUJA, p. 67.
          f. Cone subglobose, many seeds under each scale......
..........................CUPRESSUS, p. 68.
        e. Fruit a berry-like cone; leaves scalelike or awl-shaped, ternate or decussate..............JUNIPERUS, p. 74.
aa. Leaves broad and flat, netted veined (except Yucca and Washingtonia), rarely wanting....................(ANGIOSPERMS)
  b. Leaves and buds opposite or whorled.
    c. Leaves simple.
      d. Leaves lobed; fruit a double samara (key) ....
....................................ACER, p. 230.
      d. Leaves not lobed; fruit not a double samara.
        e. Leaves entire or nearly so.
          f. Stipules persistent; fruit nutlike, capsule..........
.....................CEPHALANTHUS, p. 275.

[liii]

f. Stipules absent.
  g. Leaves linear to linear-lanceolate; fruit a woody linear capsule...............CHILOPSIS, p. 273.
  g. Leaves suborbicular to elliptic.
    h. Fruit a slender capsule 6-15" long; leaves large heart-shaped...............CATALPA, p. 273.
    h. Fruit not a capsule; leaves not heart-shaped, 1-4" long.
      i. Fruit a samara with terminal wing; leaves broadly ovate to suborbicular, 1–2" long............
      ....FRAXINUS ANOMALA, p. 263.
      i. Fruit drupaceous.
        j. Leaves about 1" long, pubescent; drupe blue-black..............FORESTIERA, p. 269.
        j. Leaves over 1" long, glabrous; drupes mostly white or red............CORNUS, p. 255.
e. Leaves serrate.
  f. Buds covered by 2, valvate, large scales; fruit a drupe......................VIBURNUM, p. 279.
  f. Buds many-scaled; fruit a fleshy capsule enclosed in thin, scarlet aril..............EUONYMUS, p. 229.

c. Leaves compound.
  d. Leaves persistent; leaflets entire; flowers showy, purple; fruit a large, obcordate capsule.......PORLIERIA, p. 221.
  d. Leaves deciduous.
    e. Leaflets entire or finely serrate; fruit a samara with terminal wing..................FRAXINUS, p. 260.
    e. Leaflets sharply and coarsely or incisely serrate.
      f. Fruit a double samara; leaves with 3 leaflets........
      ....ACER NEGUNDO, p. 233.
      f. Fruit a capsule or drupe; leaves with 5 or more leaflets.
        g. Fruit clustered drupes; flowers small.............
        ....SAMBUCUS, p. 277.
        g. Fruit a linear capsule; flower showy.............
        ....TECOMA, p. 275.

b. Leaves and buds alternate.
  c. Leafless or usually appearing so branches with spines.
    d. Succulent plants (cactus) with numerous clustered spines.
      e. Branches and stems columnar; seed dark.............
      ....CARNEGIEA, p. 251.
      e. Branches jointed, tuberculate; seed pale.............
      ....OPUNTIA, p. 251.
    d. Woody, treelike plants, twigs terminating in spines.
      e. Leafless; twig with green thorns and black cushion-like processes; fruit a woody capsule....CANOTIA, p. 229.
      e. Leaves early deciduous, plants appearing leafless.
        f. Fruit a drupe or berry; twigs bright green; leaves minute and scalelike.

  g. Fruit a black berry.......KOEBERLINIA, p. 249.
  g. Fruit of 6–8 small drupes, HOLACANTHA, p. 249.
 f. Fruit a legume; twigs brown to pale green.
  g. Leaves simple; flowers papilionaceous............
  ....DALEA, p. 217.
  g. Leaves compound; flowers nearly regular..........
  .... CERCIDIUM, p. 211.
c. Leaves conspicuous and present during entire summer.
 d. Leaves simple.
  e. Leaves persistent or falling during the winter.
   f. Leaves lobed.
    g. Leaves pinnately lobed; fruit an achene.
     h. Leaves ⅓-½″ long, divided by several **lobes,**
     hoary-tomentose below; achene long-tipped......
     ....COWANIA, p. 185.
     h. Leaves ½-1¼″ long, 3-lobed at apex, **hoary-**
     tomentose on both surfaces; achene **not long-**
     tipped..................ARTEMISIA, p. 281.
    g. Leaves palmately lobed.
     h. Leaves 3-6 feet long, fanlike.................
     ................WASHINGTONIA, p. 285.
     h. Leaves 1½″ long........................
     ............FREMONTODENDRON, p. 247.
   f. Leaves not lobed.
    g. Fruit a drupe or berry.
     h. Leaves spinose-serrate; stipules minute.........
     ....RHAMNUS CROCEA, p. 245.
     h. Leaves entire; stipules absent or present.
      i. Flowers large (2″ across) ; buds naked........
      ....CORDIA, p. 271.
      i. Flowers less than ½″ long; buds scaly.
       j. Twigs often spinescent; fruit a drupe; flowers
       minute, not vaselike.
        k. Leaves 1-3½″ long; drupe ⅓-½″ in
        diameter.
         l. Leaves rusty brown, lanuginose **beneath**
         ....BUMELIA, p. 259.
         l. Leaves tomentulose beneath..........
         ....RHAMNUS, p. 243.
        k. Leaves under ½″ long; drupe under ¼″
        in diameter.........CONDALIA, p. 245.
       j. Twigs not spinescent; fruit berry-like.
        k. Fruit ⅓″ long, red, many-seeded, calyx
        deciduous...........ARBUTUS, p. 257.
        k. Fruit ½-1″ long, black, 3-8 seeded, calyx
        persistent at base....DIOSPYROS, p. 259.
    g. Fruit not fleshy.
     h. Fruit a nut or acorn; flowers in aments.

i. Fruit a nut enclosed in a bur...............
........................CASTANOPSIS, p. 155.
i. Fruit an acorn with a basal cup.............
......................QUERCUS, p. 136.
h. Fruit an achene or capsule, flowers with petals.
  i. Fruit a long-tipped achene; leaves ½-1″ long..
  ....CERCOCARPUS, p. 181.
  i. Fruit a capsule; leaves 1½-30″ long.
    j. Leaves 20-30″ long, parallel veins..........
    ....YUCCA, p. 283.
    j. Leaves 1½-7″ long, netted veins.
      k. Fruit a woody, 5-celled capsule; leaves
        1½-3″ long.....VAUQUELINIA, p. 171.
      k. Fruit a 2-celled capsule; leaves 2-7″ long
        ....NICOTIANA, p. 271.
e. Leaves deciduous.
  f. Leaves small, glandular, soon deciduous; twigs spines-
    cent; fruit a 1-seeded legume.........DALEA, p. 217.
  f. Leaves large, not falling until autumn.
    g. Leaves entire.
      h. Leaves linear or lanceolate; fruit a capsule;
        terminal bud absent.
        i. Capsule woody, linear; buds many-scaled;
          stipules absent...........CHILOPSIS, p. 273.
        i. Capsule soft, short; buds of 2 connate scales;
          stipules present..............SALIX, p. 114.
      h. Leaves oblong to ovate or reniform.
        i. Fruit drupaceous; leaves oblong to ovate, apex
          usually pointed.
          j. Fruit numerous in panicles; pith thick; buds
            naked....................RHUS, p. 227.
          j. Fruit usually solitary or few; pith thin; buds
            scaly.
            k. Leaves and fruit glabrous.
              l. Leaves unequal at base, acute or acumin-
                ate at apex...........CELTIS, p. 158.
              l. Leaves equal at base, rounded or apicu-
                late at apex.......BUMELIA, p. 259.
            k. Leaves and fruit silvery-scurfy..........
              ....ELAEAGNUS, p. 253.
        i. Fruit a legume; leaves broad ovate or reniform,
          apex obtuse...............CERCIS, p. 207.
    g. Leaves serrate to lobed.
      h. Leaves serrate.
        i. Fruit a pome or drupaceous.

j. Fruit compound; juice milky.............
.....................MORUS, p. 167.
j. Fruit simple; juice watery.
  k. Buds naked, terminal absent; fruit drupaceous............RHAMNUS, p. 245.
  k. Buds scaly, terminal present.
    l. Fruit a pome.
      m. Branches spiny; mature carpels bony
      ....CRATAEGUS, p. 176.
      m. Branches not spiny; mature carpels
      papery.....AMELANCHIER, p. 175.
    l. Fruit a drupe.
      m. Terminal bud present; leaves even
      at base............PRUNUS, p. 186.
      m. Terminal bud absent; leaves oblique
      at base.............CELTIS, p. 158.
i. Fruit dry, not fleshy.
  j. Plants with milky juice, fruit a 2-celled capsule...................SAPIUM, p. 225.
  j. Plants with watery juice.
    k. Leaves singly serrate; fruit a capsule.
      l. Buds of 2 connate scales; terminal ab-
      sent; scales of ament entire...........
      ....SALIX, p. 114.
      l. Buds of many scales; terminal present;
      scales of ament laciniate.............
      ....POPULUS, p. 96.
    k. Leaves doubly serrate; terminal bud ab-
    sent; fruit not a capsule.
      l. Fruit a samara; leaves oblique at base..
      ....ULMUS, p. 157.
      l. Fruit a nutlet within an involucre or
      strobile; leaves even at base.
        m. Nutlet wingless, enclosed within blad-
        der-like involucre....OSTRYA, p. 119.
        m. Nutlet more or less winged, in woody
        strobile.
          n. Strobile persistent; bud of 2 connate
          scales...........ALNUS, p. 126.
          n. Strobile deciduous; bud of many
          scales...........BETULA, p. 120.
h. Leaves lobed or deeply sinuately toothed.
  i. Fruit a capsule, juice milky or mucilaginous.
    j. Seed not woolly.......................
    ....RICINUS COMMUNIS, p. 225.

        j. Seed woolly.........GOSSYPIUM, p. 241.
      i. Fruit not a capsule, juice watery.
        j. Fruit an acorn; terminal bud present......
          ....QUERCUS, p. 136.
        j. Fruit a head of achenes; terminal bud absent................PLATANUS, p. 169.
d. Leaves compound.
  e. Fruit a legume..................(*LEGUMINOSAE*)
    f. Leaves doubly or more pinnate.
      g. Branches armed with spines or prickles.
        h. Leaves with 6 or more (rarely 4) pinnae, persistent; flowers yellow; stamens numerous, free; legume indehiscent............ACACIA, p. 201.
        h. Leaves with 2 (rarely 4) pinnae.
          i. Flowers green-white, in spikes; legume indehiscent...............PROSOPIS, p. 203.
          i. Flowers yellow, in racemes; legume dehiscent.
            j. Leaflets 4-12, leaves short, caducous........
              ....CERCIDIUM, p. 211.
            j. Leaflets 40-60, leaves elongated, persistent until autumn......PARKINSONIA, p. 209.
      g. Branches without spines or prickles.
        h. Flowers large, showy, yellow, in racemes........
          ....POINCIANA, p. 205.
        h. Flowers minute, in globose heads, whitish.
          i. Legume 6-10″ long and ⅓-½″ wide; flowers with 10 stamens........LEUCAENA, p. 199.
          i. Legume 5-8″ long and ¾-1″ wide; flowers with 12-20 stamens..........LYSILOMA, p. 199.
    f. Leaves once pinnate.
      g. Leaflets 20–46, glandular-dotted; legume ½″ long; twigs unarmed........EYSENHARDTIA, p. 215.
      g. Leaflets 3-21, not glandular-dotted; legume 1-7″ long.
        h. Leaflets 15–21; legume compressed; flowers white or pink; stipules becoming spinescent..........
          ....ROBINIA, p. 219.
        h. Leaflets 7-15; legume round; flowers blue, purple, or yellow.
          i. Flowers yellow; leaves deciduous with 8-12 leaflets...................CARAGANA, p. 207.
          i. Flowers blue or purple; leaves persistent, mostly odd pinnate.
            j. Twigs armed with sharp infrastipular spines; leaflets 10-15............OLNEYA, p. 221.

j. Twigs unarmed, leaflets 7–9...............
.....................SOPHORA, p. 213.
h. Leaflets 3; flowers red; twigs spiny...........
.....................ERYTHRINA, p. 217.
e. Fruit not a legume; leaves once pinnate.
f. Leaves 3-foliolate; fruit a broad-winged samara......
. ...PTELEA, p. 223.
f. Leaves usually many foliolate; fruit not a samara.
g. Leaflets ¼" long; rachis winged.
h. Leaflets 20-40, deciduous; Arizona.............
.......................BURSERA, p. 225.
h. Leaflets 9-19, semi-persistent; Texas...........
.......................PISTACIA, p. 227.
g. Leaflets 1" or more long; rachis not winged.
h. Buds large; fruit a nut within husk; pith chambered......................JUGLANS, p. 95.
h. Buds small; fruit not a nut; pith solid.
i. Fruit a 3-valved capsule; leaflets 5–7, serrate...
....................UNGNADIA, p. 241.
i. Fruit not a capsule.
j. Fruit twisted samaras in crowded clusters; leaves glandular toothed.................
.................AILANTHUS, p. 223.
j. Fruit a berry, drupe, or pome; leaves not glandular.
k. Fruit a small pome; stipules present, leaflets serrate............SORBUS, p. 173.
k. Fruit a berry or drupe; stipules absent.
l. Terminal bud absent; leaflets entire; berry ½" in diameter................
.................SAPINDUS, p. 239.
l. Terminal bud present; leaflets entire or serrate; drupe under ⅓" in diameter..
....................RHUS, p. 227.

MANUAL OF ROCKY MOUNTAIN TREES

Including

DESCRIPTION OF SPECIES
PLATES OF DIAGNOSTIC CHARACTERS
DISTRIBUTION MAPS
KEYS TO SPECIES

PINACEAE

THE PINES

Characteristics of the Genus *Pinus* L.

HABIT. Evergreen trees with straight, unbranched, cylindrical trunks, and whorled, spreading branches.

LEAVES. Needle-like; in fascicles or bundles of 1-5; enclosed in bud by 6-12 scales which form a persistent or soon-deciduous basal sheath; usually with several lines of stomata on each surface; juvenile leaves on young shoots differ in being spirally arranged, single, and scalelike.

FLOWERS. Monoecious; male, or pollen-producing, consisting of spirally arranged, sessile anthers, yellow, orange, or scarlet; female, or cone- and seed-producing, small, conelike bodies consisting of numerous spirally arranged, 2-ovuled scales, each subtended by a small bract.

FRUIT. A cone, usually pendent, composed of the hardened, woody scales of the flower; scales more or less thickened on the exposed terminal surface (the apophysis) with the ends of the growth of the previous year appearing as a terminal or dorsal, brown protuberance or scar (the umbo), which is often armed with a prickle; maturing in 2 (rarely 3) seasons. Seed: 2 borne at the base on inner face of each fertile scale; with thin, terminal, papery wing or wingless.

BUDS. Variable in size, shape, and color; covered by fringed or papery-margined overlapping scales; these component scales each protecting a tiny bud which, after the main bud unfolds, develops into a fascicle of leaves or occasionally into a female flower.

WOOD. Among our most important trees; extremely variable; numerous, large, easily visible resin ducts; resinous scent. Some species produce, in addition to lumber, naval stores and edible nuts.

GENERAL. The largest and most important genus of conifers, including about 80 species widely scattered over the Northern Hemisphere; 36 species are native to the United States, and 15 of these are found in the Rocky Mountain region; the North American species can be conveniently grouped into the soft or white pines, and hard, pitch, or yellow pines.

[2]

KEY TO THE SPECIES OF PINUS

I. Leaf sheath deciduous; leaves with 1 fibrovascular bundle; cone scales without prickles (except in 6); Soft Pines.
  A. Leaves in fascicles of 5.
    1. Cone scales thin, unarmed, cones long-stalked.
      a. Cones 5-11″ long, northern......1. *P. monticola*, p. 5.
      b. Cones 12-18″ long, Nevada.....2. *P. lambertiana*, p. 7.
    2. Cone scales thick, short-stalked (except in 5).
      a. Cones without prickles; seed longer than wing.
        (1) Cones 1½-3″ long, subglobose, closed; alpine and northern.................3. *P. albicaulis*, p. 9.
        (2) Cones 3-10″ long, subcylindrical, opening.
          (a) Cone scales slightly reflexed; entire region...
          ....4. *P. flexilis*, p. 11.
          (b) Cone scales strongly reflexed; stalks ½-⅔″ long; southern........................
          ....5. *P. flexilis* var. *reflexa*, p. 11.
      b. Cones with long, slender prickles; seed shorter than wing; central..................6. *P. aristata*, p. 17.
  B. Leaves in fascicles of 1-3.
    1. In 1's, stout; south-central........7. *P. monophylla*, p. 15.
    2. In 2's, stout; south-central...........8. *P. edulis*, p. 15.
    3. In 3's, slender; southern..........9. *P. cembroides*, p. 13.

II. Leaf sheath persistent (except 10); leaves with 2 bundles; cone scales with prickles; Hard Pines.
  A. Leaves in fascicles of 3, sheath deciduous; cone matures in 3 years; southern.................10. *P. leiophylla*, p. 23.
  B. Leaf sheath persistent; cone matures in 2 years.
    1. Leaves in fascicles of 2; cones unsymmetrical.
      a. Cones with distinct prickles; leaves 1-3″ long; entire region......................11. *P. contorta*, p. 25.
      b. Cones appear unarmed; leaves ¾-1½″ long, divergent; extreme north..............12. *P. banksiana*, p. 27.
    2. Leaves in fascicles of 3, 2 and 3, or 5, 4–15″ long; cones symmetrical.
      a. Leaves in 5's; cones 2-3¼″; southern................
      ....13. *P. ponderosa* var. *arizonica*, p. 21.
      b. Leaves in 3's, or 2's and 3's.
        (1) Cones 5-15″ long; leaves in 2's and 3's, 6-9″, persistent 6-9 years; purplish twigs with pineapple odor; Nevada ....14. *P. jeffreyi*, p. 21.
        (2) Cones 3-6″ long; leaves persistent 2-3 years; orange-brown twigs with resinous odor.
          (a) Leaves 4-11″, in 2's and 3's, yellow-green; throughout region....15. *P. ponderosa*, p. 19.
          (b) Leaves 8-15″, in 3's, dark green, conspicuously fringed; Arizona and New Mexico..........
          ....16. *P. engelmannii*, p. 21.

[3]

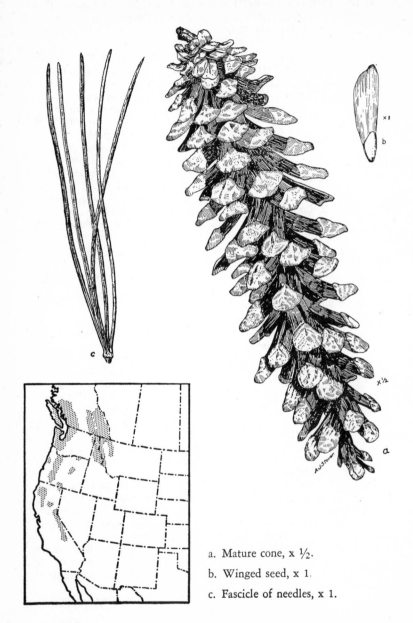

a. Mature cone, x ½.

b. Winged seed, x 1.

c. Fascicle of needles, x 1.

PINACEAE

Western White Pine
Pinus monticola Dougl.

HABIT. A tree 90–180 feet high and 2½–5 feet in diameter (max. 200 by 8 feet); on good sites a tall bole with narrow, symmetrical crown and slender, drooping branches.

LEAVES. In fascicles of 5; 2–4 inches long; slender; twisted; blue-green; persistent 3–4 years; sheath deciduous; margin with minute teeth; all sides marked by stomata.

FLOWERS. Male yellow; female red-purple in clusters.

FRUIT. Cones long-stalked; 5–15 inches long (av. 8 inches); narrow; scales thin, unarmed, with terminal umbo. Seed: ¼ inch long with wing about 1 inch long; red-brown.

TWIGS. Slender; at first rusty-pubescent, later smooth and red-brown to purple-brown. Winter buds: ½ inch long; oblong ovoid.

BARK. On young stems thin, smooth, and light gray; on mature trees rarely over 1½ inches thick in square or rectangular, dark gray plates.

WOOD. Very important; soft, light in weight, and not strong; light brown heartwood; similar to eastern white pine; planing mill products, building, construction, patterns, etc.

SILVICAL CHARACTERS. Tolerant when young, becoming intolerant with age; maturity reached in 200–350 years (extreme age, 400–500 years); reproduction generally sparse; tree windfirm with well-developed tap and lateral root system; fire, blister rust, and bark beetles cause damage.

HABITAT. Canadian zone; altitudinal range from near sea level in north to 7,000 feet; best on rich, porous, moist soils; occasionally forming pure stands but more commonly in mixture with other conifers.

GENERAL. Eastern white pine, *Pinus strobus* L. is occasionally planted in this region. It is very similar to western white pine but has shorter cones (4–8 inches long and averaging about 5 inches) and needles which are persistent 2 years.

[5]

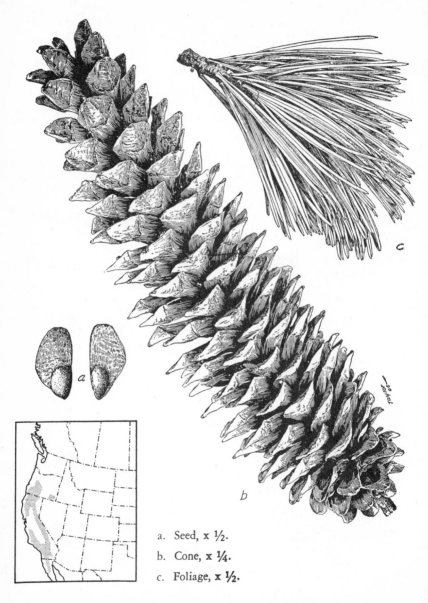

a. Seed, x ½.

b. Cone, x ¼.

c. Foliage, x ½.

PINACEAE

SUGAR PINE

Pinus lambertiana Dougl.

HABIT. The largest American pine commonly 175–200 feet high and 3–5 feet in diameter (max. 246 by 10 feet); on good sites with a long, clear bole and a short crown of large, often contorted, horizontal branches.

LEAVES. In fascicles of 5; 2–4 inches long; stouter than in white pine; twisted; blue- to gray-green; persistent 2–3 years; sheath deciduous; margin with minute teeth; often silvery with conspicuous white lines of stomata.

FLOWERS. Male yellow; female bright pink with purple margins.

FRUIT. Cones long-stalked; 10–26 inches long and 4–5 inches in diameter; scales slightly thicker and more rigid than in white pine, unarmed and with terminal umbo. Seed: ½ inch long, dark brown to black, with wing 1–1½ inches long.

TWIGS. Slender to stout; at first rusty-pubescent, later smooth and orange-brown. Winter buds: ⅓ inch long, sharp-pointed, chestnut-brown.

BARK. On young stems thin, smooth, and gray-green; on mature boles 1½–4 inches thick, in thick plate-like ridges covered with purplish to reddish scales.

WOOD. Very important; similar to white pine but coarser in texture; sash, doors, pattern work, etc.; a sweet, sugar-like substance, pinite, exudes from wounds and gives the tree its name.

SILVICAL CHARACTERS. Intolerant; maturity reached in 200–350 years (extreme age 623 years); reproduction generally sparse; tree windfirm with well developed tap and lateral root system; blister rust and bark beetles cause damage.

HABITAT. Transition zone; altitudinal range from 3,000–10,000 feet; best development on west slopes of Sierra range between 4,500–5,500 feet; in mixed stands with ponderosa and Jeffrey pines, Douglas-fir, and other conifers; on cooler, moister sites than associated pines.

[7]

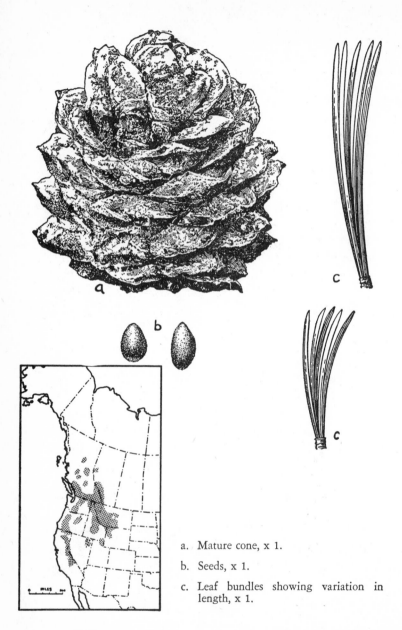

a. Mature cone, x 1.

b. Seeds, x 1.

c. Leaf bundles showing variation in
   length, x 1.

PINACEAE

WHITEBARK PINE

Pinus albicaulis Engelm.

HABIT. A tree 20–40 feet high and 1–2 feet in diameter (max. 60 by 4 feet); bole usually short and twisted; crown broad, open, irregular, with long, stout, flexible branches; at high elevation a low, spreading shrub.

LEAVES. In fascicles of 5; 1½–2½ inches long; stout and rigid; dark green; persistent 5–8 years; clustered toward the ends of the branchlets; basal sheath deciduous; margins usually smooth, but sometimes with minute, widely separated teeth; marked on back or dorsal side by 1–3 rows of stomata.

FLOWERS. Male and female scarlet; opening in July.

FRUIT. Cones short-stalked; 1½–3 inches long; subglobose; closed at maturity and ultimately disintegrating at the axis; scales thickened and often armed with stout, pointed, terminal umbos; purple-brown in color. Seed: large, ⅓–½ inch long; wingless; with thick, hard, dark brown shell.

TWIGS. Stout and tough; pubescent for 2 years or sometimes glabrous; red-brown becoming white-gray. Winter buds: ⅓–½ inch long; ovoid.

BARK. Thin, smooth, white-gray on young stems and branches; only about ½ inch thick on old trunks, and broken into narrow, brown-white, platelike scales; inner bark red-brown.

WOOD. Unimportant; light and soft, but firm; brittle when dry; sapwood thin, whitish; heartwood pale brown when freshly cut; used only locally for fuel and mine timbers.

SILVICAL CHARACTERS. Very intolerant; growth slow; maturity reached in about 250 years; reproduction rather sparse; tree very windfirm; susceptible to fire injury and subject to attack by blister rust and bark beetles.

HABITAT. Hudsonian and Canadian zones; altitudinal range from 5,000–10,000 feet in Rocky Mountain region; adapted to wide variety of soils but typically on exposed, rocky crags or cañon walls; occasionally in pure stands, but usually in mixture with other high-altitude conifers as Engelmann spruce, Lyall's larch, and limber and lodgepole pines.

a. Foliage with mature closed cone, x ⅔.
b. Upper side of cone scale with seeds, x 1.

PINACEAE

LIMBER PINE
Pinus flexilis James

HABIT. A tree 25–50 feet high and 1–3 feet in diameter (max. 85 by 6⅓ feet); bole short and sharply tapered; crown broad, open, with numerous, large, plumelike, often drooping branches; shrublike at high elevations.

LEAVES. In fascicles of 5; 1½–3 inches long, stout; rigid; dark green; persistent 5–6 years; sheath deciduous; margins with minute teeth; marked on all sides by rows of stomata.

FLOWERS. Male red; female clustered, red-purple.

FRUIT. Cones short-stalked; 3–10 inches long; subcylindrical; open at maturity; scales greatly thickened and often slightly reflexed, with terminal unarmed umbo. Seed: ⅓–½ inch long; wingless; thick, light brown shell.

TWIGS. Stout and tough; at first covered with soft, white hairs, but soon smooth and silver-white or gray. Winter buds: ⅓–½ inch long; broad ovoid and pointed.

BARK. Thin, smooth, white-gray on young stems and branches; on old trunks dark brown and plated.

WOOD. Unimportant; moderately light and soft; heartwood lemon-yellow; sapwood thin and white; used locally for rough construction, mine props, railroad ties, and fuel.

SILVICAL CHARACTERS. Very intolerant; growth usually slow; maturity reached in 200–300 years; reproduction generally sparse; tree very windfirm with long, sparsely branched taproot, later supplemented by several laterals. Fire, blister rust, and bark beetles cause serious damage.

HABITAT. Upper Sonoran to Hudsonian zones; large altitudinal range from 4,000–10,000 feet in north to 4,500–11,500 feet in Colorado; adapted to wide variety of sites, but typical of summits, ridge tops, and rocky foothills; occasionally in pure stands, but typically scattered with other conifers.

GENERAL. The variety *reflexa* Engelm., growing from southern Texas to northern Arizona and south into Mexico, differs from the species in having strongly reflexed cone scales. This variety has been called *Pinus strobiformis* Engelm.

[11]

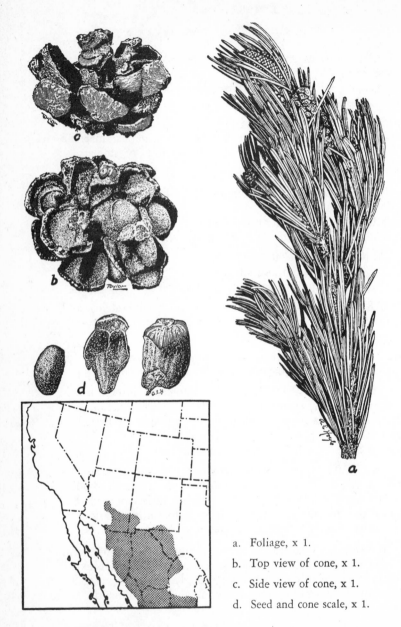

a. Foliage, x 1.

b. Top view of cone, x 1.

c. Side view of cone, x 1.

d. Seed and cone scale, x 1.

PINACEAE

MEXICAN PINYON. NUT PINE
Pinus cembroides Zucc.

HABIT. A tree 10–40 feet high and 1–2 feet in diameter (max. 50 by 3 feet); bole rapidly tapering and often divided with a spreading, rounded crown, giving the tree a bushy appearance.

LEAVES. In fascicles of 3, or 2 and 3 (rarely from 1 to 5); 1–2 inches long; moderately slender (less than 1 mm.); blue-green; incurved; sharp-pointed; persistent 3–4 years; margins with minute teeth; no rows of stomata on dorsal surface; fascicle sheath only partially deciduous.

FLOWERS. Male yellow in crowded clusters; female dark red.

FRUIT. Cone 1–2½ inches long; ovoid to globose; scales few and unarmed; yellow-brown; maturing in August or September of second season and shedding seed soon after; immature cones with stalk ¼–⅓ inch long. Seed: ½–¾ inch long with rudimentary terminal wing; shell cannot be cracked with teeth.

TWIGS. Moderately stout; light orange-colored, ultimately becoming dark brown. Winter buds: Apex long tapering.

BARK. Rarely over ½ inch thick on mature trees; irregularly divided into flattened connecting ridges separated by shallow fissures; superficially scaly; light red-brown.

WOOD. Unimportant; moderately light; rather hard; brittle, cross-grained, fine-textured; light yellow heartwood; thin, whitish sapwood; used locally for fuel, ties, and fence-posts; of less importance than the large, oily seeds which are an important article of food among the Indians and Mexicans.

SILVICAL CHARACTERS. Very intolerant in all but seedling stage; growth slow; maturity reached in 250–350 years; reproduction generally sparse and scattered; tree very windfirm with extensive, shallow to moderately deep root system.

HABITAT. Upper Sonoran zone; altitudinal range, from 4,800–8,000 feet; hot, arid, gravelly mountain slopes and cañon sides; occasionally in small pure groves, but usually in mixture with junipers and scrub oaks.

[13]

PINYON

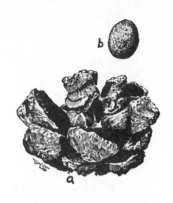

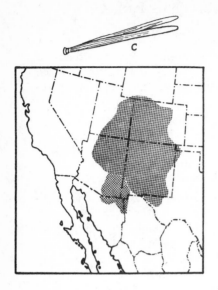

a. Mature cone opened, x 1.

b. Seed, x 1.

c. Needles, x 1.

SINGLELEAF PINYON

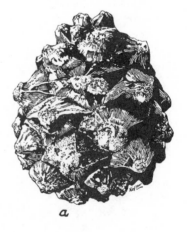

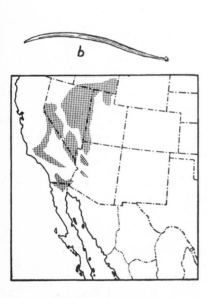

a. Mature cone closed, x 1.

b. Needle, x 1.

PINACEAE

PINYON. COLORADO PINYON

Pinus edulis Engelm. [*Pinus cembroides* var. *edulis*
(Engelm.) Voss.]

A tree similar in appearance to *Pinus cembroides* but differing from it in distribution and the following characters:

LEAVES. In fascicles of 2, or less frequently of 1 or 3; $\frac{3}{4}$–$1\frac{1}{2}$ inches long; stout (greater than 1 mm.) and rigid; yellow-green; incurved; sharp-pointed; persistence not definite; falling off from the third to the ninth year; margins entire; rows of stomata on all sides (4–6 rows on dorsal surface) fascicle sheath only partially deciduous at base.

FRUIT. Immature cones short-stalked (less than $\frac{1}{8}$ inch); seed easily cracked with teeth.

WINTER BUDS. Apex short-pointed.

HABITAT. Upper Sonoran zone; altitudinal range from 5,000–9,000 feet; arid, shallow, rocky soils of foothills, mesas and cañon walls; occasionally in pure groves, but usually in mixture with juniper, oak, or yellow pine.

* * *

SINGLELEAF PINYON

Pinus monophylla Torr. and Frem.

[*Pinus cembroides* var. *monophylla* (Torr. and Frem.) Voss.]

A tree similar in appearance to *Pinus edulis* but differing from it in distribution and leaf characters.

LEAVES. Usually single, but sometimes in fascicles of 2, about $1\frac{3}{4}$ inches long; stout and rigid; pale, glaucous green; incurved; sharp-pointed; persistence not definite, falling off from the fourth to twelfth year; margins entire; rows of stomata on all sides; fascicle sheath only partially deciduous.

HABITAT. Upper Sonoran zone; altitudinal range from 2,000–7,000 feet; arid, gravelly slopes and mesas; differs from other pinyons in frequently forming extensive pure stands, otherwise in mixture with juniper or chaparral.

[15]

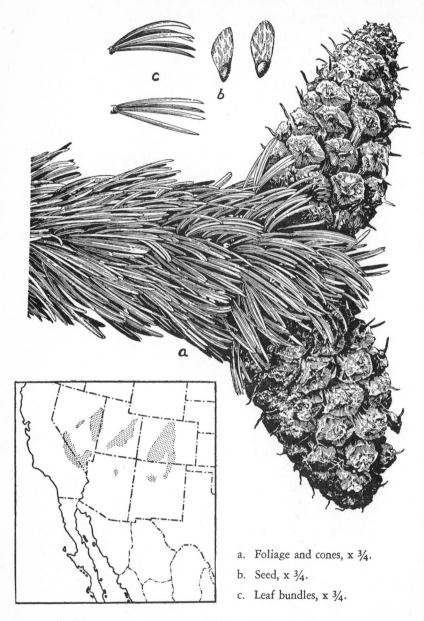

a. Foliage and cones, x ¾.

b. Seed, x ¾.

c. Leaf bundles, x ¾.

PINACEAE

BRISTLECONE PINE. FOXTAIL PINE
Pinus aristata Engelm.

HABIT. An alpine tree 30–40 feet high and 1–2 feet in diameter (max. 60 by 3 feet); bole short, stocky, and commonly malformed; crown dense, irregular, bushy in appearance, and frequently clothing the stem nearly to the ground; at high elevations a prostrate shrub.

LEAVES. In fascicles of 5; 1–1½ inches long; stout and curved; deep green; persistent for 10–17 years; in dense, often appressed, clusters; sheath deciduous; lustrous on back, marked on lower or ventral surfaces by numerous rows of stomata; usually showing conspicuous whitish exudations of resin.

FLOWERS. Male dark orange-red; female purple.

FRUIT. Cones short-stalked, 3–3½ inches long; ovoid-oblong; open at maturity; scales thin with thickened tips, with dark chocolate-brown apophysis; umbo dorsal, with long, bristle-like, fragile, incurved prickle; often covered with brown, shiny droplets of resin. Seed: ¼ inch long; light brown, often mottled; with long terminal wing.

TWIGS. Stout; light orange-colored, becoming nearly black; long tufts of foliage at ends; glabrous, or at first puberulous. Winter buds: ⅓ inch long, oblong-ovoid, brown.

BARK. Thin, smooth, and gray-white on young stems; ½–¾ inch thick on mature trunks, red-brown, and shallowly furrowed and ridged.

WOOD. Unimportant; a light, moderately soft, narrow-ringed, brittle wood; sapwood thin and whitish; heartwood pale brownish-red; used locally for fuel and mine props.

SILVICAL CHARACTERS. Very intolerant; growth slow; maturity reached in 200–250 years with extreme ages of 3000–4000 years; reproduction sparse and scattered; tree windfirm.

HABITAT. From typical Hudsonian to Transition zones; altitudinal range from 7,500–10,800 feet; typical of exposed sites and dry, thin, rocky soils; rarely in pure, open groves, usually in mixture with limber pine, ponderosa pine, white fir and Engelmann spruce.

[17]

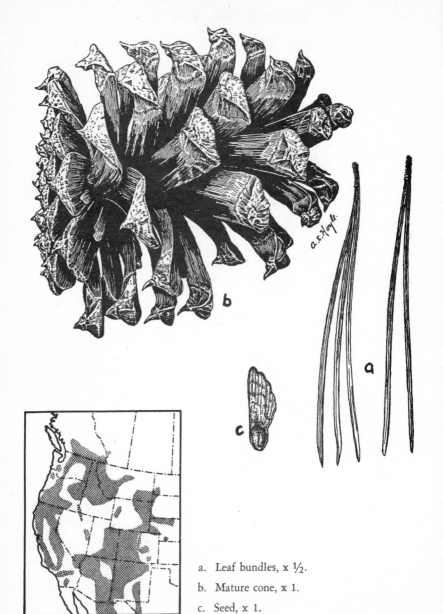

a. Leaf bundles, x ½.
b. Mature cone, x 1.
c. Seed, x 1.

PINACEAE

PONDEROSA PINE. WESTERN YELLOW PINE
Pinus ponderosa Laws.

HABIT. A tree 150–180 feet high and 3–4 feet in diameter (max. 232 by 8 feet on Pacific coast); bole symmetrical, clear; crown short conical or flat-topped.

LEAVES. In fascicles of 3, or 2 and 3 (rarely from 1–5); 4–11 inches long (mostly 5–7 inches); stout; dark to yellow-green; persistent until third year; cross section shows 2–5 resin ducts; basal sheath $\frac{1}{4}$–$\frac{3}{4}$ inch long, persistent.

FLOWERS. Male yellow; female red, clustered or paired.

FRUIT. Subsessile; $2\frac{1}{2}$–6 inches long; ovoid to ellipsoidal; basal scales usually remaining attached to twig when cones shed; umbo dorsal and armed with prickles. Seed: $\frac{1}{4}$ inch long; brown-purple, often mottled; wing 1 inch long.

TWIGS. Stout; orange-colored, becoming nearly black; turpentine odor when bruised. Winter buds: about $\frac{1}{2}$ inch long; oblong to ovoid; often covered with resin.

BARK. Brown to black and deeply furrowed on young trees; on old trunks 2–4 inches thick; yellow-brown to cinnamon-red, and broken into large, flat plates.

WOOD. Very important; variable from light, soft, and fine-textured to moderately heavy, hard, and coarse-textured; sapwood white and very thick with properties of white pine; heartwood light brown; wide variety of uses including construction, planing mill products, railroad ties, and mine timbers.

SILVICAL CHARACTERS. Intolerant; growth generally rather slow; maturity reached in 350–500 years (extreme age recorded is 660 years); reproduction abundant and vigorous; long taproot; fire and bark beetles cause greatest damage, while mistletoe and several fungi are also destructive.

HABITAT. Transition zone; large altitudinal range, varying from 2,000–7,000 feet in northern Idaho to 5,000–8,000 feet in Arizona; adapted to wide range of soils; exceedingly drought resistant; in open pure stands or more commonly the most abundant tree in mixed coniferous stands.

GENERAL. The Rocky Mountain variety is known as *Pinus ponderosa* var. *scopulorum* Engelm.

[19]

ARIZONA PINE

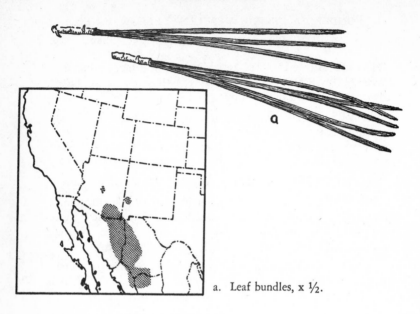

a. Leaf bundles, x ½.

APACHE PINE

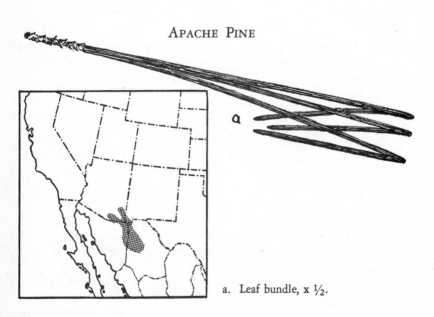

a. Leaf bundle, x ½.

PINACEAE

ARIZONA PINE

Pinus ponderosa var. *arizonica* (Engelm.) Shaw.
(*Pinus arizonica* Engelm.)

A tree similar in most of its characteristics to *Pinus ponderosa,* and differing from it in the following ways:

HABIT. A tree 75–90 feet high and 2–3 feet in diameter (max. 120 by 4 feet.)

LEAVES. Mostly in fascicles of 5 (rarely 2–5 on same tree); 5–7 inches long; rigid; dark yellow-green; cross section shows 3 resin ducts.

FRUIT. Never more than 2–3¼ inches long.

HABITAT. Transition zone; altitudinal range from 6,000–8,000 feet; frequently in pure stands at lower elevations, but at higher levels commonly in mixture with Chihuahua, Apache, and ponderosa pines, Arizona cypress, and scrub oaks.

APACHE PINE

Pinus engelmannii Carr. (*Pinus latifolia* Sarg.)

A tree similar in most of its characteristics to *Pinus ponderosa,* and differing from it in the following ways:

HABIT. A tree 50–60 feet high and 1–2 feet in diameter (max. 75 by 3 feet.)

LEAVES. In fascicles of 3 (occasionally 2–5); 8–15 inches long, (mostly about 10 inches); dark green; with conspicuously fringed margins; persistent 2 years; cross section shows 11–14 resin ducts; basal sheath ¾–1 inch long.

HABITAT. Transition zone; altitudinal range 5,500–8,200 feet; otherwise similar to Arizona pine.

GENERAL. Some authors consider this tree a synonym or variety of *Pinus ponderosa;* it is characterized during its first few years by development of a very deep taproot and little height growth.   *   *   *

The Jeffrey pine, *Pinus jeffreyi* Grev. and Balf., is another species closely allied to *Pinus ponderosa.* Entering this region only in western Nevada, it is characterized by cones 5–15 inches long, leaves 4–9 inches long and persistent 6–9 years, and non-resinous buds on purplish twigs which have an odor like pineapple when crushed. The related and rare *P. washoensis* M. & S. has been reported in Washoe County, Nevada.

[21]

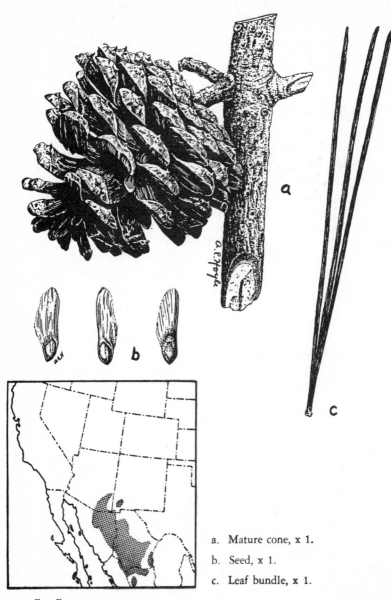

a. Mature cone, x 1.

b. Seed, x 1.

c. Leaf bundle, x 1.

[22]

PINACEAE

CHIHUAHUA PINE

Pinus leiophylla var. *chihuahuana* (Engelm.) Shaw
(*Pinus chihuahuana* Engelm.)

HABIT. A tree rarely over 40–50 feet high and 2 feet in diameter (larger in Mexico); bole fairly straight and clear for ½–⅔ of its length, crown a narrow pyramid or rounded.

LEAVES. In fascicles of 3; 2–4 inches long; slender; pale glaucous green; persistent for 4 years; margins with minute teeth; marked by 6–8 rows of stomata on all sides; cross section shows 2 resin ducts; basal sheath deciduous.

FLOWERS. Male yellow; female green; exceptional in that they do not appear until July.

FRUIT. Long-stalked; 1½–2 inches long; ovoid; light chestnut-brown in color and lustrous; often remaining closed several years; scales slightly thickened, their umbos armed with minute, recurved, deciduous prickles; exceptional in that fruit matures in September of third year. Seed: ⅛ inch long; thin, dark brown shell; wing ⅓ inch long.

TWIGS. Slender; bright orange-brown becoming dull red-brown with age. Winter buds: ½ inch long; oblong-ovoid; brown.

BARK. ⅞–1½ inches in thickness on mature trees; color varies from a blackish-brown to bright red-brown; deeply and narrowly furrowed with broad, flat ridges between, the latter covered with thin, closely appressed scales.

WOOD. Unimportant; similar to ponderosa pine in properties and substituted for it in Mexico; in United States used locally for firewood.

SILVICAL CHARACTERS. Intolerant; growth slow; maturity reached in 250–300 years; often forming coppice by growth of shoots from stumps of cut trees; reproduction generally sparse although seed produced abundantly.

HABITAT. Transition zone; altitudinal range from 5,500–8,200 feet (usually between 6,000–7,000 feet); on dry, rocky, gravelly slopes and benches; occasionally in pure open stands, or with Arizona, Apache, and ponderosa pines.

GENERAL. The Mexican *Pinus leiophylla* Schiede & Deppe is characterized by having needles in fascicles of fives.

[23]

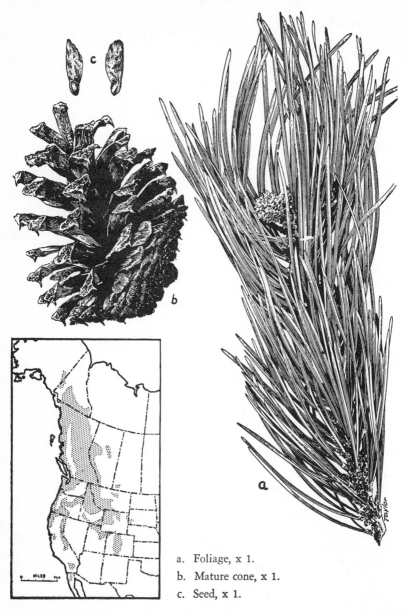

a. Foliage, x 1.
b. Mature cone, x 1.
c. Seed, x 1.

PINACEAE

LODGEPOLE PINE

Pinus contorta var. *latifolia* Engelm.
(*Pinus murrayana* Grev. and Balf.)

HABIT. A tree 70–80 feet high and $1\frac{1}{4}$–$2\frac{1}{2}$ feet in diameter (max. 150 by 3 feet); long, clear, slender, cylindrical bole; short, narrow, rounded or pyramidal crown.

LEAVES. In fascicles of 2; 1–3 inches long; stout; often twisted; bright yellow-green; persistent 4–6 years; margins with minute teeth, marked on all faces by 6–10 rows of stomata; basal sheath persistent.

FLOWERS. Orange-red; male in spikes; female clustered.

FRUIT. Subsessile; $\frac{3}{4}$–2 inches long; ovoid to subcylindrical; opening at maturity or frequently remaining closed and on the tree for many years; unsymmetrical; apophysis flattened, or those at base knoblike; umbo dorsal and armed with long, recurved, often deciduous prickle. Seed: $\frac{1}{6}$ inch long; thin, dark red-brown shell, often mottled; wings $\frac{1}{2}$ inch long.

TWIGS. Moderately slender; light orange-brown, becoming black. Winter buds: $\frac{1}{4}$ inch long, ovoid, dark chestnut-brown, resinous.

BARK. Very thin, rarely over $\frac{2}{5}$ inch thick; orange-brown to gray; covered by thin, loosely appressed scales.

WOOD. Moderately important; soft and uniform; fine-textured; sapwood thick, whitish; heartwood pale brown; tangential surface with many indentations; used for construction lumber, railroad ties, telephone poles, and mine timbers.

SILVICAL CHARACTERS. Intolerant, but recovers well from suppression; growth slow; maturity reached in about 200 years; shallow root system, trees not windfirm; reproduction vigorous, typically forming dense stands following fires; fire, bark beetles, and mistletoe cause damage; susceptible to sun-scald.

HABITAT. Canadian zone; altitudinal range from 6,000–11,000 feet; adapted to variety of soil types (except those of limestone origin), but best on moist, well-drained loams; in pure, dense, even-aged stands, or in mixture with various conifers.

GENERAL. The species proper, *Pinus contorta* Dougl., commonly called Shore Pine, is a stunted, short-leaved, twisted-cone form restricted to the Pacific Coast.

[25]

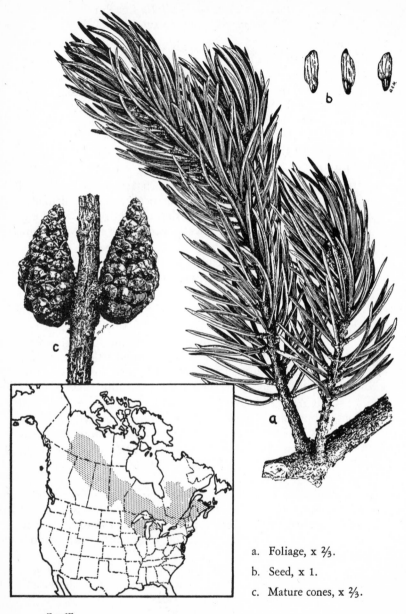

a. Foliage, x 2/3.

b. Seed, x 1.

c. Mature cones, x 2/3.

PINACEAE

JACK PINE. SCRUB PINE

Pinus banksiana Lamb. (*Pinus divaricata* D.M. de C.)

HABIT. Under favorable conditions, a tree 70–80 feet high and 1–1¼ feet in diameter (max. 90 by 2 feet), but usually much smaller; bole is often crooked and scraggly in appearance from long-persistent, dead lower branches; crown varies from open and symmetrical to irregular and scrubby.

LEAVES. In fascicles of 2; ¾–1½ inches long; divergent; stout; often twisted; yellow-green; persistent 2–3 years; margins with minute teeth; basal sheath persistent.

FLOWERS. Male yellow; female dark purple; clustered.

FRUIT. Sessile; 1½–2 inches long; oblong-conic; unsymmetrical and often strongly incurved; erect; often remaining closed and on branches for many years; scales irregularly developed, thin and stiff; umbo dorsal, unarmed or with minute deciduous prickle. Seeds: 1/12 inch long, triangular, black and roughened; wing about ⅓ inch long.

TWIGS. Thin, tough, and flexible; smooth and yellow-green first year, becoming rough and dark red-brown. Winter buds: ¼ inch long, ovoid and rounded; pale cinnamon-brown

BARK. Thin; dark red-brown; narrow, shallow ridges separating into closely appressed scales.

WOOD. Not important; light and soft, not strong; close-grained; sapwood thick and creamy-white; heartwood yellow-brown; used for fuel, posts, and cheap grades of lumber.

SILVICAL CHARACTERS. Very intolerant; growth moderately rapid; short-lived tree, maturity being reached in about 60 years and deterioration starting soon after (trees 150 years old have been found); root system widespreading and moderately deep, with a taproot; reproduction vigorous; very drought-resistant; fire and fungi cause damage.

HABITAT. Canadian zone; growing at low altitudes, from 100–1,200 feet; essentially a Canadian tree, extending farther north than any other pine; typical of sterile sandy soils; mostly in pure stands; where its distribution overlaps that of lodgepole pine, jack pine is found at the lower elevations.

[27]

PINACEAE

THE LARCHES

Characteristics of the Genus *Larix* Mill.

HABIT. Tall, pyramidal trees; open crowns, with slender, irregularly disposed, horizontal or pendulous branches; dwarfed, short, spurlike lateral branchlets.

LEAVES. Deciduous, needle-shaped or linear; produced in dense false whorls or clusters on spurlike lateral branches; solitary and spirally arranged on new shoots; numerous lines of stomata on all surfaces; 2 resin canals in cross section.

FLOWERS. Monoecious, terminal, single, appearing with leaves; male naked, globose to oblong, consisting of several yellow, spirally arranged scales, each bearing two pollen sacs; female erect, consisting of few or many rounded, red-purple scales in the axes of much longer scarlet bracts, each scale bearing 2 small inverted ovules.

FRUIT. Woody, erect, short-stalked cones; maturing in one season; cone scales thin, persistent, concave, longer or shorter than their long-pointed bracts. Seed: 2 under each scale; triangular and light brown; large terminal wing.

TWIGS. Smooth and glaucous, or pubescent. Winter buds: subglobose, small, nonresinous, with accrescent inner scales which mark lateral spur branches with prominent ringlike scars.

WOOD. Rather strong and durable; small, scattered resin ducts; thin, white sapwood and sharply defined, red to russet-brown heartwood.

SILVICAL CHARACTERS. Intolerant, slow-growing, and found on a variety of habitats; extensive forests occasionally destroyed by larch sawfly (*Nematus erichsonii*).

GENERAL. This genus contains about 10 species scattered through the Northern Hemisphere. In North America 3 species are native. The European larch (*Larix decidua* Mill.), an important tree, has been planted in the United States for ornamental purposes. It can be identified by its puberulous cones, ¾–1½ inches long, with inserted bracts and 40–50 suborbicular scales.

[28]

KEY TO THE SPECIES OF LARIX

I. Cones small, ½-¾" long, with bracts inserted; twigs slender, covered at first with glaucous bloom; eastern and far northern.................................1. *Larix laricina,* p. 31.

II. Cones larger, 1-2" long, with bracts exserted; twigs stout, at first pubescent.

  A. Twigs with pale pubescence, brittle; bark thick, red-brown, plated and deeply furrowed; cones 1-1½" long; needles flatly 3-angled; western.........2. *Larix occidentalis,* p. 33.

  B. Twigs densely woolly, tough; bark thin, gray-scaly, and obscurely furrowed; cones 1½-2" long; needles 4-angled; western alpine.............................3. *Larix lyallii,* p. 35.

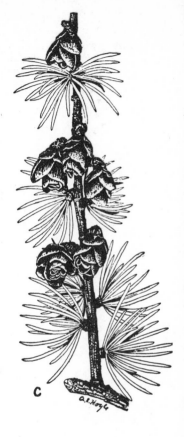

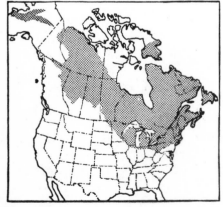

a. Foliage, x 1.

b. Seed, x 1.

c. Branchlet with cones, x 1.

PINACEAE

TAMARACK. EASTERN LARCH

Larix laricina (Du Roi) K. Koch.

HABIT. A tree seldom over 50 feet high and 12–14 inches in diameter in the northern Rocky Mountain region; long, clear, cylindrical bole; and an open, pyramidal, irregular crown with slender horizontal branches.

LEAVES. Linear; triangular in cross section; $\frac{3}{4}$–$1\frac{1}{4}$ inches long; bright blue-green; falling in September or October; in clusters of 12–20.

FLOWERS. Male subglobose and sessile; female oblong and short-stalked.

FRUIT. $\frac{1}{2}$–$\frac{3}{4}$ inch long; short-stalked, oblong to subglobose, chestnut-brown, and falling during second year; cone scales less than 20, slightly longer than broad, erose at margin, glabrous and lustrous and twice as long as their bracts. Seed: $\frac{1}{8}$ inch long with light chestnut-brown wings about $\frac{1}{4}$ inch long.

TWIGS. Slender, smooth, glaucous at first, becoming orange-brown during first year. Winter buds: conspicuous, globose, small, lustrous, and dark red.

BARK. Thin and smooth on young stems; $\frac{1}{2}$–$\frac{3}{4}$ inch thick, red-brown and scaly on mature trunks.

WOOD. Heartwood yellow-brown, medium texture, strong, hard, heavy, and durable; not widely used, chief uses being poles, railroad ties, and rough lumber.

SILVICAL CHARACTERS. Intolerant; growth moderate, maturity being reached in 100–200 years; reproduction vigorous on favorable sites; shallow root system; larch sawfly and fire cause serious damage.

HABITAT. Hudsonian and Canadian zones; altitudinal range from 600–1,700 feet; restricted to sphagnum bogs or swamps in southern part of range and making best growth on moist beaches and well-drained uplands further north; chiefly with black spruce, also balsam fir, aspen, birch, and jack pine; extending northward to limits of tree growth.

* * *

Alaska larch, *Larix alaskensis* Wight., restricted to coastal Alaska, is closely related to *Larix laricina,* and is not considered distinct in this text.

[31]

a. Seed, x 1.

b. Branchlet with cones, x 1.

PINACEAE

WESTERN LARCH

Larix occidentalis Nutt.

HABIT. A tree 140–180 feet in height and 3–4 feet in diameter; long, clear, cylindrical bole, frequently with a swollen butt; short, open, irregular, pyramidal crown of small, few, horizontal branches.

LEAVES. Linear, flatly triangular in cross section, 1–1¾ inches long, light pale green becoming yellow, and falling in early autumn, in clusters of 14–30.

FLOWERS. Male short, oblong; female oblong, subsessile.

FRUIT. 1–1½ inches long, short-stalked, oblong, purple-red to red-brown, falling during first year; cone scales broader than long, sometimes toothed at reflexed apex, usually white woolly on the outside, and shorter than exserted long-tipped bracts. Seed: ¼ inch long, with thin, fragile wings ½ inch long.

TWIGS. Stout, brittle, at first with a pale pubescence, soon becoming glabrous and orange-brown. Winter buds: ⅛ inch in diameter, subglobose, chestnut-brown.

BARK. Thin and scaly on young stems; up to 4–6 inches thick, plated, and deeply furrowed on old trunks; red-brown to cinnamon-red.

WOOD. Heartwood red-brown, coarse-textured, heavy, hard, strong, and durable; similar to Douglas-fir for which it is sometimes sold; lumber, poles, ties, etc.

SILVICAL CHARACTERS. Intolerant; growth rather slow, maturity being reached in 300–400 years (trees over 700 years reported); reproduction vigorous, competing with lodgepole pine on burned areas; windfirm with deep, wide-spreading root system; fungi and mistletoe often cause damage.

HABITAT. Transition zone; altitudinal range 2,000–7,000 feet; best development on deep, moist, porous soils of mountain slopes and valleys, but does well on dry, gravelly slopes; in nearly pure stands or with Douglas-fir, western white, ponderosa and lodgepole pines, western hemlock, Engelmann spruce, and alpine and grand fir.

[33]

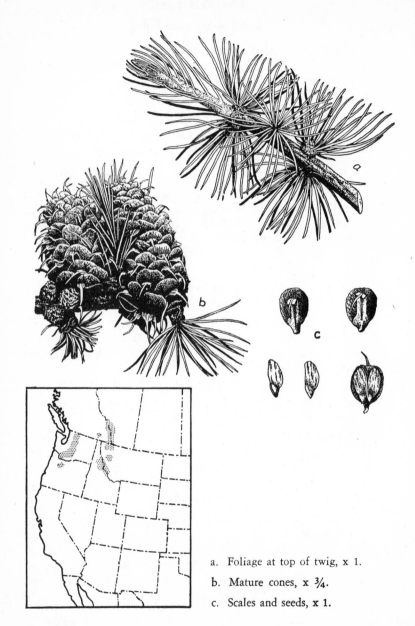

a. Foliage at top of twig, x 1.

b. Mature cones, x ¾.

c. Scales and seeds, x 1.

PINACEAE

SUBALPINE LARCH
Larix lyallii Parl.

HABIT. A small, timber-line tree 25–50 feet in height and 1–2 feet in diameter (max. 80 by 3 feet); bole short and tapering, often bent; crown very irregular, open, pyramidal, with long, willowy, often drooping branches.

LEAVES. Linear, 4–angled, 1–1½ inches long, pale blue-green, becoming bright yellow and falling in autumn, in clusters of 30–40 or more.

FLOWERS. Male short, oblong; female ovoid to oblong.

FRUIT. 1½–2 inches long, subsessile or slender-stalked, ovoid, acute, red-purple, falling during first year; cone scales broader than long, and erose-fringed at margin, covered with matted hair on lower surface, and shorter than exserted, purple, bristle-pointed bracts. Seed: ⅛ inch long, with lustrous light red wings ¼ inch long.

TWIGS. Stout, tough, densely woolly, ultimately nearly black. Winter buds: ⅛ inch long, prominent, with scales fringed with long, white, matted hairs.

BARK. Thin, ash-gray, and unbroken on young trees; becoming ½–⅞ inch thick, purple-brown or red-brown, and shallowly furrowed with flat, loose-scaly ridges.

WOOD. Similar to western larch but little used because of poor form, small size, and inaccessibility.

SILVICAL CHARACTERS. Intolerant; growth slow, attaining maturity at 400–500 years of age and reaching ages of 650–700 years; reproduction generally scanty; windfirm with widespreading root system.

HABITAT. Hudsonian zone, altitudinal range from 4,000–8,000 feet; prefers northern aspects and sheltered vales in regions of heavy snows that fall early and remain late; will grow on poor rocky soil where moisture is abundant; in small, pure groves or with alpine fir, Engelmann spruce, mountain hemlock, and whitebark pine; appears hardier than these associates, ascending higher and showing greater vigor.

[35]

PINACEAE

The Spruces

Characteristics of the Genus *Picea* Dietr.

HABIT. Evergreen trees with sharp-pointed, pyramidal crowns, and straight, tapering trunks; branches in regular whorls.

LEAVES. Spirally arranged, linear, sessile, stiff, and single; extending from all sides of twigs; persistent 7–10 years, but deciduous when dried; mostly 4–angled; when falling, leaving basal peglike projections (sterigmata) on the twig.

FLOWERS. Monoecious, catkin-like, solitary; male, or pollen-bearing, axillary, yellow to red or purple, ¾–1 inch long, consisting of numerous spirally arranged scales, each bearing two pollen sacs; female, or cone- and seed-producing, terminal, erect, yellow-green or red, ¾–1¼ inches long, consisting of numerous 2–ovuled, bracted scales.

FRUIT. Woody, pendent cone; matures in one season; borne mostly near top of crown; scales numerous, thin, unarmed, persistent, much longer than bracts. Seed: 2 under each fertile scale, small, compressed; highly buoyant with thin wing.

TWIGS. Roughened by sterigmata. Winter buds: ovoid or conical, of overlapping scales, and usually not resinous.

BARK. Thin and scaly (furrowed on old trunks in one species).

WOOD. Light, soft, resilient, fine-textured, long-fibered and straight-grained; small, scattered resin ducts; not resinous; high satiny luster; strong for weight; highly important for paper pulp, lumber, boxes, etc.

SILVICAL CHARACTERS. Tolerant; no taproot and generally shallow-rooted. Natural enemies: fire, leaf aphis (*Adelges abietis*) which causes conelike gall, spruce budworm (*Harmologa fumiferana*), which often destroys young stands, and white pine weevil (*Pissodes strobi*).

HABITAT. Cool, moist sites; typically in swampy areas or along the margins of streams and lakes.

GENERAL. This genus contains about 40 species, largely restricted to cooler regions in the Northern Hemisphere. In North America there are 7 indigenous species. The Norway spruce, *Picea abies* (L.) Karst., characterized by cones 4–7 inches long, is commonly planted throughout the United States.

[36]

KEY TO THE SPECIES OF PICEA

I. Cone scales rounded at apex, margin smooth or erose, 2 resin ducts in cross section of leaf; northern.

  A. Cones ovoid, purple, ½-1½″ long, on strongly incurved stalks, persistent many years; cone scales stiff and rigid, smooth or erose at margin; branchlets rusty pubescent; needles blunt at apex..............1. *Picea mariana*, p. 39.

  B. Cones oblong-cylindric, brown, 1-2½″ long, nearly sessile, falling during first year; cone scales soft and flexible, smooth at margin; branchlets glabrous; needles pointed...........
..................................2. *Picea glauca*, p. 41.

II. Cone scales truncate or acute at apex, margin erose, cones oblong-cylindric, brown; 1 or no resin ducts in cross section of leaf.

  A. Cones 1-2½″ long, persistent 1 year; branchlets minutely pubescent; needles flexible, acute, but not very prickly to touch, no resin duct in cross section; buds ⅛-¼″ long with scales usually appressed; bark on mature trees thin and scaly; through Rocky Mountain region....................
...........................3. *Picea engelmannii*, p. 43.

  B. Cones 2¼-4½″ (mostly about 3½‴) long, persistent 2 years; branchlets glabrous; needles stiff, bristle-pointed and sharp to touch; 1 resin duct in cross section; buds ¼-½″ long with scales usually reflexed; bark on mature trees thick and deeply furrowed; central Rockies only...................
..............................4. *Picea pungens*, p. 45.

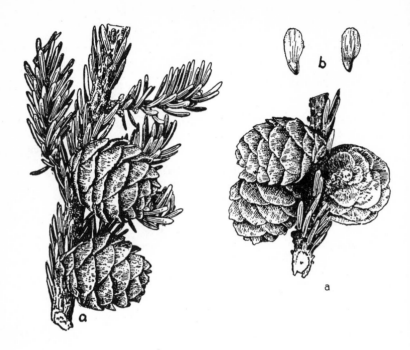

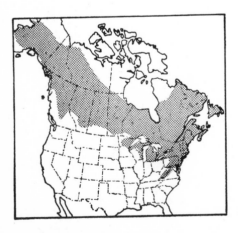

a. Branchlet with cones, x 1.

b. Seed, x 1.

PINACEAE

BLACK SPRUCE

Picea mariana (Mill.) B.S.P.

HABIT. A tree sometimes 40–80 feet high and ⅔–3 feet in diameter, but commonly much smaller; short slender bole usually pruning poorly; crown open, conical, more or less irregular.

LEAVES. Spreading in all directions; ¼–¾ inch long; pale blue-green and glaucous; blunt at apex; more or less incurved; hoary on upper surface from broad bands of stomata; lustrous and slightly stomatiferous below; 2 resin ducts in cross section.

FLOWERS. About ½ inch long; male red; female purple.

FRUIT. ½–1½ inches long; ovoid; on strongly incurved, short stalks; cone scales stiff, brittle, rigid, rounded, smooth or erose at apex, puberulous, and dull gray-brown; persistent many years. Seed: ⅛ inch long, dark brown, with pale brown oblique wing ¼–⅜ inch long.

TWIGS. Rusty-pubescent and rather slender; at first green, becoming dull red-brown. Winter buds: ⅛ inch long, ovoid, acute, light red-brown, puberulous.

BARK. Thin, ¼–½ inch thick; gray-brown; separated into thin, closely appressed scales or flakes; inner bark often olive-green.

WOOD. Not important except for pulp; used interchangeably with white spruce.

SILVICAL CHARACTERS. Very tolerant, recovering from suppression at an advanced age; growth slow; tree rather short-lived, attaining an age of 200 years; shallow, spreading root system; reproduction good on moist sites; lower branches often take root, forming clusters of small trees.

HABITAT. Hudsonian and Canadian zones; typical of cold sphagnum bogs and swamps, but also found on dry slopes in Northwest; altitudinal range from 100–3,500 feet; with white spruce and tamarack, reaches northern limit of tree growth; in dense, pure stands, or in mixture with tamarack, balsam fir, white spruce, white birch, aspen, etc.

[39]

a. Branchlet with cone, **x 1.**

b. Seed, x 1.

PINACEAE

WHITE SPRUCE

Picea glauca (Moench) Voss. (*Picea canadensis* B.S. & P.)

HABIT. A tree 60–70 feet high and 1½–2 feet in diameter (max. 120 by 4 feet); slender symmetrical bole; crown narrowly to broadly pyramidal with long, thick branches.

LEAVES. Tending to be crowded on upper side of branch by twisting of those on lower side; ⅓-¾ inch long; blue-green, occasionally with whitish tinge; rigid acute tips; odor pungent when crushed; 2 resin ducts in cross section.

FLOWERS. Male pale red to yellow; female with red or yellow-green scales.

FRUIT. 1–2½ inches long; oblong-cylindrical; nearly sessile; cone scales flexible, rounded and smooth at apex; light green or reddish before shedding seed, and becoming light brown and falling soon after. Seed: ⅛ inch long, pale brown, oblique wing ¼–⅜ inch long.

TWIGS. Glabrous, or in far Northwest downy; rather slender; orange-brown; skunklike odor when bruised. Winter buds: ⅛–¼ inch long; ovoid, obtuse, and chestnut-brown.

BARK. Thin, ¼–½ inch thick; ash-brown to silvery, separated into irregular thin plates or scales.

WOOD. Important in Northeast; used for pulp, construction lumber, boxes and crates, sounding boards, etc.

SILVICAL CHARACTERS. Tolerant of considerable shade, recovers from suppression well; growth slow, but faster than black spruce; tree attains age of 250–300 years; reproduction abundant on moist sites; shallow, spreading root system.

HABITAT. Hudsonian and Canadian zones; typical of low, damp woods, and banks of streams and lakes; altitudinal range from sea level to 5,000 feet; frequently gives way to black spruce or tamarack on wet sites, and to lodgepole pine on dry sites; often forms pure, dense forests, but also in mixture with black spruce, fir, birch, poplars, and willows.

GENERAL. The Western White Spruce, *Picea glauca* var. *albertiana* (S. Brown) Sarg., is the form found in the Rocky Mountain region. It is characterized by somewhat shorter and broader cones and a narrow crown.

[41]

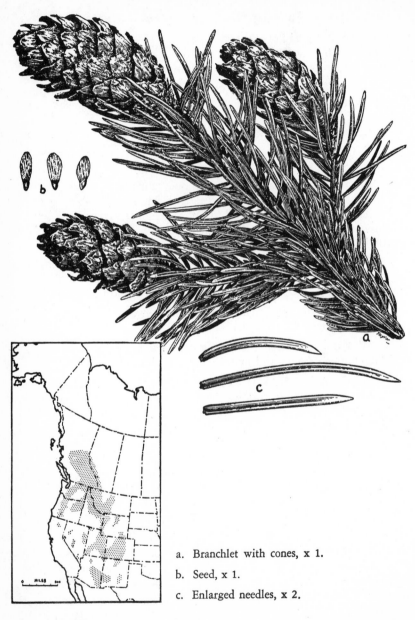

a. Branchlet with cones, x 1.

b. Seed, x 1.

c. Enlarged needles, x 2.

PINACEAE

ENGELMANN SPRUCE
Picea engelmannii Parry.

HABIT. A tree 60–120 feet high and 1½–3 feet in diameter (max. 165 by 5 feet); bole long and clear, cylindrical; crown compact, somewhat scraggly, narrowly pyramidal, with short, whorled branches. A prostrate shrub at high elevations.

LEAVES. Tending to be crowded on the upper side of the branch by the curving of those on the lower side; 1–1⅛ inches long; blue-green, occasionally with whitish, glaucous bloom; blunt or acute tips (not very sharp to touch); flexible; no resin ducts in cross section.

FLOWERS. Male dark purple; female bright scarlet.

FRUIT. 1–2½ inches long; oblong-cylindrical; sessile or short-stalked; cone scales flexible, variable in outline and erose-dentate at apex; light chestnut-brown; falling during autumn or winter of first season. Seed: ⅛ inch long, nearly black; broad, oblique wing ½ inch long.

TWIGS. Minutely pubescent (visible with hand lens); rather stout; orange-brown to gray-brown. Winter buds: ⅛–¼ inch long; broadly ovoid to conic; pale chestnut-brown; but scales usually appressed.

BARK. Thin, ¼–½ inch thick; cinnamon-red to purple-brown; broken into large, thin, loosely attached scales.

WOOD. Properties similar to white spruce; this is the longest-fibered and lightest weight spruce, but at present not widely used because inaccessible; lumber, telephone poles, railroad ties, mine timbers, and fuel.

SILVICAL CHARACTERS. Tolerant and recovering well from prolonged suppression; growth generally rather slow because of short summer season; a long-lived tree, reaching ages of 350–500 or more years; reproduction abundant and vigorous; shallow, spreading root system.

HABITAT. Hudsonian and Canadian zones; varying from 1,500–5,000 feet in the northern Rockies to 10,000–12,000 feet in the southern Rockies; rich, loamy soils with abundance of moisture; in pure stands or in mixture with alpine fir, lodgepole pine, and other conifers growing at high elevations.

[43]

a. Branchlet with cone, x ¾.

b. Seed, x 1.

c. Needles, x 1½.

PINACEAE

BLUE SPRUCE. COLORADO SPRUCE

Picea pungens Engelm. [*Picea parryana* (André) Sarg.]

HABIT. A tree 80–100 feet high and 1–2 feet in diameter (max. 150 by 4 feet); bole symmetrical, tapering, knotty; crown typically dense and conical when young, becoming thin, ragged and pyramidal in age, and extending to the ground on open grown species. The State Tree of Colorado.

LEAVES. Extending at nearly right angles from all sides of twig: 1–1¼ inches long; blue-green, frequently with a silvery, glaucous bloom which persists for 3-4 years on young trees; rigid, tipped with long, bristle-sharp point; 1 resin duct in an angle of leaf in cross section.

FLOWERS. Male yellow, tinged with red; female pale green.

FRUIT. 2¼–4½ (mostly 3½) inches long, oblong-cylindrical; sessile or short-stalked; cone scales tough, stiff, spreading, with erose margins; shiny, light chestnut-brown; not falling until fall of second season. Seed: ⅛ inch long, dark chestnut-brown; broad oblique wing about ½ inch long.

TWIGS. Glabrous; stout and rigid; orange-brown to gray-brown. Winter buds: ¼–½ inch long; broadly ovoid and obtuse; light chocolate-brown; bud scales usually reflexed.

BARK. Pale to dark gray; thin and scaly on young trunks, becoming ¾–1½ inches thick and deeply furrowed with rounded ridges on old trunks.

WOOD. Rather similar to white spruce but brittle, knotty, and of little value. The chief use of this tree is for ornamental planting.

SILVICAL CHARACTERS. Moderately tolerant, but least so of spruces; slow-growing, long-lived; reproduction generally scanty because of dense ground cover; widespread, moderately deep root system and decidedly windfirm.

HABITAT. Transition and Canadian zones, but mostly below the Engelmann spruce belt; varying from 6,000–9,000 feet in the north to 8,000–11,000 feet in the south; rich, moist soils, typically on stream banks; never abundant; in scattered pure groves or singly in mixture with ponderosa pine, Douglas-fir, alpine fir, Engelmann spruce, and hardwoods.

PINACEAE

The Hemlocks

Characteristics of the Genus *Tsuga* (Endl.) Carr.

HABIT. Tall, broadly pyramidal, evergreen trees; long, slightly tapering trunks; pyramidal or conical crown with scattered, slender, horizontal, and often pendulous branches; leading shoots characteristically drooping.

LEAVES. Spirally arranged, often appearing 2-ranked by a twist of the petioles; linear; single; abruptly petiolate; flattened or rounded; persistent 3–6 years and leaving conspicuous, woody, persistent bases (sterigmata) when they fall; deciduous in drying; usually grooved above, with 2 conspicuous bands of stomata below; 1 centrally located resin duct in cross section.

FLOWERS. Monoecious, single, on twigs of previous season; male, or pollen-bearing, axillary, globose, of numerous short stamens; female, or cone- and seed-bearing, terminal, erect, of numerous, circular scales of nearly the same length as their membranous bracts.

FRUIT. Woody, pendent cones; maturing in one season; scales thin, rounded, entire-margined, several times longer than bracts. Seed: 2 under each scale; small, light, and widely disseminated; long, terminal, obovate wing; dotted with small, resin vesicles.

TWIGS. Slender; round; roughened by persistent leaf bases. Winter buds: small, nonresinous, ovoid to globose.

BARK. Rough, hard, ridged, deeply furrowed; clear chocolate-red color when broken; containing tannin.

WOOD. Moderately soft; moderately strong; resin ducts normally absent; light to red-brown; considered inferior to pine and Douglas-fir.

SILVICAL CHARACTERS. Tolerant trees; requiring abundant moisture; seldom attaining ages of more than 500 years; shallow, widespreading root system.

GENERAL. This genus contains 10 or more species widely scattered through North America and Asia. In North America there are 4 native species, 2 western and 2 eastern.

[46]

KEY TO THE SPECIES OF TSUGA

I. Leaves flat, obtuse, lustrous and grooved above, stomatiferous below, mostly 2-ranked; cones ovoid; ¾-1″ long, light brown....
.............................1. *Tsuga heterophylla*, p. 49.

II. Leaves rounded, bluntly pointed, stomatiferous on both surfaces, extending from all sides of twig; cones oblong-cylindric, mostly over 2″ long, yellow-green to purple 2. *Tsuga mertensiana*, p. 51.

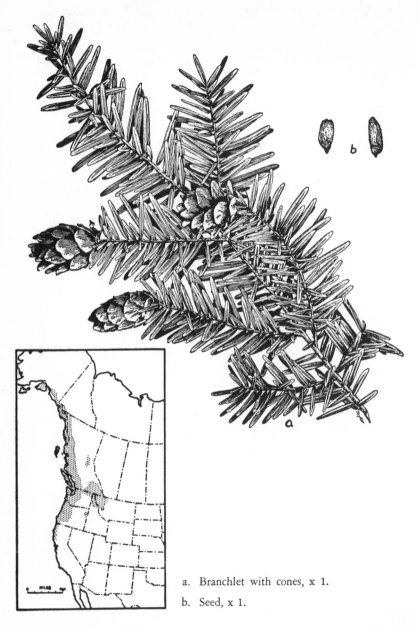

a. Branchlet with cones, x 1.

b. Seed, x 1.

PINACEAE

WESTERN HEMLOCK

Tsuga heterophylla (Raf.) Sarg.

HABIT. A tree 125–175 feet high and 2–4 feet in diameter (max. 259 by 9 feet); tall, clear trunk; short, open, pyramidal crown with typically drooping terminal leader.

LEAVES. Flattened; 1/4–3/4 inch long; dark, shiny green and grooved above, 2 broad bands of stomata below; abrupt, slender petiole; mostly 2–ranked; rounded or blunt at apex.

FLOWERS. Male yellow; female red or purple with rounded bracts shorter than scales.

FRUIT. 3/4–1 inch long, ovoid, light brown, scales suborbicular, wavy-margined. Seed: 1/16 inch long; ovoid; 1/3 as long as narrow, straw-colored wing.

TWIGS. Slender; pubescent for 5–6 years; pale yellow-brown becoming dark red-brown; drooping. Winter buds: ovoid, 1/16 inch long, blunt, bright chestnut-brown.

BARK. Thin (1–1 1/2 inches) even on largest trees; young bark scaly, russet-brown; on old trunks hard, dark russet-brown with furrows separating wide flat ridges; inner bark dark red streaked with purple; used for its tannin content.

WOOD. Superior in quality to eastern hemlock; one of 4 major timber-producing species of Pacific Northwest; uniform texture and not very harsh or splintery; suitable for all uses but heavy construction, and most important pulpwood species of region.

SILVICAL CHARACTERS. Tolerant throughout life; growth rapid, comparing favorably with Douglas-fir, seldom attaining age of over 500 years; reproduction very abundant and vigorous; shallow, widespreading root system; susceptible to fire injury, and butt rot common in old trees.

HABITAT. Transition and Canadian zones; altitudinal range from sea level to 7,000 feet; prefers deep, moist, porous soils, but hardy in drier situations; in pure, dense stands or mixed at lower levels with Douglas-fir, silver and grand firs, giant arborvitae, and hardwoods; and at higher levels with noble fir, Alaska cedar, mountain hemlock, western white and lodgepole pines.

[49]

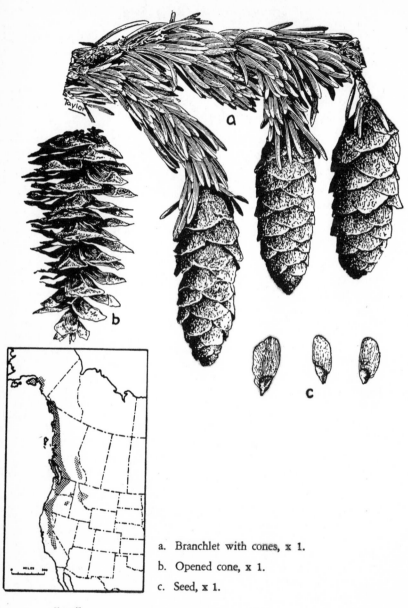

a. Branchlet with cones, x 1.

b. Opened cone, x 1.

c. Seed, x 1.

PINACEAE

MOUNTAIN HEMLOCK. BLACK HEMLOCK
Tsuga mertensiana (Bong.) Carr.

HABIT. An alpine tree 75–100 feet high and 2½–3½ feet in diameter; trunk tapering and long clear, or knotty and malformed; crown open, pyramidal, with slender, drooping branches and drooping terminal leader; a sprawling shrub at timber line.

LEAVES. Semicircular in cross section; ½–1 inch long; pale bluish-green and stomatiferous on all surfaces; upper surface often keeled or grooved; abruptly narrowed into straight or twisted petiole; extending from all sides of twig or crowded toward upper side; bluntly pointed.

FLOWERS. Male purple on slender drooping stems; female purple or green, slender-tipped bracts longer than scales.

FRUIT. ½–3½ inches long, (mostly over 2 inches); oblong-cylindric; yellow-green to purple; scales oblong-obovate and spreading at right angles or reflexed when mature. Seed: ⅛ inch long; ¼ as long as wing.

TWIGS. Thin or stout; dense, short, pale, pubescence for 2–3 years; light red-brown, becoming gray-brown and scaly. Winter buds: conical, ⅛ inch long, acute, red-brown, outer scales with awl-like tip.

BARK. Thin (1–1½ inches), early broken and rough on young trees; on old trunks hard, purplish to red-brown, with deep, narrow furrows separating narrow, rounded ridges; contains large quantities of tannin.

WOOD. Little used and inferior in quality to western hemlock; light, soft, not strong, and close-grained.

SILVICAL CHARACTERS. Tolerant; growth slow; trees over 500 years of age seldom found; reproduction generally abundant; shallow, widespreading root system.

HABITAT. Hudsonian and Canadian zones; altitudinal range from sea level (Alaska) to 11,000 feet, but mostly near timber line; at its best on cool, moist, deep soils of northern exposure, moisture being essential; in pure stands or in mixture with alpine fir, alpine larch, Engelmann spruce, whitebark, lodgepole, and western white pines.

[51]

a. Branchlet with cones, x 1.
b. Seed, x 1.

PINACEAE

Douglas-fir

Pseudotsuga taxifolia var. *glauca* (Mayr) Sudw.
[*Pseudotsuga menziesii* (Mirb.) Franco]

HABIT. An evergreen tree rarely more than 130 feet high and 3 feet in diameter in the Rocky Mountains; narrow, compact, pyramidal crown, with irregularly disposed branches.

LEAVES. Linear, single, more or less flattened, spirally arranged, and petiolate; ¾–1¼ inches long; grooved above and stomatiferous below; persistent 5–8 years or longer.

FLOWERS. Monoecious; male orange-red; female red-green.

FRUIT. Pendent, woody cones; 2–4½ inches long, oblong-ovoid, maturing in one season; scales thin, rigid, rounded, much shorter than their long, exserted, 3-lobed bracts. Seed: ¼ inch long, with large, rounded, terminal wing.

TWIGS. Slender, pubescent, orange-brown, becoming gray-brown. Winter buds: ¼ inch long, characteristically long conical, sharp-pointed, lustrous, brown.

BARK. Smooth gray-brown and with resin blisters on young trees; becoming thick (4–6 inches), rough, with red-brown ridges separated by deep furrows.

WOOD. Highly variable from yellowish, narrow-ringed, moderately light and soft, to red-brown, wide-ringed, with weak spring wood and very dense summer wood. Extremely valuable and widely used for lumber, ties, poles, etc.

SILVICAL CHARACTERS. Not very tolerant but more so than Rocky Mountain associates; reproduction abundant and vigorous; well-developed, widespreading, lateral root system.

HABITAT. Transition and Canadian zones; altitudinal limit in the Rocky Mountains from about 4,000 feet in the north to 11,000 feet in the south; adapted to variety of soils but best on moist, deep, porous soils of northern exposure; will endure considerable drought; in pure stands or mixed with Rocky Mountain conifers.

GENERAL. While not commonly accepted in this country, European taxonomists separate this species into 11 species. Only the species proper, growing in the coastal states, and the Rocky Mountain variety *glauca* are recognized in this text.

[53]

PINACEAE

THE FIRS

Characteristics of the Genus *Abies* Mill.

HABIT. Tall, pyramidal, evergreen trees; dense, spirelike crowns; slender, horizontal, whorled branches; and straight, gradually tapering trunks.

LEAVES. Spirally arranged, linear, sessile, and single; usually flat and blunt; extending from all sides of twig but mostly appearing 2-ranked by a twist near their base; persistent for 7–10 years; usually grooved above and with stomatiferous lines below; 2 resin canals in cross section; when falling leaving a conspicuous, smooth, circular scar on twig.

FLOWERS. Monoecious, axillary, single; male, or pollen-bearing, numerous on lower sides of lower crown branches, oval or cylindrical, with yellow to scarlet anthers; female, or cone- and seed-bearing, on upper side of topmost branches, erect, globose to oblong, consisting of numerous, imbricated, 2-ovuled scales much shorter than their bracts.

FRUIT. Woody, erect cones; maturing in one season; scales thin, fan-shaped, and falling at maturity from the central, spikelike axis which persists many years. Seed: 2 under each scale; large, thin wing; peculiar, conspicuous resin-vesicles.

TWIGS. Smooth, glabrous, or pubescent. Winter buds: small, mostly subglobose or ovoid, with thin, loosely imbricated scales and usually thickly covered with resin.

BARK. Young bark thin, smooth, with numerous blister-like resin pockets; old bark thicker and often furrowed.

WOOD. Rocky Mountain species with light-colored, often coarse-grained, rather weak and brittle wood; no resin ducts; not durable; only little used for inferior lumber and pulp. Canada balsam obtained from resin blisters of one species.

SILVICAL CHARACTERS. Tolerant, moisture-loving trees, of fast to slow growth, and moderately long-lived.

GENERAL. This genus contains about 35 species widely scattered through North and Central America, Europe, Asia, and northern Africa. In North America there are 9 indigenous species, 5 of these occurring in the Rocky Mountain region.

KEY TO THE SPECIES OF ABIES

I. Cones large (6-9" long), egg-shaped; needles 4-sided; western Nevada.
  A. Bracts inserted.....................1. *Abies magnifica*, p. 61.
  B. Bracts exserted and reflexed...............................
    ....2. *Abies magnifica* var. *shastensis*, p. 61.
II. Cones smaller (2-5" long), oblong-cylindric; bracts shorter than scales; needles of lower branches flattened.
  A. Cones dark purple; scales longer than broad; leaves of lower branches not over 1¾" long.
    1. Leaves dark green above, stomatiferous only below, 2-ranked on lower branches; bark of old trees with thin, easily detached scales; northern Canada to northeastern United States.................3. *Abies balsamea*, p. 57.
    2. Leaves stomatiferous on both surfaces, crowded and nearly erect; mature bark not scaly.
      a. Mature bark hard, tough, smooth and gray, becoming dark, with shallow fissures at base of trunk; cone scales wedge-shaped at base; entire region...............
      ....4. *Abies lasiocarpa*, p. 59.
      b. Mature bark soft and corky, yellow-white; cone scales mostly halberd-like at base, southern..............
      ....5. *Abies lasiocarpa* var. *arizonica*, p. 61.
  B. Cones yellow to green-purple; scales broader than long; leaves of lower branches over 1½" long.
    1. Leaves on lower branches distinctly 2-ranked and scattered, 1½-2" long, lustrous, dark green and deeply grooved above, 2 bands of stomata below; northern......
    ....6. *Abies grandis*, p. 65.
    2. Leaves on lower branches obscurely 2-ranked or spreading from all sides of twig, crowded, 2-3" long, pale green and stomatiferous above and below; mostly central and southern......................7. *Abies concolor*, p. 63.

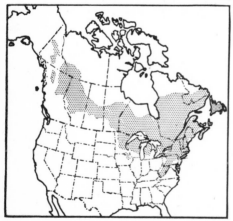

a. Lower crown branchlet.

b. Branchlet with cone, x 1.

c. Upper and lower sides of cone scale, x 1.

d. Seed, x 1.

PINACEAE

BALSAM FIR

Abies balsamea (L.) Mill.

HABIT. A medium-sized tree 40–60 feet high and 1–1½ feet in diameter (max. 85 by 2 feet); a dense, dark green, narrowly pyramidal crown with a slender spirelike tip.

LEAVES. On lower branches 2-ranked, ¾–1½ inches long, scattered, flattened, blunt, or notched; on upper branches shorter, spreading, and crowded; dark green above, silvery-banded below.

FLOWERS. Male of yellow anthers; female of orbicular purple scales.

FRUIT. 2–4 inches long, oblong-cylindric, dark purple; scales longer than broad, and twice as long as short, pointed bracts. Seed: ¼ inch long, with broad purple-brown wings.

TWIGS. Slender; finely pubescent and yellow-green; becoming smooth and gray to purple. Winter buds: subglobose, ⅛–¼ inch long, with orange-green scales.

BARK. Thin, ash-gray, smooth except for numerous resin blisters on young trees; becoming ½ inch thick, red-brown, and broken into thin scales.

WOOD. Soft and brittle; used for pulp, boxes, etc.; resin in bark blisters is source of Canada balsam.

SILVICAL CHARACTERS. Tolerant (less so than spruce), recovering well from suppression; growth generally rapid; a short-lived tree reaching an age of 150 years, but generally defective before 90 years; reproduction plentiful and aggressive; shallow root system; lower branches sometimes take root, producing new trees.

HABITAT. Canadian and Hudsonian zones; entering the Rocky Mountain region only in northern Canada, altitudinal range from sea level to 5,600 feet; demands abundant soil moisture and humid atmosphere; forms pure stands in swamps, but does best on adjacent flats in association with spruce; on higher sites in mixture with spruce, hemlock, and broad-leafed species.

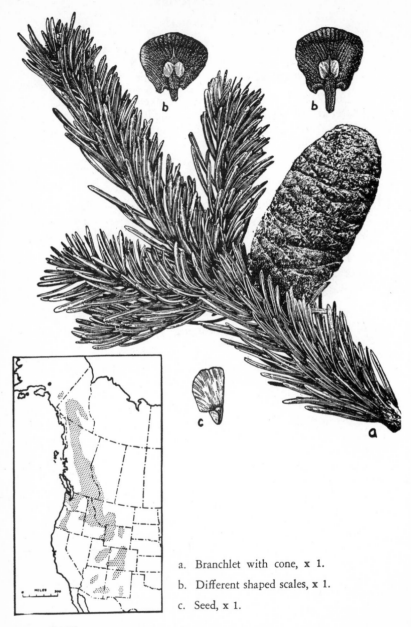

a. Branchlet with cone, x 1.

b. Different shaped scales, x 1.

c. Seed, x 1.

PINACEAE

SUBALPINE FIR

Abies lasiocarpa (Hook.) Nutt.

HABIT. A tree 60–100 feet high and 1½–2 feet in diameter (max. 160 by 3 feet); a dense, narrowly pyramidal, spire-like crown often extending to the ground, with short, thick branches; a prostrate shrub at timber line.

LEAVES. On lower branches, 1–1¾ inches long (mostly about 1 inch), flattened, blunt or notched; on upper branches ½ inch long and pointed; deep blue-green; crowded and nearly erect by a twist at their base; stomatiferous on both surfaces (less conspicuous above).

FLOWERS. Male dark indigo-blue; female dark violet-purple.

FRUIT. 2–4 inches long, oblong-cylindric, dark purple; scales mostly longer than broad and 3 times longer than long-tipped bracts. Seed: ¼ inch long, with dark lustrous wings.

TWIGS. Stout, pubescent, and pale orange-brown; becoming smooth and gray or silver-white. Winter buds: subglobose, ⅛–¼ inch long, with light orange-brown scales.

BARK. Thin, gray, smooth except for numerous resin blisters on young trees; becoming ¾–1½ inches thick, shallowly fissured and roughened by thickened, closely appressed, cinnamon-red scales.

WOOD. Similar to balsam fir but little used except for fuel.

SILVICAL CHARACTERS. Tolerant (of its associates, only Engelmann spruce and mountain hemlock are more so); growth not rapid, trees 15 inches in diameter often over 175 years old; reproduction abundant and vigorous; shallow root system; lower branches sometimes taking root.

HABITAT. Canadian and Hudsonian zones; growing from 3,500 feet to timber line in the north and from 10,500 feet to timber line in the south; in cool, moist sites, and best in deep, loose, moist soil; in restricted pure stands or commonly with Engelmann spruce, lodgepole, whitebark, limber, or bristle-cone pines, alpine larch, cork fir, and aspen.

[59]

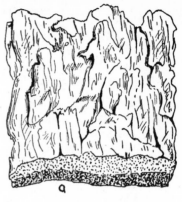

a. Soft, corky bark, x ½.

RED FIR

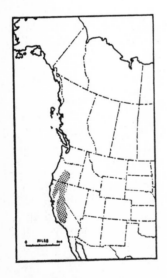

a. Lower crown needles, x ¾.

PINACEAE

CORKBARK FIR. CORK FIR

Abies lasiocarpa var. *arizonica* (Merr.) Lemm. *(Abies arizonica* Merr.)

This tree is more correctly considered a variety of the alpine fir, and differs from it in the following characters:

HABIT. A small tree of the southern Rocky Mountains from 50–75 feet in height and 1–1½ feet in diameter.

FRUIT. Cones generally longer and narrower than alpine fir; cone scales often halberd-like at base while those of alpine fir are mostly wedge-shaped. As there are intergrading forms, these differences are not consistent and cannot always be relied upon.

BARK. The soft, corky, yellow-white to ash-gray trunk bark readily separates this species from all other firs, although intergrading forms are found between this bark and the typical bark of alpine fir.

HABITAT. Canadian and Hudsonian zones; altitudinal range between 8,000–10,000 feet; often growing with or displacing alpine fir; typically on thin, gravelly, or rocky soils. An unimportant tree commercially.

* * *

CALIFORNIA RED FIR

Abies magnifica A. Murr.

This large fir enters the Rocky Mountain region only along the western edge of Nevada, being primarily a Pacific Coast species. It can be readily distinguished from other Rocky Mountain species by its large, egg-shaped cones (6–9 inches long), and crowded, 4-angled needles which are stomatiferous on all surfaces. The Shasta Red Fir, *Abies magnifica* var. *shastensis* Lemm.; with a similar distribution, differs from the pecies in having exserted, reflexed bracts.

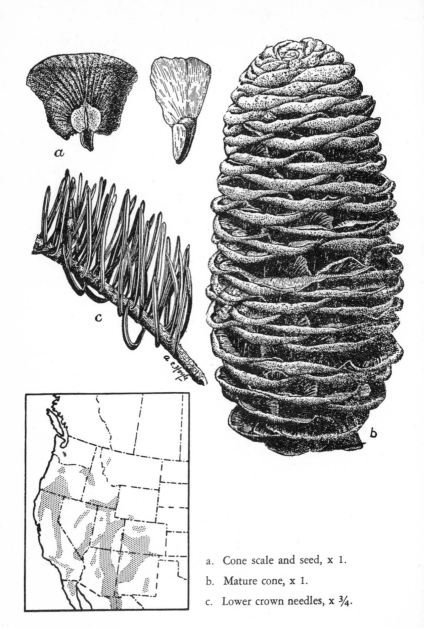

a. Cone scale and seed, x 1.

b. Mature cone, x 1.

c. Lower crown needles, x ¾.

PINACEAE

White Fir

Abies concolor (Gord. & Glend.) Hoopes

HABIT. A tree in the Rocky Mountain region 80–100 feet high and 1½–2½ feet in diameter; a dense conelike crown with heavily foliaged, long-persisting, short branches.

LEAVES. On lower branches 2–3 inches long, flat, straight, and acute at apex; on fertile branches, or on old trees, ¾–1½ inches long, thick, keeled above, usually curved, acute or rarely notched at apex; silver-blue to silver-green; crowded; more or less obscurely 2-ranked or extending from all sides of twig; stomatiferous above and below.

FLOWERS. Male rose to dark red; female with broad, round scales.

FRUIT. 3–5 inches long, oblong, bright yellow to olive-green or purple; scales much broader than long, and twice as long as short-tipped bracts. Seed: ⅓–½ inch long, yellow-brown with rose-tinted broad wing.

TWIGS. Moderately stout, smooth, yellow-green to brown-green and ultimately gray-brown. Winter buds: subglobose, ⅛–¼ inch long, yellow-brown.

BARK. Thin, gray, smooth except for numerous resin blisters on young trees; becoming 4–7 inches thick, ash-gray, hard and horny, with deep furrows and wide ridges.

WOOD. Similar to balsam fir; widely used for lumber, packing cases, or butter tubs.

SILVICAL CHARACTERS. Tolerant, although slightly less so than alpine fir; growth moderately rapid, maturity being reached in about 300 years; reproduction generally abundant and aggressive; root system normally shallow; severely damaged by mistletoe, with heart rot and wind shake common defects.

HABITAT. Transition and Canadian zones; altitudinal range from 6,000–11,000 feet; best development on moist, rich, light soils on northern slopes of benches and cañons; this species requires less moisture than other western firs, existing surprisingly well on poor, dry, shallow sites; seldom in pure stands, usually with ponderosa and limber pine, Douglas-fir, alpine fir, Engelmann spruce, and aspen.

[63]

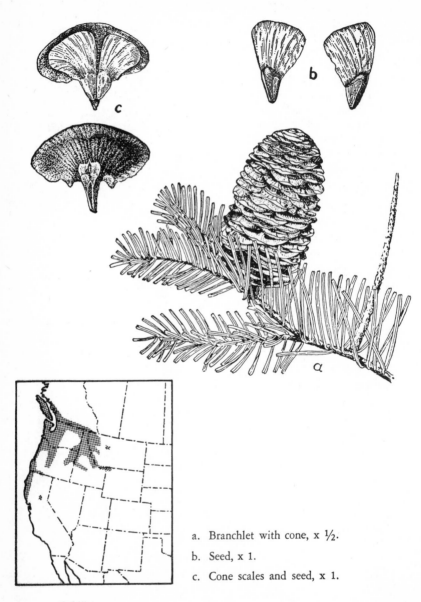

a. Branchlet with cone, x ½.

b. Seed, x 1.

c. Cone scales and seed, x 1.

PINACEAE

Grand Fir. Lowland White Fir

Abies grandis (Dougl.) Lindl.

HABIT. A tree in the Rocky Mountain region reaching 120 feet in height and 3 feet in diameter; rather open domelike crown, on old trees appearing wider in the middle because of the drooping of the lower branches.

LEAVES. On lower branches 1½–2 inches long, scattered, distinctly 2-ranked; on fertile branches 1–1½ inches long, more crowded, obscurely 2-ranked or nearly erect; blunt, flat, lustrous dark yellow-green and grooved above, white with 2 bands of stomata below.

FLOWERS. Male pale yellow; female light yellow-green.

FRUIT. 2–4½ inches long, cylindrical, yellow-green to green-purple; scales ⅓ broader than long, and 3–4 times longer than short-tipped bracts. Seed: ⅜ inch long, light brown, with straw-colored wing about ¾ inch long.

TWIG. Slender, yellow-green to orange-brown, puberulous becoming glabrous in second year. Winter buds: subglobose, ⅛–¼ inch long.

BARK. Thin, gray-brown, smooth except for resin blisters and chalky white blotches on young trees; becoming 2–3 inches thick, red-brown, plated or divided into flat ridges separated by deep furrows.

WOOD. Similar to balsam fir, but with disagreeable odor, and so known as "stinking fir"; lumber and interior finish.

SILVICAL CHARACTERS. Moderately tolerant, but less so than associated firs; growth moderate, maturity being reached in about 200 years; reproduction abundant if sufficient moisture and protection against frost present; windfirm with deep, spreading root system; subject to attack by spruce budworm and stringy brown-rot fungus.

HABITAT. Transition and Canadian zones; altitudinal range from sea level to 5,000 feet; on deep, moist, alluvial soils along streams or on mountain slopes; in limited pure stands, or more frequently in mixed hardwood and coniferous forests with ponderosa, western white, and lodgepole pines, Douglas-fir, western larch, alpine fir, Engelmann spruce, etc.

[65]

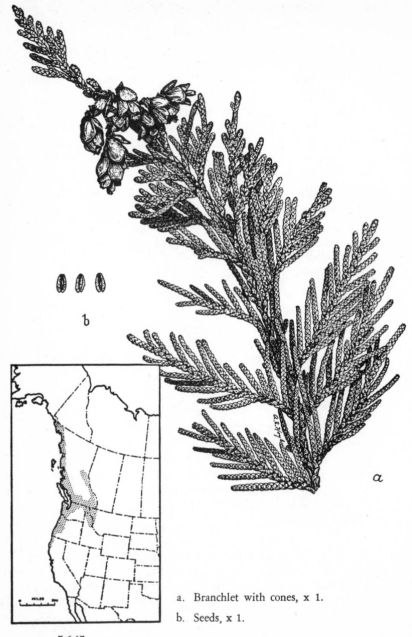

a. Branchlet with cones, x 1.

b. Seeds, x 1.

[66]

PINACEAE

WESTERN REDCEDAR. GIANT ARBORVITAE

Thuja plicata Donn.

HABIT. A large tree, 150–200 feet high and 4–8 feet in diameter (max. 250 by 16 feet); tapering, fluted trunk; irregular crown of horizontal or drooping branches.

LEAVES. Small, scalelike; persistent 2–5 years; decussate the facial leaves flattened, grooved; the lateral leaves rounded or keeled; lustrous dark yellow-green.

FLOWERS. Monoecious; terminal; dark brown; male with 3–6 pairs of decussate stamens; female 8–12 scaled.

FRUIT. Leathery or sub-woody erect cones; ½ inch long; ovoid-oblong; maturing in one season; scales 8–12 (only 6 being fertile), thin, spine-tipped. Seed: ⅛ inch long, brown, with lateral wings each about as wide as seed.

TWIGS. Slender; flattened; leaf-covered; in long drooping sprays. Winter buds: minute, naked, inconspicuous.

BARK. Thin (½–1 inch); fibrous; narrow interlacing ridges; cinnamon-red to gray-brown on old trunks.

WOOD. Widely used where durability rather than strength is required; sapwood white; heartwood reddish, soft, fragrant; shingles, siding, interior trim, boats, poles, etc.

SILVICAL CHARACTERS. Tolerant; growth rather rapid; trees over 1,000 years old reported; reproduction generally plentiful; shallow, widespreading root system; fire and pecky heart rot cause serious damage.

HABITAT. Transition and Canadian zones; altitudinal range 2,000–7,000 feet in Rocky Mountains; on rich soils with abundant moisture; in mixed coniferous stands.

GENERAL. The eastern arborvitae or white-cedar, *Thuja occidentalis* L., and the oriental arborvitae, *Thuja orientalis* L. are often planted in this region for ornamental purposes.

a. Male flowers, x ½.

b. Fruiting branch, x ½.

c. Seed, x 1.

PINACEAE

CALIFORNIA INCENSE-CEDAR

Libocedrus decurrens Torr.

HABIT. A medium-sized tree 80–120 feet high and 3–4 feet in diameter (max. 186 by 8 feet); tapering, often fluted trunk covered for up to half its length with lustrous, irregular foliage.

LEAVES. Small, scale-like; decussate; facial leaves flattened; the lateral keeled and almost ensheathing facial leaves; oblong-ovate; $\frac{1}{8}$–$\frac{1}{2}$ inch long; persistent 3–5 years; glandular; aromatic when crushed; fronds usually in a vertical plane.

FLOWERS. Monoecious; terminal; male oblong, golden, with 12–16 decussate 4-celled anthers; female oblong, yellow-green, of 6 scales, the inner 2 each bearing 2 erect ovules.

FRUIT. Leathery, pendent cones; $\frac{3}{4}$–$1\frac{1}{2}$ inches long; oblong; 6-scaled, with 2 becoming greatly enlarged and spreading at maturity; maturing in one season. Seed: $\frac{1}{3}$–$\frac{1}{2}$ inch long, in pairs on fertile scales, unequally laterally winged, straw-colored.

TWIGS. Slender; flattened; leaf-covered; in long sprays which are more often in a vertical plane than in a horizontal plane. Winter buds: minute, naked, inconspicuous.

BARK. Thin, smooth to scaly, and gray-green on young stems, becoming 3–8 inches thick, yellow-brown to cinnamon-red, fibrous, and deeply furrowed on old trees.

WOOD. Chief source of pencil stock; would be highly important for many uses except for prevalence of pecky rot; sapwood white; heartwood reddish, soft, fragrant.

SILVICAL CHARACTERS. Tolerant; growth rather slow; maturity reached in about 300 years; reproduction abundant and vigorous; moderately deep lateral root system; fire and pecky rot caused by *Polyporus amarus* cause extensive damage.

HABITAT. Transition zone; altitudinal range 1,000–9,000 feet; on cool, moist soils; in mixed stands with sugar, ponderosa, Jeffrey, and white pine, white fir, and Douglas-fir.

[69]

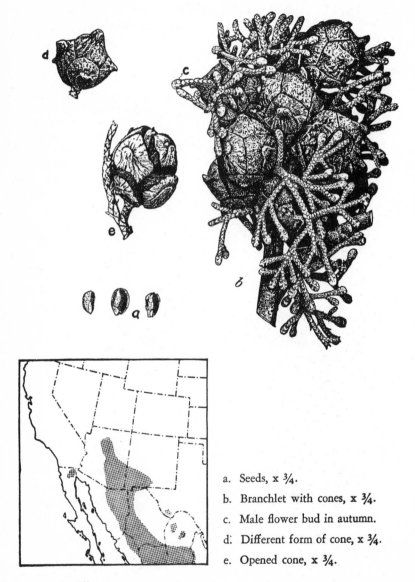

a. Seeds, x ¾.

b. Branchlet with cones, x ¾.

c. Male flower bud in autumn.

d. Different form of cone, x ¾.

e. Opened cone, x ¾.

PINACEAE

ARIZONA CYPRESS

Cupressus arizonica Greene

HABIT. Under favorable conditions a tree 50–60 feet high and 1–2½ feet in diameter (max. 80 by 4 feet); trunk short, limby, sharply tapering; crown dense, sharply conical (broad and rounded on poor sites) of short, stout, long-persisting, horizontal branches.

LEAVES. Scale-like, pointed, 1/16 inch long; silvery gray-green; dying and turning red-brown the second year and falling about 4 years later; commonly without glands or pits on back; giving off a skunklike odor when bruised.

FLOWERS. Male oblong, obtuse, yellow; female subglobose.

FRUIT. ¾–1 inch in diameter, subglobose, dark red-brown on stout stalks; of 6–8 peltate scales, each with stout, incurved, prominent boss; maturing during second summer and remaining on tree many years. Seed: 1/16–1/8 inch long, oblong to triangular, deep red-brown; thin, narrow, lateral wings.

TWIGS. 4-angled, dark gray, loose-scaly bark with smooth, reddish inner bark visible below. Winter buds: minute, inconspicuous, naked.

BARK. Loose-scaly on young trunks and branches, showing smooth reddish inner bark below; on old trunks 1¼ inches thick, fibrous, deeply furrowed and ridged, dark red-brown.

WOOD. Slightly aromatic; durable; heartwood light brown; sapwood straw-colored; soft and light, splitting easily; used locally for fence posts, mine timbers, etc.

SILVICAL CHARACTERS. Tolerant throughout life; growth slow; trees seldom found over 400 years old; in places repeated fires have destroyed stand; reproduction generally scanty, although seed produced abundantly every year, as conditions seldom favorable for germination.

HABITAT. Transition zone; altitudinal range from 4,500–8,000 feet; best growth on moist, gravelly, north slopes and benches, but hardy on dry, sterile, rocky sites; commonly in pure, open stands, but occasionally with Arizona pine and huckleberry oak.

a. Male flower bud in autumn.

b. Foliage and cones, x 1.

c. New shoot showing large form of leaves, x 1.

d. Seed, x 1.

e. Seed, x 2.

[72]

PINACEAE

SMOOTH CYPRESS

Cupressus arizonica var. *bonita* (Sudw.) Lemm.
(*Cupressus glabra* Sudw.)

HABIT. A tree 25–30 feet high and 10–14 inches in diameter; trunk tapering and upper portion sometimes divided into several branches; crown compact, conical, of strongly upright, stout, long-persistent branches.

LEAVES. Scale-like, pointed, $\frac{1}{16}$ inch long; glaucous, blue-green; dying and turning red-brown the second year and falling about 4 years later; with prominent, oblong or circular gland or pit on keeled back of nearly every leaf.

FLOWERS. Male oblong, obtuse, yellow; female subglobose.

FRUIT. $\frac{3}{4}$–1 inch in diameter, subglobose, dark red-brown, on stout stalks; peltate scales, each with stout, incurved boss (becoming less conspicuous on very old cones than it does in Arizona cypress); maturing second summer and often remaining on tree unopened for 14–18 years. Seed: $\frac{3}{16}$–$\frac{5}{16}$ inch long, oblong to triangular, deep red-brown; thin, narrow lateral wings.

TWIGS. Slender, 4-angled, dark gray, loose-scaly bark with smooth, reddish inner bark visible below. Winter buds: minute, inconspicuous, naked.

BARK. Thin, smooth, dark red-brown; superficially scaly on old trunks and becoming dark gray and fibrous.

WOOD. Slightly aromatic; durable; heartwood light brown; sapwood straw-colored; rather heavy and hard; used locally for fence posts, mine timbers, etc.

SILVICAL CHARACTERS. Tolerant throughout life; growth slow; reaching age of at least 200–250 years; reproduction generally scanty although seed produced abundantly every year, as conditions are seldom favorable for germination.

HABITAT. Transition and Upper Sonoran zones; altitudinal range from 3,700–7,000 feet; best growth on moist, sheltered slopes and benches, but hardy on dry, rocky soils; not abundant; in pure open stands or in mixture with nut pines, Arizona cypress, and oaks.

[73]

PINACEAE

THE JUNIPERS
Characteristics of the Genus *Juniperus* L.

HABIT. Evergreen, aromatic small trees or shrubs.

LEAVES. Persistent, sessile, aromatic; needle-like or awl-shaped on young growth; of three types on older growth; (1) ternate, spreading, jointed at base, and entirely needle-like or subulate; (2) decussate, appressed, decurrent, and entirely scalelike; (3) a combination of the preceding types.

FLOWERS. Dioecious (rarely monoecious); minute and inconspicuous; male yellow, solitary, of numerous ternate or decussate stamens; female of 3–8 decussate or ternate pointed scales, some or all bearing 1 or 2 ovules.

FRUIT. A berry-like, succulent, indehiscent cone, formed by coalescence of flower scales; subtended by persistent flower bracts; maturing in 1–3 years. Seed: 1–12 in cone, ovoid, unwinged, marked at base by a scar (hilum).

BUDS. Small, scaly, or naked and covered by leaves.

BARK. Thin, soft, shreddy (brittle, thick and divided into nearly square plates in one species).

WOOD. Durable; weak; close-grained; aromatic; heartwood red-purple to brown; sapwood whitish.

SILVICAL CHARACTERS. Exceedingly variable; mostly slow-growing; long-lived; seed disseminated by birds or mammals.

GENERAL. This genus contains 40–60 species widely scattered through the Northern Hemisphere, with 14 species native to the United States. Of the 12 species occurring in the Rocky Mountain region, 2 appear only as small shrubs:

(1) The dwarf juniper, *Juniperus communis* L., while circumpolar and extending through the region, attains tree size in North America only in southern Illinois; this species has ternate leaves, 1/3–1/2 inch long, which are all needle-like, and axillary flowers; the prostrate, high mountain form has been designated *J. communis* var. *montana* Ait. (*J. communis* var. *sibirica* Rydb.).

(2) The shrubby red cedar, *Juniperus sabina* var. *prostrata* Loud. (*J. horizontalis* Moench) entering Montana from the north, differs from dwarf juniper in having closely appressed, decussate leaves, 1/8–1/4 inch long.

[74]

KEY TO THE SPECIES OF JUNIPERUS

I. Leaves all needle-like or awl-shaped, $\frac{1}{3}$-$\frac{1}{2}$" long; buds scaly; a small shrub..........................1. *J. communis*, p. 74.

II. Leaves on mature branches scalelike, $\frac{1}{8}$" long or less; buds indistinct, naked; flowers terminal.

    A. Creeping shrub; Montana to Canada......2. *J. sabina*, p. 74.

    B. Small trees or large shrubs.

        1. Trunk bark in thick, squarish plates; fruit red-brown, $\frac{1}{2}$" long, usually 4-seeded, ripening in 2 years; southwest.............................3. *J. deppeana*, p. 87.

        2. Trunk bark fibrous and shreddy.

            a. 4-12 seeds in berry ($\frac{1}{3}$-$\frac{1}{4}$" long, red-brown, ripening in 2 years); drooping branchlets; Texas and Mexico....
.................................4. *J. flaccida*, p. 89.

            b. 1-3 seeds in berry; branchlets rarely drooping.

                (1) Berry bright red, $\frac{1}{4}$" long, 1-seeded; southwest.

                    (a) Seed with large, dark ridge band and 3 concavities..............5. *J. erythrocarpa*, p. 91.

                    (b) Seed different ....6. *J. pinchotii*, p. 91.

                (2) Berry dull red-brown or blue.

                    (a) Fruit red-brown; heartwood brown; seed single.

                        [(1)] Seed enclosed, with large hilum.

                            [(a)] Fruit $\frac{1}{4}$-$\frac{1}{3}$" long...........
.......7. *J. osteosperma*, p. 85.

                            [(b)] Fruit $\frac{1}{2}$-$\frac{3}{4}$" long...8. *J. utahensis*, var...*megalocarpa*, p. 85.

                        [(2)] Seed exposed at tip.................
............9. *J. gymnocarpa*, p. 81.

                  (b) Fruit bluish.

                        [(1)] Heartwood red; leaf margin smooth; berry 1-3 seeded...................
...........10. *J. scopulorum*, p. 79.

                      [(2)] Heartwood brown; leaves toothed (under lens).

                          [(a)] Berry with 2-3 thick-shelled seeds; Idaho and west.......
......11. *J. occidentalis*, p. 77.

                      [(b)] Berry with 1-2 thin-shelled seeds.

                          (1) Seed 1 (rarely 2), pale brown; leaves gray-green, acute, glandular; bark gray; south and central........
12. *J. monosperma*, p. 81.

                        (2) Seed 1-2, dark chestnut-brown; leaves blue-green, obtuse; bark red-brown; Texas and Mexico........
.......13. *J. ashei*, p. 83.

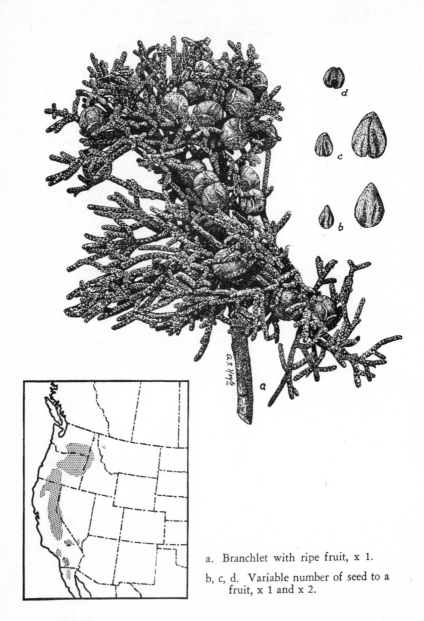

a. Branchlet with ripe fruit, x 1.

b, c, d. Variable number of seed to a
fruit, x 1 and x 2.

PINACEAE

SIERRA JUNIPER. WESTERN JUNIPER
Juniperus occidentalis Hook.

HABIT. In the Rocky Mountain region from a bushy shrub to a tree 15–30 feet high and seldom over 10 inches in diameter; short, conical, straight trunk; broad, rounded, open crown, extending nearly to ground, composed of enormous, nearly horizontal branches.

LEAVES. Ternate or decussate; closely appressed (may spread slightly at tip on young shoots); scalelike; about $\frac{1}{8}$ inch long; acute or acuminate; gray-green; conspicuously glandular-pitted on back; denticulately fringed.

FLOWERS. Dioecious; male stout, obtuse, of 12–18 stamens; female with ovate, acute, spreading scales, mostly obliterated from the fruit.

FRUIT. Glaucous; blue-black; berry-like; globose or ovoid; $\frac{1}{4}$–$\frac{1}{3}$ inch in diameter; flesh sweet, resinous, but scanty; skin tough, only slightly marked near top by tips of flower scales; maturing in 2 years. Seed: 2–3 in each cone; ovoid, acute, rounded and deeply grooved or pitted on back; flattened on inner surface; about $\frac{1}{8}$ inch long; thick, bony shell.

TWIGS. Stout, rounded, bright red-brown after leaves fall, and papery-scaly. Winter buds: naked, leaf-covered.

BARK. Thin ($\frac{1}{2}$–$1\frac{1}{4}$ inches); stringy; bright cinnamon-red; divided by shallow furrows into wide, flat ridges, which are superficially scaly.

WOOD. Heartwood pale brown tinged with red; sapwood white and thick; light, soft and brittle; like other brown-wooded junipers, exceedingly durable; used locally for posts and fuel.

SILVICAL CHARACTERS. Intolerant; growth slow; exceedingly long-lived, the largest trees probably 800–1,000 years or older; enormous long, large roots make it windfirm on most exposed sites; reproduction scanty although seed produced abundantly.

HABITAT. Upper Sonoran to Hudsonian zones; altitudinal range in Rocky Mountains between 2,000–9,000 feet (mostly above 6,000 feet); on exposed, dry, rocky, mountain slopes where few other species exist; usually in pure, very open stands.

[77]

a, b. Variable number of seed in fruit,
x 1 and x 2.

c. Branchlet with ripe fruit, x 1.

PINACEAE

ROCKY MOUNTAIN JUNIPER

Juniperus scopulorum Sarg.

HABIT. From a bushy shrub on exposed sites to a tree 40–55 feet high and 15–30 inches in diameter; trunk short and stout, often dividing near the ground; crown typically irregular and rounded, of thick, long, ascending branches, but in protected sites of long, slender, drooping branches.

LEAVES. Decussate; closely appressed; scalelike; about $\frac{1}{8}$ inch long; acute or acuminate; pale to dark green; obscurely glandular on back; smooth margins.

FLOWERS. Dioecious; male with about 6 stamens; female with spreading acute scales.

FRUIT. Glaucous; clear blue; berry-like; globose; $\frac{1}{4}$–$\frac{1}{3}$ inch in diameter; sweet, resinous flesh; thin skin maturing in 2 years. Seed: 1–2 (sometimes 3) in each cone; angled and acute; conspicuously grooved; marked at base with short, 2-lobed hilum; hard, bony outer coat.

TWIGS. Slender, leafy, 4-angled; becoming smooth, round, and pale brown. Winter buds: naked, leaf-covered.

BARK: Thin, soft, fibrous, stringy; red-brown or gray-brown; divided by shallow furrows into flat interlacing ridges, which are broken on the surface into persistent, shredded scales.

WOOD. Heartwood dull red or bright red and streaked with white; sapwood thick and white; durable, light, soft; could be substituted for eastern red cedar; used locally for posts and fuel; suitable for pencils and chests.

SILVICAL CHARACTERS. Moderately tolerant, appearance of trees in shaded situations differing markedly from open-grown species; growth very slow; ages of 300 years probably reached; deep, compact, uniformly spreading root system; reproduction rather sparse although seed produced abundantly.

HABITAT. Upper Sonoran and Transition zones; largest distribution of any western juniper; altitudinal range in Rocky Mountain region from 5,000–9,500 feet; very drought resistant; in pure stands or mixed with pinyon and ponderosa pine, Douglas-fir, oak, and narrowleaf cottonwood.

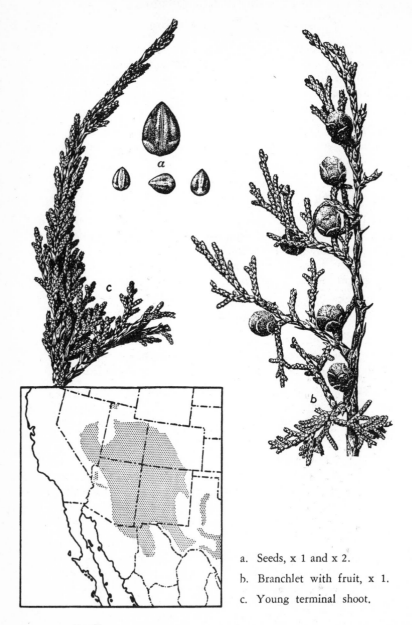

a. Seeds, x 1 and x 2.
b. Branchlet with fruit, x 1.
c. Young terminal shoot.

[80]

PINACEAE

ONE-SEED JUNIPER

Juniperus monosperma (Engelm.) Sarg.

[*Juniperus mexicana* var. *monosperma* (Engelm.) Cory.]

HABIT. A spreading shrub or small, profusely branched tree; rarely over 50 feet high and from 1–2 feet in diameter; crown open and very irregular; shrubby on desert sites as a result of large branches usually leaving the trunk at the root collar at or below the surface of the ground.

LEAVES. On old twigs decussate (rarely ternate), scalelike, slightly spreading at tips, ⅛ inch long, acute, gray-green, thickened and rounded on back, denticulately fringed, usually glandular; on vigorous shoots ternate, awl-shaped, ⅓–⅝ inch long, conspicuously glandular on back.

FLOWERS. Dioecious; male with 8–10 stamens; female with spreading, pointed scales.

FRUIT. Glaucous; copper-colored (rarely blue); berry-like; subglobose; ⅛–¼ inch long; thin-fleshed; maturing in one year. Seed: 1 (rarely 2) in each cone; ovoid; often 4-angled; obtuse; marked at base by small 2-lobed hilum.

TWIGS. Slender, leafy, 4-angled, becoming round, red-brown, and loosely scaly. Winter buds: naked, leaf-covered.

BARK. Thin (¼–¾ inch), soft, fibrous, stringy; ash-gray; separated by narrow, deep furrows into narrow, flat ridges.

WOOD. Heartwood yellow-brown to red-brown; sapwood white; durable; rather heavy and hard; used for posts and fuel.

SILVICAL CHARACTERS. Intolerant with age; growth slow; probably reaching age of 500 years; reproduction scanty.

HABITAT. Upper Sonoran zone; altitudinal range from 3,500–7,000 feet; growing on very dry, rocky, high desert plains and mountain slopes; in pure, open stands or with Utah, Pinchot's, and alligator junipers, pinyon and ponderosa pines.

GENERAL. A Southwestern form with a single seed exposed at the apex, formerly given specific rank as open-seed juniper (J. gymnocarpa (Lemm.) Cory is now considered a form of *J. monosperma.*)

a. Variable forms and numbers
   of seed in fruit, x 1 and x 2.

b. Branchlet with fruit, x 1.

PINACEAE

Mexican Juniper. Ashe Juniper

Juniperus ashei Buchholz (*Juniperus mexicana* Spreng.)
[*Juniperus sabinoides* (H.B.K.) Nees.]

HABIT. A spreading shrub or small tree; normally 12–20 feet high and 8–12 inches in diameter (max. 35 by 1½ feet); trunk short, crooked, and generally divided near the ground into large, ascending branches; often a many-stemmed shrub on dry, exposed sites; crown irregular and mostly open.

LEAVES. On old twigs decussate, scalelike, $\frac{1}{16}$ inch long, sharp-pointed, roughish and prickly to touch, dark blue-green, thickened and keeled on back, denticulately fringed, mostly without glands; on vigorous shoots ternate, lanceolate, ¼–½ inch long, rigid, sharp-pointed.

FLOWERS. Dioecious; male with 12–18 stamens; female with ovate, acute, spreading scales.

FRUIT. Glaucous; deep blue; berry-like; subglobose; ¼–½ inch long; thin, pungent, sweet flesh; thick, tough skin; maturing in one season. Seed: 1–2 in each cone; ovoid; acute; slightly grooved at top; marked at base with low, narrow hilum; thin outer coat.

TWIGS. Slender, leafy, 4-angled; becoming round and light red-brown or ash-gray. Winter buds: naked, leaf-covered.

BARK. Thin (¼–½ inch), stringy and fibrous; brown or red-brown; furrowed and ridged or scaly.

WOOD. Heartwood cinnamon-brown and streaked; sapwood very thin and whitish; light, rather hard, brittle, very narrow-ringed, and durable; used for poles, posts, light traffic railroad ties, and fuel.

SILVICAL CHARACTERS. Very tolerant in youth, becoming less so with age; growth slow; rather long-lived; reproduction plentiful with abundant seed produced.

HABITAT. Upper Sonoran zone; altitudinal range in the United States from 600–2,000 feet; here it occurs in dense, pure, often almost impenetrable stands (cedar breaks), or in mixture with Pinchot and one-seed junipers, Mexican walnut, oaks, elm, and hackberry; on dry, rocky, gravelly, or sandy soils.

[83]

a. Narrow side of seeds, x 1 and x 2.

b. Broad side of seeds, x 1 and x 2.

c. Branchlet with ripe fruit, x 1.

PINACEAE
Utah Juniper
Juniperus osteosperma (Torr.) Little
[*Juniperus utahensis* (Engelm.) Lemm.]

HABIT. A spreading shrub or small tree; rarely over 20 feet high or 12 inches in diameter; trunk single, or many-stemmed just above the ground; crown rounded.

LEAVES. On old twigs decussate, scalelike, ⅛ inch long, acute or acuminate, pale yellow-green, minutely toothed, usually glandular, long persistent; on vigorous shoots ternate, awl-shaped, much larger, sharp-pointed.

FLOWERS. Usually monoecious, sometimes dioecious; male with 18–24 stamens; female with acute, spreading scales.

FRUIT. Glaucous; red-brown; berry-like; subglobose; ¼–⅓ inch long; thin, dry, sweet flesh; smooth, tough skin; maturing in 2 years. Seed: 1 (rarely 2) in each cone; ovoid; sharply angled; acute; marked to the middle by a conspicuous hilum; hard, bony outer coat.

TWIGS. Slender, rounded, stiff-looking; yellow-green with thin red-brown scales. Winter buds: naked, leaf-covered.

BARK. Thin (¼–⅜ inch); ash-gray to gray-white; divided into long, thin, persistent, fibrous scales.

WOOD. Heartwood light yellow-brown; sapwood thick and white; very durable; used locally for fuel and fence posts.

SILVICAL CHARACTERS. Intolerant with age; growth slow; probably reaching age of 300 years; reproduction scanty although seed produced abundantly.

HABITAT. Upper Sonoran zone; altitudinal range from 5,000–7,000 feet; on dry, rocky to sandy, desert foothills and mountain slopes; mostly in pure stands or with one-seed juniper, singleleaf pinyon, and desert shrubs.

A form often considered a variety of the Utah juniper is the bigberry juniper (*Juniperus utahensis* var. *megalocarpa* Sarg.). This is a rare tree restricted to the south rim of the Grand Canyon and to the Sacramento River Valley in southwestern New Mexico; it can be identified by its large fruit (½–¾ inch in diameter). *Juniperus knightii* A. Nels., reported from the Red Desert of Wyoming, is considered a synonym of *J. osteosperma.*

[85]

a. Variable forms and numbers of seed in fruit, x 1 and x 2.

b. Branchlet with ripe fruit, x 1.

PINACEAE

ALLIGATOR JUNIPER

Juniperus deppeana Steud. (*Juniperus pachyphloea* Torr.)

HABIT. A spreading shrub or small to medium-sized tree, 30–50 feet high and 18–32 inches in diameter (max. 60 by 6 feet); trunk short; crown broad, compact, with long, stout, spreading branches.

LEAVES. On old twigs decussate, scalelike, ⅛ inch long, acute, blue-green, minutely toothed, small but conspicuously glandular; on vigorous shoots linear-lanceolate, keenly pointed, pale blue-green.

FLOWERS. Monoecious; male with 10–12 stamens; female with ovate, acuminate, spreading scales.

FRUIT. More or less glaucous; dark red-brown; berry-like; subglobose; ⅓–½ inch long; thick, dry, mealy flesh; thin skin, often with knobby protuberances; usually marked with short tips of flower scales; occasionally opening and discharging the seed at apex; maturing in 2 years. Seed: 1–4 (usually 4) in each cone; acute or obtuse, distinctly grooved; conspicuously swollen on back; marked at base by short, 2-lobed hilum; thick outer shell.

TWIGS. Slender; 4-angled in leaf, becoming red-brown, smooth or rarely scaly. Winter buds: naked, leaf-covered.

BARK. Very characteristic; ½–4 inches thick; red-brown or gray-brown; deeply furrowed, with flat ridges cut into nearly square plates 1–2 inches across, giving tree its common name.

WOOD. Heartwood clear red-brown, often streaked with yellow; sapwood thin and white; durable, light, soft, and brittle; much used locally for fuel and fence posts, suitable for pencils.

SILVICAL CHARACTERS. Intolerant; growth slow; very long-lived, probably reaching 500–800 years; reproduces plentifully; stumps sprout vigorously.

HABITAT. Upper Sonoran and Transition zones; altitudinal range from 4,500–8,400 feet; extremely hardy and drought resistant; typically on dry, sterile, rocky soils; of frequent occurrence in scattered, pure stands or more commonly mixed with nut pines and oaks.

[87]

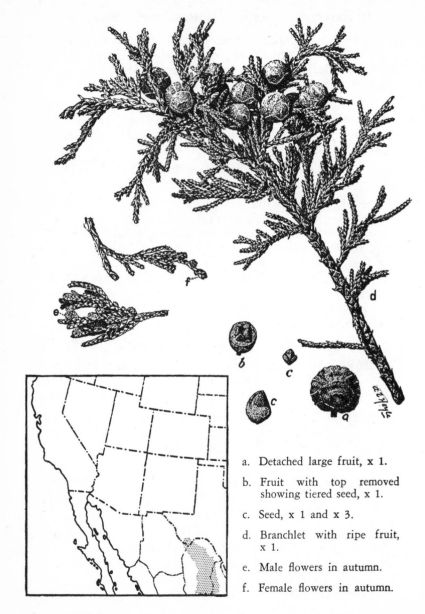

a. Detached large fruit, x 1.

b. Fruit with top removed showing tiered seed, x 1.

c. Seed, x 1 and x 3.

d. Branchlet with ripe fruit, x 1.

e. Male flowers in autumn.

f. Female flowers in autumn.

PINACEAE

DROOPING JUNIPER

Juniperus flaccida Schlecht.

HABIT. A spreading shrub or a small tree from 8–30 feet high and 3–20 inches in diameter; trunk straight and clear on better sites; crown open, pyramidal, of widespreading, ascending, graceful branches ending in slender, drooping branchlets.

LEAVES. On old twigs decussate, scalelike, ⅛ inch long, acuminate and long-pointed, slightly spreading at apex and prickly, light yellow-green, dying on branch and turning cinnamon-red, minutely toothed, with or without glands; on vigorous shoots ternate or opposite, ovate-lanceolate ¼–½ inch long, bristle-pointed.

FLOWERS. Dioecious; male of 16–20 stamens; female with acute or acuminate spreading scales.

FRUIT. More or less glaucous; dull red-brown; berrylike; subglobose; ⅓–⅝ inch long; thick, hard, dry, resinous flesh; close, firm skin, often with knobby protuberances, distinctly marked by tips of flower scales; maturing in 2 years. Seed: 4–12 in each cone; in several tiers; irregularly shaped; pointed; often abortive; ⅛–¼ inch long.

TWIGS. Slender; drooping; thin, loosely scaly, bright, cinnamon-brown bark. Winter buds: naked, leaf-covered.

BARK. ½–1½ inches thick; red-brown (externally gray); firm; fibrous, and separating into long, narrow, loosely attached scales.

WOOD. Heartwood clear yellow-brown; sapwood thick and white; durable; rather heavy and hard; used locally for posts, mine timbers, and fuel.

SILVICAL CHARACTERS. Tolerant; growth slow; long-lived, probably reaching 400–500 years; reproduction fair on good sites.

HABITAT. Upper Sonoran and Transition zones; essentially a Mexican tree with altitudinal range from 6,000–8,000 feet; best in moist cañons but hardy on dry, rocky, exposed sites; in small, pure groups or mixed with alligator juniper, Mexican pinyon, and hardwoods.

[89]

a. Branchlet with fruit, x 1.

b. Seed, x 1 and x 4.

PINACEAE

PINCHOT JUNIPER. REDBERRY JUNIPER
Juniperus pinchotii Sudw.

HABIT. A spreading shrub with several stems 1–12 feet tall, or small tree rarely 20 feet high and 1 foot in diameter; open, irregular crown with stout, widespreading branches.

LEAVES. On old twigs ternate, scalelike, $\frac{1}{16}$ inch long, obtusely pointed, dark yellow-green and turning light red-brown before falling, glandular-pitted and keeled on back, margins entire; on vigorous shoots linear-lanceolate, spreading, thin, acuminate, $\frac{1}{4}$–$\frac{1}{3}$ inch long.

FLOWERS. Dioecious; male not seen; female with spreading pointed scales.

FRUIT. Bright red (rarely copper-colored); berry-like; subglobose; $\frac{1}{4}$ inch long; thick, dry, mealy, resinous flesh; thin skin; maturing in one year. Seed: 1 seed in each cone (rarely 2); bluntly pointed; ovoid; deeply grooved; $\frac{1}{8}$–$\frac{1}{4}$ inch long; irregularly marked by usually 2-lobed hilum.

TWIGS. Thick to rather slender; with dark, gray-brown, scaly bark. Winter buds: naked, leaf-covered.

BARK. Thin; gray-brown; shallowly furrowed and separating into long, narrow, persistent scales; inner bark dull brown.

WOOD. Heartwood light brown, slightly tinged with red; sapwood light-colored; only moderately durable; rather soft; close-grained; used for posts and fuel.

SILVICAL CHARACTERS. Intolerant; rather slow-growing; reproduction sparse, although seed produced abundantly; stumps sprout vigorously and repeatedly, enabling tree to exist in region of common grass fires; related to *Juniperus gigantea* K. Koch of Mexico.

HABITAT. Upper Sonoran zone; altitudinal range from about 2,000–5,000 feet; on dry, grassy cañon bottoms or rocky, mountain slopes; local and rare; associated with *J. monosperma*. The Arizona distribution shown for this species is uncertain.

* * *

A related form with a bright red fruit, but differing in that the single seed is marked by a large dark-colored ridge band and 3 concavities, has been reported from southwestern Texas and Coahuila, Mexico, and named the Redberry juniper, *Juniperus erythrocarpa* Cory.

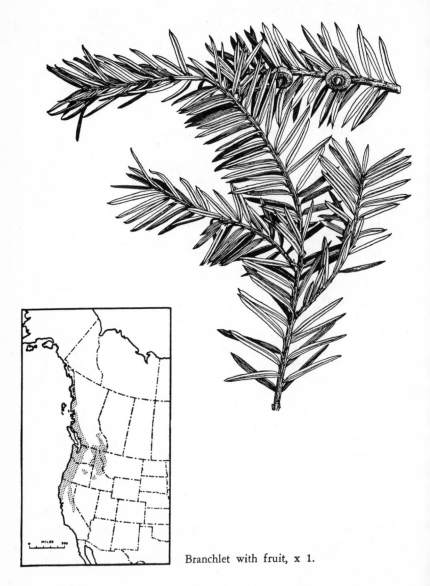

Branchlet with fruit, x 1.

TAXACEAE

PACIFIC YEW. WESTERN YEW
Taxus brevifolia Nutt.

HABIT. A small tree or large shrub, 20–50 feet high and 1–2 feet in diameter; limby, often fluted or malformed trunks; large, open, conical crown, with long, slender, drooping branches; a sprawling shrub near timber line.

LEAVES. Persistent; linear-lanceolate; spirally arranged, appearing 2-ranked; ½–1 inch long; sharp-pointed; petiolate; green above, paler beneath.

FLOWERS. Dioecious, solitary axillary, on twigs of previous season, surrounded by scales of bud; male in globose heads of 6–14 stamens each with 5–9 anthers, yellowish; female single, greenish, of several scales, the apical scale bearing a solitary erect ovule with a basal disk.

FRUIT. A single, erect, ovoid-oblong seed with a hard, bony shell; ⅓ inch long; exposed at apex, but partially or entirely surrounded by, but free from, the thickened, scarlet, fleshy aril-like disk of the flower; maturing in one season.

TWIGS. Slender, drooping. Winter buds: small, ovoid, obtuse; of numerous overlapping scales.

BARK. Very thin (¼ inch), scaly, dark red-purple.

WOOD. Heavy, hard, strong; often with spiral grain; durable; heartwood bright orange to rose-red; sapwood thin, yellow; unimportant, but used for bows, canoe paddles, fence posts, and turned articles.

SILVICAL CHARACTERS. Most tolerant forest tree of northwest; growth slow; maturity reached in 250–350 years; reproduction scanty to rare; deep, widespreading root system; largest trunks often with spiral grain and hollow butt.

HABITAT. Transition to Hudsonian zone; altitudinal range from 2,000–8,000 feet; on deep, moist soils; in small groups or singly as an occasional understory tree in mixed coniferous forests.

GENERAL. This genus contains about 5 species in Asia and North America. Three species are native to the United States.

a. Leaves, x ⅓.
b. Fruit, x 1.
c. Pistillate flowers, x 1.
d. Staminate flowers, x ⅔.

JUGLANDACEAE

LITTLE WALNUT. TEXAS BLACK WALNUT

Juglans microcarpa Ber. (*Juglans rupestris* Engelm.)

HABIT. A shrub or small tree seldom over 20–30 feet high and 18–30 inches in diameter; trunk often crooked; bushy, round-topped crown with large, stout branches.

LEAVES. Alternate; unequally pinnately compound; with 17–23 (rarely 13 or 15), narrow-lanceolate, acuminate, often falcate leaflets 2–3 inches long and ⅓–⅔ inch wide; finely serrate or nearly entire; thin; light green; mostly glabrous; deciduous; rachis round, grooved; stipules absent.

FLOWERS. Regular; monoecious; staminate in slender, axillary aments 3–4 inches long, with yellow-green, 3–5 lobed calyx and about 20 stamens; pistillate in few-flowered, terminal spikes with 1–3-celled ovary free only at apex; appearing after the unfolding of the leaves.

FRUIT. Drupaceous, consisting of a fleshy, indehiscent husk enclosing a hard, thick-walled nut; ½–¾ inch in diameter; subglobose; pubescent; tipped with remnant of calyx.

TWIGS. Rather slender; round; pubescent and orange-red at first, becoming glabrous and ash-gray; marked by pale lenticels and large, 3–lobed leaf scars; pith partitioned into chambers. Winter buds: terminal ¼–½ inch long, scaly, compressed, tomentose; lateral ⅛ inch long, pubescent.

BARK. Rather thick; dark; furrowed and scaly ridged.

WOOD. Heavy; hard; not strong; durable; diffuse-porous; heartwood dark brown; sapwood thick, whitish; unimportant; stumps used for veneer.

SILVICAL CHARACTERS. Lower and Upper Sonoran zones; intolerant; borders of streams on desert, mountain sites; in rocky soils, often of limestone origin; deep taproot.

* * *

The Arizona walnut or Nogal, *Juglans major* (Torr.) Heller (*J. rupestris* var. *major* Torr.), with larger, usually 9–13 (rarely 15–19), oblong-lanceolate to ovate, coarsely serrate leaflets and fruit 1–1½ inches in diameter, is the form found in western New Mexico, Arizona, and Colorado. Both distributions are included on the map. The eastern black walnut, *Juglans nigra* L., is extensively planted in this region and can be recognized by its larger fruit (1½–2 inches in diameter.)

[95]

SALICACEAE

The Poplars and Cottonwoods

Characteristics of the Genus *Populus* L.

HABIT. Mostly large, fast-growing, short-lived deciduous trees with bitter bark.

LEAVES. Alternate; simple; usually ovate or ovate-lanceolate; entire, dentate, or lobed; pinnately veined; turning yellow before falling in autumn; petioles mostly long and often laterally compressed; stipules present, falling as leaves unfold.

FLOWERS. Regular; dioecious; both sexes in drooping aments; appearing from separate buds, before the leaves; individual flowers solitary, apetalous, inserted on broad, cup-shaped disk, subtended by dilated, lobed, and often laciniate scale or bract; staminate with 4 to many stamens; pistillate a single, 1-celled, usually sessile ovary with 2–4 placentas and 2–4 stigmas on a usually short style.

FRUIT. A 1-celled, 2–4-valved capsule containing numerous seeds. Seed: small, tufted with long silky hairs, extremely light and buoyant; vitality transient and germination must take place within few days.

TWIGS. Slender to stout; round or angled; mostly olive-brown to lustrous red-brown; marked by persistent ringlike or deltoid leaf scars; pith homogeneous, stellate in cross section. Winter buds: terminal present, resinous or nonresinous, covered by several imbricated scales; lateral similar and not much smaller; flower buds conspicuously larger.

BARK. Astringent; light-colored; deeply furrowed or smooth.

WOOD. Light; soft; weak; brittle; diffuse-porous; not durable; heartwood light brown to whitish; used for pulp and light weight lumber.

SILVICAL CHARACTERS. Intolerant; fast-growing; short-lived; reproduction widespread and abundant; stumps and roots sprout vigorously; extensive, widespreading root systems; mostly moisture-loving trees.

GENERAL. This genus contains about 35 species scattered over the Northern Hemisphere and in Northern Africa; 13 to 15 species are native to North America, and 7 of these are listed as occurring in the Rocky Mountain region. Species cultivated in the Rocky Mountain region include European White Poplar, *P. alba,* L., Carolina poplar, *P.* X *canadensis* Moench., and Lombardy poplar, *P. nigra* var *italica* Muen.

[96]

KEY TO THE SPECIES OF POPULUS

I. Petioles not flattened laterally; leaves mostly at least ⅓ longer than broad, without definite translucent border.
  A. Leaves ovate to ovate-lanceolate, whitish below; terminal bud ¾–1″ long, ovoid, resinous-sticky.
    1. Ovary and capsule usually pubescent, mostly subglobose, 3-valved; stigmas 3; stamens 40–60, anthers purple; leaves ⅓ or less longer than broad; Pacific region........
    ....1. *P. trichocarpa,* p. 99.
    2. Ovary and capsule glabrous, ovoid-oblong, 2-valved; stigmas 2; stamens 20–30 with pink anthers; leaves mostly twice as long as broad; through northern North America......................2. *P. balsamifera,* p. 101.
  B. Leaves lanceolate to ovate-lanceolate, green on both surfaces; terminal bud less than ¾″ long, slender.
    1. Leaves lanceolate to ovate-lanceolate; petioles ⅓ length of blade or less; buds 5-scaled, aromatic, rather sticky...
    ....3. *P. angustifolia,* p. 103.
    2. Leaves ovate- to rhombic-lanceolate; petioles at least ½ length of blade; buds 6–7–scaled, nonaromatic, not sticky........................4. *P.* X *acuminata,* p. 105.
II. Petioles flattened laterally; leaves little or no longer than broad, with definite translucent border (except in 5).
  A. Leaves broadly ovate to suborbicular, 1–3″ in diameter, finely serrate; bark smooth; buds conical; stigmas 2, filiform.....
  ....5. *P. tremuloides,* p. 107.
  B. Leaves deltoid, 2–4″ long, coarsely serrate; bark furrowed; buds ovoid; stigmas 3–4, broad.
    1. Pedicels longer than capsules; leaves with not more than 10 teeth on a side; Texas, New Mexico, to central Colorado.................6. *P. fremontii wislizenii,* p. 109.
    2. Pedicels shorter than capsules; leaves with more than 10 teeth on a side.
      a. Buds puberulous; leaves with glands at apex of petiole; eastern foothills of Rocky Mountains.................
      ....7. *P. sargentii,* p. 111.
      b. Buds glabrous; leaves without glands at apex of petiole; western New Mexico and Utah to California..
      ....8. *P. fremontii,* p. 113.

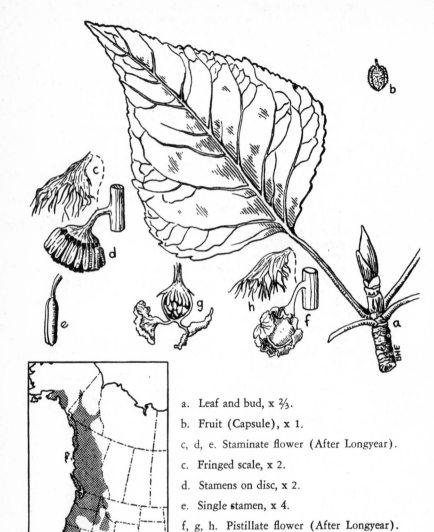

a. Leaf and bud, x ⅔.

b. Fruit (Capsule), x 1.

c, d, e. Staminate flower (After Longyear).

c. Fringed scale, x 2.

d. Stamens on disc, x 2.

e. Single stamen, x 4.

f, g, h. Pistillate flower (After Longyear).

f. Single flower, x 2.

g. Cross section of ovary with stigmas attached.

h. Fringed scale, x 2.

SALICACEAE

BLACK COTTONWOOD

Populus trichocarpa Torr. & Gray

HABIT. The largest of American poplars and the largest broad-leaved tree in the Pacific Northwest; in the Rocky Mountain region it is seldom more than 100 feet high; long, clear, cylindrical trunk; crown open, rounded.

LEAVES. Ovate to ovate-lanceolate; 5–6 inches long and 3–4 inches wide; apex acute to long-acuminate; base rounded or slightly cordate; margin finely crenate to crenate-serrate; rather thick and leathery; dark green and glabrous above, silver-white to pale green or rusty-brown below; petioles round, long.

FLOWERS. Aments stalked, villose-pubescent to glabrous; bracts filiformly lobed; staminate in dense aments, each flower with 40–60, long-stalked, purple stamens; pistillate in loose aments, disk cup-shaped, ovary usually hoary-tomentose and subglobose with 3 nearly sessile, lobed stigmas.

FRUIT. Capsules subglobose; $\frac{1}{3}$ inch long; 3-valved; nearly sessile; mostly pubescent. Seed: $\frac{1}{12}$ inch long.

TWIGS. Moderately slender; round or slightly angled; glabrous or pubescent and red-brown at first, becoming glabrous and dark gray; marked by numerous orange lenticels and roughened by greatly enlarged and thickened elevated leaf scars. Winter buds: terminal $\frac{3}{4}$ inch long and $\frac{1}{4}$ inch broad; ovoid; curved; long-pointed; orange-brown; with 6–7 scales; covered by fragrant, yellow-brown resin.

BARK. Smooth and greenish on young stems; becoming pale gray, 1–$2\frac{1}{2}$ inches thick, deeply and sharply furrowed.

SILVICAL CHARACTERS. Upper Sonoran to Canadian zones; very intolerant; shallow-rooted; on moist sandy or gravelly sites; in pure stands or in mixture with conifers.

GENERAL. According to Sudworth, the black cottonwood is replaced by the variety, *Populus trichocarpa* var. *hastata* (Dode) Henry, in the southern part of its range. Other taxonomists do not recognize the variety, holding that the differences between it and the species are too variable to be valid. The distribution of both species and variety is included on the map.

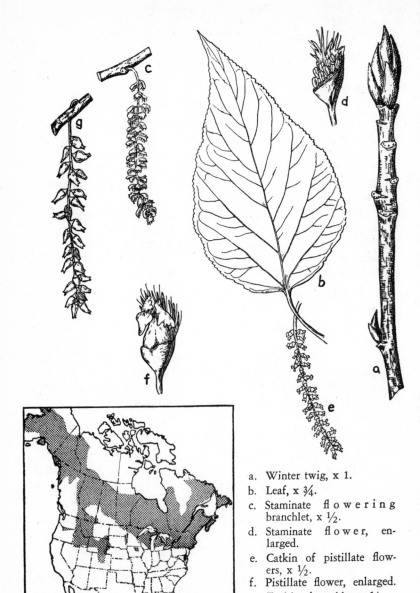

a. Winter twig, x 1.
b. Leaf, x ¾.
c. Staminate flowering branchlet, x ½.
d. Staminate flower, enlarged.
e. Catkin of pistillate flowers, x ½.
f. Pistillate flower, enlarged.
g. Fruiting branchlet, x ½.

SALICACEAE

BALSAM POPLAR

Populus balsamifera L. (*Populus tacamahacca* Mill.)

HABIT. A medium-sized tree seldom over 60-80 feet high and 1–3 feet in diameter; long, cylindrical trunk; open, narrow, irregular, pyramidal crown with rather erect branches.

LEAVES. Broadly ovate to ovate-lanceolate; 3–6 inches long and 2–4 inches broad; apex abruptly acute to acuminate; base rounded or cordate; finely crenate-serrate; thin and firm; lustrous dark green and glabrous above, much paler, conspicuously veined and commonly with rusty blotches below; petioles round, slender, pubescent and 2–3½ inches long.

FLOWERS. Aments long-stalked; bracts filiformly lobed; staminate in dense aments, each flower having 20–30 light red, short-stalked stamens; pistillate becoming 4-5 inches long, each glabrous ovary with 2 large, nearly sessile stigmas.

FRUIT. Capsules ovoid; ¼–⅓ inch long; 2-valved; glabrous; short-stalked. Seed: light brown, ¹⁄₁₂ inch long.

TWIGS. Moderately stout; round; red-brown and glabrous or pubescent at first, becoming lustrous and gray or orange-brown; marked by bright orange lenticels and roughened by thickened leaf scars. Winter buds: terminal 1 inch long, ⅓ inch broad; ovoid; terete; long-pointed; chestnut-brown; covered by 5 scales; saturated by fragrant, amber-colored resin.

BARK. On young trunks smooth or roughened by dark protuberances and green-brown to red-brown; on large trunks deeply furrowed, widely ridged, and gray to gray-black.

SILVICAL CHARACTERS. Canadian and Hudsonian zones; intolerant; characteristic of moist alluvial bottom-lands and stream banks; reaching greatest size in northwestern Canada.

GENERAL. The variety *candicans* (Ait.) Stout, differs from the species in having leaves which are usually broader, cordate at the base, pubescent beneath along the veins and with pubescent petioles. The ornamental form of this variety is called the Balm-of-Gilead poplar and is known only in pistillate form. It is thought to be either a hybrid or a clon from a single pistillate tree.

[101]

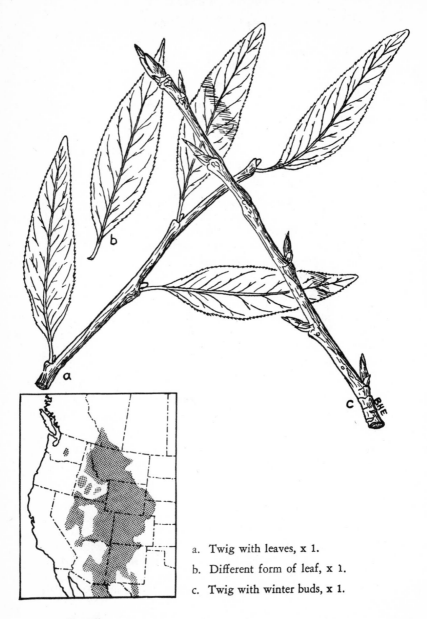

a. Twig with leaves, x 1.
b. Different form of leaf, x 1.
c. Twig with winter buds, x 1.

SALICACEAE

Narrowleaf Cottonwood

Populus angustifolia James

HABIT. A medium-sized tree 50–70 feet high and 12–20 inches in diameter; crown open and pyramidal with rather slender, erect branches.

LEAVES. Lanceolate to ovate-lanceolate, rarely elliptical or obovate; 2–4 inches long and ½–1½ inches wide, on vigorous shoots sometimes 6–7 inches long and 1½ inches wide; apex long-tapering and acute or rounded; cuneate or rounded at base; finely to coarsely serrate; slightly revolute margin; thin and firm; bright yellow-green above, paler and usually glabrous below; petioles short (less than ⅓ length of blade), slender, somewhat flattened on upper side.

FLOWERS. Aments densely flowered, glabrous, short-stalked, 1–2½ inches long; bracts light brown, glabrous, scarious, deeply filiformly lobed; staminate with 12–30 short-stalked, large, red stamens; pistillate with cup-shaped disk, each ovary with style ending in 2 oblique stigmas.

FRUIT. Capsules broadly ovoid; ¼ inch long; thin-walled; 2-valved; often abruptly contracted above middle; short-pointed; short-stalked; on cup-shaped disk. Seed: light brown, hairy, nearly ⅛ inch long.

TWIGS. Slender; round; yellow-green or orange, becoming ash-gray; marked by pale lenticels and small, oval leaf scars. Winter buds: terminal ¼–¾ inch long, slender, long-pointed, with usually 5 scales, chestnut-brown, resinous and somewhat aromatic.

BARK. Light yellow-green; ¾–1 inch thick; smooth except near base of old trees where it is divided by shallow furrows into broad ridges.

SILVICAL CHARACTERS. Upper Sonoran, Transition, and Canadian zones; decidedly intolerant; short-lived; on banks of streams at altitudes of 5,000–10,000 feet; frequently planted as street tree in Rocky Mountain region, especially at high altitudes.

[103]

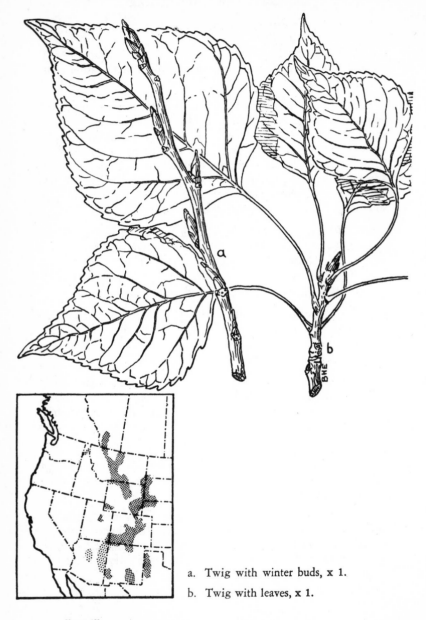

a. Twig with winter buds, x 1.

b. Twig with leaves, x 1.

SALICACEAE

LANCELEAF COTTONWOOD
Populus X *acuminata* Rydb.

HABIT. A medium-sized tree about 40 feet high and 1–2 feet in diameter (larger under cultivation); dense, rounded crown with large spreading and ascending branches.

LEAVES. Rhombic-lanceolate to ovate; 2–4 inches long and ¾–2 inches wide; apex abruptly acuminate; base narrowed and usually cuneate; coarsely crenate-serrate; rather thick and leathery; dark green and lustrous above, dull green below; petioles nearly round, slender, 1–3 inches long.

FLOWERS. Aments slender, short-stalked, loosely flowered, 2–3 inches long; bracts light brown, scarious, glabrous, deeply filiformly lobed; staminate with wide oblique disk containing 15–20 short-stalked, red stamens; pistillate with deep, cup-shaped disk, ovary glabrous and broadly ovoid with nearly sessile, irregularly lobed stigmas.

FRUIT. Capsules oblong-ovoid; about ⅓ inch long; thin-walled; acute; 3- or rarely 2-valved; on short, slender stalks. Seed: light brown, hairy, about 1/12 inch long.

TWIGS. Slender; round or slightly 4-angled; pale yellow-brown; roughened by elevated, oval, horizontal leaf scars. Winter buds: terminal about ⅓–¾ inch long, narrow, glabrous, acuminate, with 6–7 scales, light chestnut-brown, rather resinous and nonaromatic.

BARK. Nearly white and smooth on young trunks; on old trees gray-brown, ½ inch thick, deeply divided into flat ridges.

SILVICAL CHARACTERS. Upper Sonoran and Transition zones; very intolerant; along stream banks in rather arid habitats; sometimes planted as shade tree in Rocky Mountain region.

GENERAL. *Populus* X *acuminata* has come to be regarded as a hybrid between *P. angustifolia* and *P. sargentii* with wide distribution within their overlapping ranges. Where recorded outside the range of *P. sargentii*, as in Arizona, it is thought to be a hybrid between *P. angustifolia* and some other broad-leaved species.

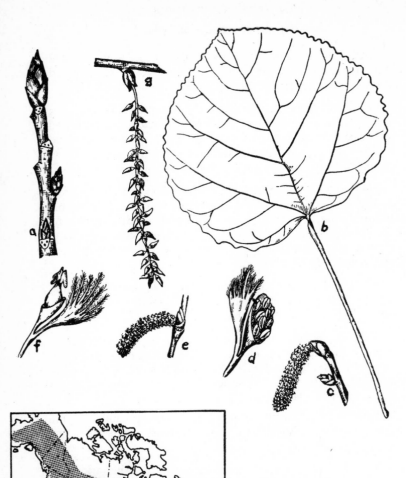

a. Winter twig, x 2.

b. Leaf, x 1.

c. Staminate flowering branchlet, x ½.

d. Staminate flower, enlarged.

e. Pistillate flowering branchlet, x ½.

f. Pistillate flower, enlarged.

g. Fruiting branchlet, x ½.

SALICACEAE

QUAKING ASPEN. POPLAR

Populus tremuloides Michx.

HABIT. A small to medium-sized tree seldom over 50–60 feet high and 1–2 feet in diameter; loose, rounded crown with slender, often contorted branches.

LEAVES. Semiorbicular or broadly ovate to rhombic; 1½–3 inches in diameter; apex abruptly acute to acuminate; base rounded; finely crenate-serrate with glandular teeth; thin and firm; green and lustrous above, dull or pale below; glabrous; turning golden yellow in autumn; petioles flattened, 1½–3 inches long.

FLOWERS. Aments 1½–3 inches long, the pistillate gradually becoming longer; bracts deeply 3–5-lobed and fringed with long hairs; staminate with entire, oblique disk containing 6–12 stamens; pistillate with crenate disk, each ovary with short style and 2, erect, 2-lobed, slender, red stigmas.

FRUIT. Capsules narrowly conical; ¼ inch long; curved; 2-valved; gray-hairy when opening. Seed: light brown, 1/32 inch long.

TWIGS. Slender; round; bright red-brown and lustrous, becoming gray; marked by orange lenticels and roughened by elevated leaf scars. Winter buds: terminal ¼–½ inch long, conical, sharp-pointed, red-brown, covered by 6-7 visible scales, sometimes slightly resinous.

BARK. Smooth; green-white to cream-colored; often marked by dark, wartlike protuberances; becoming dark and furrowed near base of old trunks.

SILVICAL CHARACTERS. Canadian and Hudsonian zones; shallow-rooted; exceedingly intolerant; a prolific seeder, reproducing vigorously on cut-over or burned-over areas and forming a protective canopy for more tolerant species; in the Rocky Mountains reproduction is largely from suckers.

GENERAL. Some authors consider the western form a separate variety. *P. tremuloides* var. *aurea* (Tides.) Daniels, however it differs from the species by relatively trivial characters.

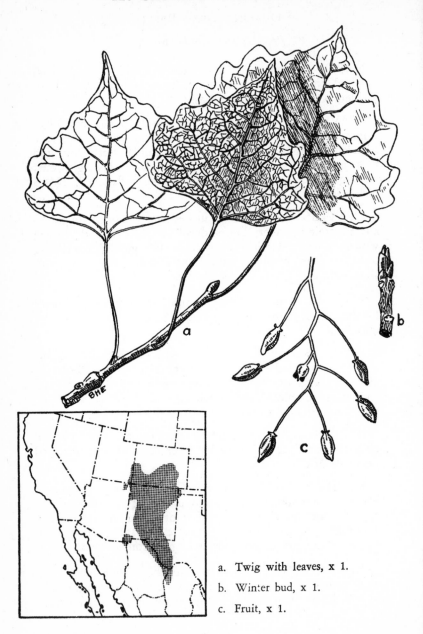

a. Twig with leaves, x 1.

b. Winter bud, x 1.

c. Fruit, x 1.

SALICACEAE

RIO GRANDE COTTONWOOD

Populus fremontii var. *wislizenii* S. Wats.

[*Populus wislizenii* (S. Wats.) Sarg.]

HABIT. A large tree from 40–100 feet high and 2–4 or more feet in diameter; broad, rather flat crown with large, wide-spreading branches.

LEAVES. Broadly deltoid; 2–2½ inches long and 3 inches wide (larger on vigorous shoots); apex abruptly short or long-pointed; base entire and truncate or cordate; coarsely and irregularly serrate with usually less than 10 teeth on each side of blade; thick and leathery; glabrous; yellow-green and lustrous above, paler below; turning bright lemon-yellow before falling; petioles flattened, slender, glabrous, 1½–2 inches long, without glands at apex.

FLOWERS. Aments 2–4 inches long, the pistillate becoming 4–5 inches; bracts scarious, light red, divided into elongated filiform lobes at apex; staminate disk broad and stamens numerous with large anthers and short filaments; pistillate disk cup-shaped, enclosing the long-stalked, ovoid ovary to the middle; stigmas 3, crenulate lobed, on short style.

FRUIT. Capsules oblong-ovoid; ¼ inch long; thick-walled; acute; 3- or 4-valved; slightly ridged; pedicels slender, ½–¾ inch long; rachis slender, glabrous, sparsely fruited. Seed: light brown, hairy tufted.

TWIGS. Stout; round; glabrous; light orange-brown, becoming gray; roughened by elevated leaf scars. Winter buds: terminal ⅓–⅗ inch long, ovoid, acute, brown, lustrous, puberulous, resinous but nonaromatic.

BARK. Thick; pale gray-brown; deeply furrowed into wide, flat, connecting ridges.

SILVICAL CHARACTERS. Lower and Upper Sonoran zones; intolerant; short-lived; along streams in an arid region; widely planted as a shade tree in Texas and New Mexico.

* * *

Palmer Cottonwood, *Populus palmeri* Sarg., is a similar form in central to west Texas.

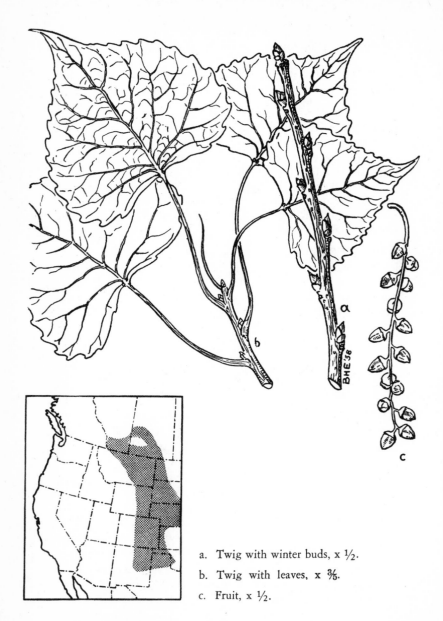

a. Twig with winter buds, x ½.

b. Twig with leaves, x ⅗.

c. Fruit, x ½.

SALICACEAE

PLAINS COTTONWOOD

Populus sargentii Dode

(*Populus deltoides* var. *occidentalis* Rydb.)

HABIT. A large tree 60–90 feet high and often 6–7 feet in diameter; broad, open crown with stout, erect, and spreading branches.

LEAVES. Broadly deltoid; 3–4 inches long and usually slightly longer than broad; apex abruptly contracted into slender, acuminate point (rarely rounded); base truncate or slightly cordate; coarsely crenate-serrate; thick and firm; glabrous; light green and lustrous; petiole flattened, slender, $2\frac{1}{2}$–$3\frac{1}{2}$ inches long, usually with 2 small glands at apex.

FLOWERS. Aments short-stalked, glabrous, not very densely flowered; bracts light brown, scarious, fringed at apex, small and appressed at base of pistillate flower; the staminate with broad disk containing 20 or more short-stalked, yellow stamens; the pistillate with small, cup-shaped disk enclosing base of subglobose ovary which bears 3–4, broad-lobed stigmas.

FRUIT. Capsules oblong-ovoid, about $\frac{2}{5}$ inch long and 3–4 times longer than pedicel; thin-walled; gradually or abruptly narrowed to blunt apex. Seed: light brown, hairy, about $\frac{1}{16}$ inch long.

TWIGS. Stout; round or angular; glabrous and light.yellow; conspicuously roughened by elevated leaf scars. Winter buds: terminal $\frac{1}{2}$ inch long, conical, acute, olive-green to brown, puberulous, coated with amber-colored, nonaromatic resin.

BARK. Gray and smooth on young trunks; on old trees gray, thick, deeply furrowed, and broadly ridged.

SILVICAL CHARACTERS. Upper Sonoran zone; intolerant; short-lived; the common cottonwood of stream banks in the eastern foothills of the Rocky Mountains from Canada to New Mexico; often planted as shade tree in Rocky Mountain region.

GENERAL. Much resembling the eastern cottonwood, *P. deltoides* var. *virginiana* (Cast.) Sudw., with which, in general appearance, it was long confused.

FREMONT COTTONWOOD

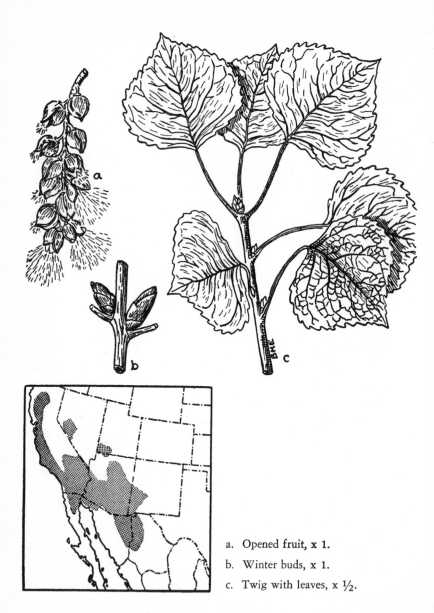

a. Opened fruit, x 1.
b. Winter buds, x 1.
c. Twig with leaves, x ½.

[112]

SALICACEAE

Fremont Cottonwood

Populus fremontii S. Wats.

HABIT. A large tree occasionally 100 feet high and 4–6 feet in diameter; wide, open crown with stout branches.

LEAVES. Deltoid or reniform; 2–2½ inches long and 2½–3 inches wide; apex abruptly contracted into short point; base entire and cordate or cuneate; coarsely serrate; thick and firm; glabrous; bright yellow-green; petioles flattened, yellow, 1½–3 inches long, without glands at apex.

FLOWERS. Staminate aments densely flowered, 1½-2 inches long, disk broad with 60 or more large red stamens; pistillate aments sparsely flowered, bracts filiformly lobed, large and dilated, disk cup-shaped, enclosing base of ovoid ovary which bears 3 or rarely 4 broad, lobed stigmas.

FRUIT. Capsules ovoid; ⅓–½ inch long; thick-walled; acute or obtuse; 3- or rarely 4-valved; short-stalked. Seed: light brown, hairy, nearly ⅛ inch long.

TWIGS. Stout; round; mostly glabrous and pale yellow, becoming yellow-gray; only slightly roughened by 3-lobed leaf scars. Winter buds: glabrous; terminal ⅓–½ inch long, ovoid, acute, light green, much larger than lateral.

BARK. Smooth and gray-brown on young trees; on old trunks 1½–2 inches thick, dark, deeply furrowed, and ridged.

SILVICAL CHARACTERS. Lower and Upper Sonoran zones; very intolerant; short-lived; along streams in arid regions.

GENERAL. Sargent has differentiated 4 varieties, namely: *pubescens* (with pubescent twigs) in Utah, Nevada, and California; *thornberii* (with ellipsoidal capsules, shorter pedicels, smaller disk, and more·numerous teeth on leaves) in southern Arizona and New Mexico; *toumeyi* (with large disks and long-pointed leaves shallowly cordate at base) in Arizona; and *macrodisca* (with long disks nearly enclosing fruit) in southwestern New Mexico.

SALICACEAE

THE WILLOWS

Characteristics of the Genus *Salix* L.

HABIT. Shrubs or less frequently trees; latter often with several trunks from greatly extended rootstalk.

LEAVES. Alternate; simple; commonly lanceolate; margins entire or toothed; pinnately veined; sessile or short-petioled; stipules small and soon falling, except on vigorous shoots where they are leaflike and persistent.

FLOWERS. Regular; dioecious; in terminal and axillary aments, appearing with or before the leaves; individual flowers solitary, apetalous, on glandlike disk, subtended by pubescent, entire to dentate, deciduous or persistent scale or bract; staminate with 1–2 or 3–12 stamens inserted on base of bract; pistillate a single, 1-celled, sessile or stalked ovary, containing 4–8 ovules on each of 2 placentas, style short, terminating in 2, short, 2-parted stigmas.

FRUIT. A 1-celled, 2-valved, acuminate capsule. Seed: small, dark brown, tufted with long, silky hairs, buoyant, maturing in late spring, of transient vitality.

TWIGS. Slender to stout; round; tough; often easily separated at junction with branch; marked by elevated leaf scars; pith homogeneous, terete. Winter buds: terminal absent; lateral covered by 2 connate scales which appear as a single, caplike scale.

BARK. Astringent; scaly; variously colored.

WOOD. Light, soft; weak; usually brittle; not durable; heartwood pale brown, often tinged with red; used to small extent for athletic goods and charcoal.

SILVICAL CHARACTERS. Intolerant; fast-growing; remarkable vitality and sprouting vigorously from stumps or cuttings; usually swamp or moisture-loving plants.

GENERAL. This genus contains about 170 species scattered over the Northern Hemisphere, with about 70 species native to North America; identification of the various species is difficult; while 13 species native to the Rocky Mountain region occasionally reach tree size, there is only one, *Salix amygdaloides*, which can typically be considered a tree; the key includes the 13 species occasionally attaining tree size.

KEY TO THE SPECIES OF SALIX OCCASIONALLY REACHING TREE SIZE IN THE ROCKY MOUNTAIN REGION

I. Stamens 3 to 12; filaments free; flower bracts deciduous.
   A. Leaves green below; petioles eglandular at base.
      1. Capsule hairy; twigs yellow-gray....1. *S. gooddingi* Ball.
      2. Capsule glabrous; twigs red to purple..2. *S. nigra* Marsh.
   B. Leaves pale or bluish below; ovary and capsules glabrous.
      1. Petioles without glands at base of leaf.
         a. Twigs easily separable, flower bracts entire; throughout region...............3. *S. amygdaloides* Anderss.
         b. Twigs firmly attached; flower bracts toothed.
            (1) Leaves silver-white below; capsules short-stalked; stamens usually 3; Southwest...................
                ....4. *S. bonplandiana* H.B.K.
            (2) Leaves glaucous or yellow-hairy below; capsules long-stalked; stamens 4–6; Southwest............
                ....5. *S. laevigata* Bebb.
      2. Petioles glandular; twigs separable; flower bracts toothed; entire region.....................6. *S. lasiandra* Benth.
II. Stamens 2.
   A. Bracts deciduous, yellowish; filaments free, more or less hairy; stipe of ovary much shorter than bract.
      1. Leaves ⅓–1⅓" long, linear; stigmas linear; southwestern.............................7. *S. taxifolia* H. B. K.
      2. Leaves over 1⅓" long, mostly linear-lanceolate; stigmas short.
         a. Leaves white-hairy below; stipules minute or wanting; entire region.....................8. *S. exigua* Nutt.
         b. Leaves nearly glabrous below; stipules large, deciduous; eastern....................9. *S. interior* Rowlee.
   B. Bracts persistent, darker; filaments glabrous.
      1. Stipe of ovary longer than bract; filaments free.
         a. Ovary and capsule glabrous; bracts dark brown, hairy at base; northern....10. *S. mackenzieana* (Hook.) Barr.
         b. Ovary and capsule hairy; bracts light, hairy; entire region ....11. *S. bebbiana* Sarg.
      2. Stipe of ovary and capsule much shorter than bract.
         a. Filaments somewhat united; capsules glabrous; Southwest ....12. *S. lasiolepis* Benth.
         b. Filaments free; capsule pubescent; entire region.......
            ....13. *S. scouleriana* Barr.

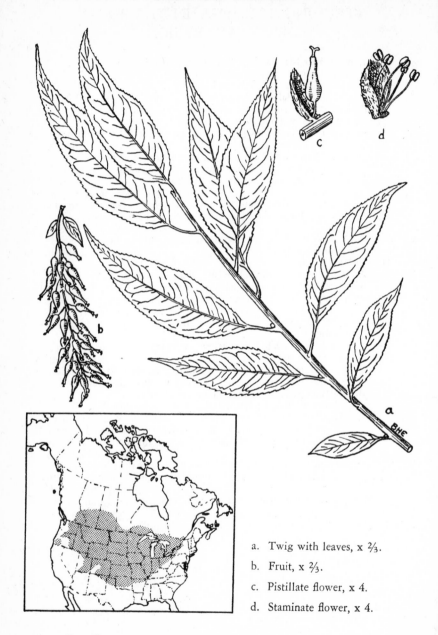

a. Twig with leaves, x ⅔.

b. Fruit, x ⅔.

c. Pistillate flower, x 4.

d. Staminate flower, x 4.

SALICACEAE

Peachleaf Willow

Salix amygdaloides Anderss.

HABIT. A tree rarely 60–70 feet high and 2 feet in diameter; trunk single, columnar; rather narrow, rounded crown with straight, ascending branches.

LEAVES. Lanceolate to ovate-lanceolate; 2–5 inches long and ¾–1¼ inches wide; apex long acuminate; cuneate or rounded and often unequal at base; finely serrate; thin and firm; light green and lustrous above, pale and glaucous below; petioles slender, round, ½-¾ inch long, without glands at base of leaf.

FLOWERS. Aments stalked, hairy, slender, 2–3 inches long; bracts yellow, entire, densely hairy on inner surface; staminate with 3–9 stamens, filaments free and hairy at base; pistillate with long-stalked, glabrous, oblong-conic ovary with short style and notched stigmas.

FRUIT. Capsules globose-conic; ¼ inch long; long-stalked; glabrous; light yellow-red. Seed: minute, hairy-tufted.

TWIGS. Slender; glabrous, lustrous, dark orange or red-brown, becoming light orange-brown; marked by scattered pale lenticels; easily separable from branch. Winter buds: ⅛ inch long, broadly ovoid, swollen on one side, dark brown.

BARK. Brown, often tinged with red; ½-¾ inch thick; divided by irregular furrows into broad, flat, connecting ridges.

SILVICAL CHARACTERS. Upper Sonoran and Transition zones; intolerant; reproduction not abundant; in moist sites along banks of streams.

GENERAL. This willow is the only species native to the Rocky Mountain region which is typically a tree; other species occasionally attain tree size, but they are typically shrubs; the variety, *Salix amygdaloides* var. *wrightii* (Anderss.) Schneid., a southwestern form, differs from the species chiefly in its yellow or yellow-brown glabrous branches.

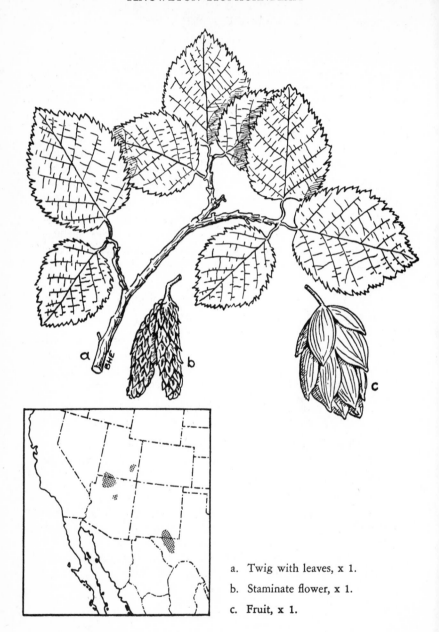

a. Twig with leaves, x 1.

b. Staminate flower, x 1.

c. Fruit, x 1.

BETULACEAE

KNOWLTON HOPHORNBEAM. IRONWOOD
Ostrya knowltonii Cov.

HABIT. A small tree 20–30 feet high and 12–18 inches in diameter; trunk frequently dividing; crown narrow, round-topped with slender, pendulous, often contorted branches.

LEAVES. Alternate; simple; elliptic to ovate; 1–2 inches long and 1-1½ inches wide; acute or round at apex; margins sharply serrate; thin and tough; dark yellow-green and pilose above, pale and soft-pubescent below; deciduous; turning dull yellow in autumn; petioles ⅛–¼ inch long, slender, hairy; stipules ½ inch long and wide, yellow-green, fugacious.

FLOWERS. Regular; monoecious; perianth absent; appearing with leaves; staminate in long, clustered, persistent aments, each flower composed of 3–14 stamens crowded on a hairy receptacle and attached to base of ovate, green and red scale; pistillate in erect, loose, terminal aments, in pairs at base of leaflike scale, enclosed in hairy sacklike involucre, single ovule in each cell of 2-celled ovary.

FRUIT. Small (¼ inch long), 1-celled, 1-seeded, ovoid, flat, unwinged nut; enclosed in enlarged (1 inch long), pale, membranaceous, involucre of flower; in loose, suspended strobiles 1–1½ inches long, resembling clusters of hops.

TWIGS. Slender; round; dark green and hoary-tomentose at first, becoming dark brown and glabrous; marked by numerous pale lenticels. Winter buds: terminal absent; lateral ⅛ inch long, pointed, ovoid, dark brown-red, scaly.

BARK. Thin (⅛ inch); light gray, tinged with red; separating into loose, platelike scales; inner bark bright orange.

WOOD. Heavy; hard; strong; close-grained; diffuse-porous; heartwood light red-brown; sapwood thin; unimportant.

SILVICAL CHARACTERS. Upper Sonoran and Transition zones; restricted and rare on cañon slopes in the pinyon belt.

GENERAL. *O. baileyi* Rose (shown on the map in Texas and New Mexico) is very similar to and often considered a synonym of *O. knowltonii;* the eastern species, *O. virginiana* (Mill.) Koch., entering this region in the foothills of South Dakota and in northwestern Nebraska, differs from the southwestern species in its larger oblong-lanceolate leaves.

[119]

BETULACEAE

THE BIRCHES

Characteristics of the Genus *Betula* L.

HABIT. Deciduous, graceful trees and shrubs; crown on young trees narrow, pyramidal, symmetrical; branches short and slender, more or less erect on young trees and becoming horizontal or pendulous on older trees.

LEAVES. Alternate; simple; mostly ovate to triangular; serrate, dentate, or lobulate; petioled; stipules fugacious; scarious.

FLOWERS. Regular; monoecious; apetalous; appearing before or with leaves; staminate in 1–3-clustered, long, pendulous aments produced early the previous season, every bract with 3 individual flowers, each of 4 stamens adnate to a 4-parted calyx; pistillate in solitary, small, slender aments appearing on ends of spurlike lateral branches below the staminate flowers, individual flowers naked, in clusters of 3, and subtended by 3-lobed bract.

FRUIT. Small, compressed, laterally winged nutlet; in erect or pendent strobiles; scales deciduous from persistent cone axis at maturity, releasing the nutlets.

TWIGS. Slender; round; marked by horizontal lenticels and small leaf scars; spur shoots with paired leaves commonly present on old growth; pith small, round, homogeneous. Winter buds: terminal absent, lateral with imbricated scales; twig lengthening by one of upper lateral buds.

BARK. Smooth; resinous; marked by horizontally elongated lenticels; often peeling off in thin, papery layers.

WOOD. Rather heavy and hard; diffuse-porous; some species highly valued for timber.

SILVICAL CHARACTERS. Mostly short-lived and adapted to planting on poor, sandy or boggy soil; many used for ornamental planting because of handsome foliage and showy bark.

GENERAL. This genus contains about 40 species of trees and shrubs scattered through the Northern Hemisphere; the European white birch (*Betula pendula* Roth.) and especially its cut-leaf, weeping variety (*dalecarlica* Schn.) are often planted in this country.

[120]

KEY TO THE SPECIES OF BETULA

I. Bark separating freely into papery layers.
  A. Bark red-brown or nearly white; branchlets densely glandular; leaves rhombic to deltoid-ovate; Alaska.............. ....1. *Betula papyrifera* var. *humilis*, p. 125.
  B. Bark cream-white or occasionally orange-brown; branchlets not glandular, or sparingly so; leaves ovate; northern (one locality in Colorado)..........2. *Betula papyrifera*, p. 123.
    1. Leaves 3" or longer.....................var. *commutata*.
    2. Leaves not over 2½".
      a. Strobile 1–1½" long, scales puberulous, middle lobe much longer than lateral lobes; northern Montana and Idaho into Canada...................var. *subcordata*.
      b. Strobile 1" long, scales glabrous but ciliate, middle lobe scarcely longer than lateral lobes; Alaskan coast.. ....var. *kenaica*.
II. Bark not separating into thin layers; branchlets glandular.
  A. Leaves truncate or rounded at broad base, acute or acuminate at apex; strobiles 1–1¼" long and ½" wide; through region.....................3. *Betula occidentalis*, p. 125.
  B. Leaves cuneate at base, acute or rounded at apex; strobiles ½–¾" long and ⅛" wide.
    1. Leaves coarsely serrate, 1–1½" long; Canadian and Alaskan shrub or small tree....4. *Betula X eastwoodiae*, p. 125.
    2. Leaves crenate-dentate, less than ½" long; low, alpine shrub extending south to Colorado................... ....5. *Betula glandulosa*, p. 125.

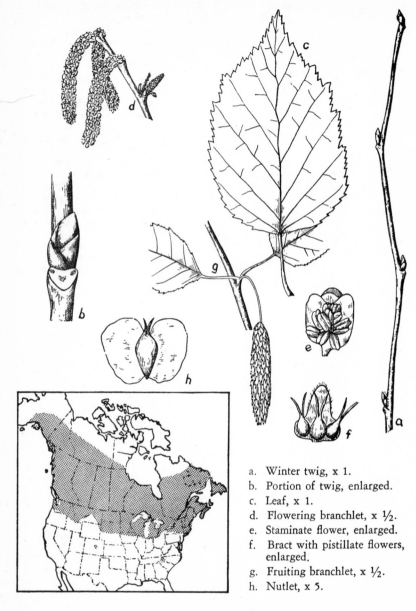

a. Winter twig, x 1.
b. Portion of twig, enlarged.
c. Leaf, x 1.
d. Flowering branchlet, x ½.
e. Staminate flower, enlarged.
f. Bract with pistillate flowers, enlarged.
g. Fruiting branchlet, x ½.
h. Nutlet, x 5.

BETULACEAE

Paper Birch

Betula papyrifera Marsh.

HABIT. A tree 60–70 feet high and 2–3 feet in diameter (rarely larger); old trees with open crowns and short, pendulous branches.

LEAVES. Ovate; 2–5 inches long and 1–2¼ inches wide; acute or abruptly acuminate; coarsely, irregularly, and usually doubly serrate; thick and firm; dull dark green and glabrous above, light yellow-green, black-glandular and glabrous or puberulous below; turning light, clear yellow in autumn; petioles stout, ½–¾ inch long, yellow, glandular; stipules light green, ovate, acute, ciliate on margins.

FLOWERS. Staminate aments ¾–1¼ inches long during winter, becoming 3–4 inches long, slender, brownish, pendent; pistillate aments about 1½ inches long, slender, erect, greenish; styles bright red.

FRUIT. Nut narrower than its wing, ellipsoidal, ⅟₁₆ inch long; strobiles 1½ inches long, cylindric, glabrous, long-stalked; scales lobed, hairy on margins.

TWIGS. At first green, hairy, and marked by scattered, orange-colored, oblong lenticels; becoming dark orange-brown, lustrous, and ultimately covered with white papery bark. Winter buds: ¼ inch long, obovoid, acute, dark chestnut-brown, glabrous.

BARK. Cream-white; separating into thin, papery layers; marked by long, narrow, raised lenticels; inner bark orange.

WOOD. Moderately heavy; hard; strong; tough; close-grained; heartwood light brown, tinged with red; sapwood thick, whitish; used for pulp, lumber, turned articles, and fuel.

SILVICAL CHARACTERS. Canadian zone; intolerant; short-lived; shallow roots; reproduction vigorous, taking over extensive areas following fire; rich or sandy soils.

GENERAL. Two varieties [*subcordata* (Rydb.) Sarg., and *commutata* (Reg.) Fern.] are differentiated in the Rocky Mountain region; similar Alaskan forms have been designated as *Betula papyrifera* var. *kenaica* (Evans.) Henry, and *Betula papyrifera* var. *humilis* Fern & Raup. These 4 varieties have been included in the Key and distribution map.

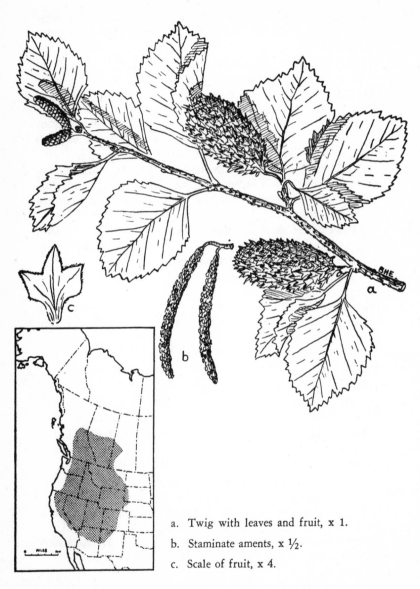

a. Twig with leaves and fruit, x 1.

b. Staminate aments, x ½.

c. Scale of fruit, x 4.

BETULACEAE

WATER BIRCH. RED BIRCH

Betula occidentalis Hook. (*Betula fontinalis* Sarg.)

HABIT. A shrub or small tree 20–25 feet high and 12–14 inches in diameter; broad, open crown with ascending branches; frequently in crowded, dense thickets.

LEAVES. Ovate; 1–2 inches long and ¾–1 inch wide; acute or acuminate; sharply and often doubly serrate; sometimes slightly lobed; thin and firm; glabrous; dark dull green above, pale yellow-green and minutely glandular below; turning dull yellow in autumn; petioles stout, ⅓–½ inch long, light yellow, glandular-dotted; stipules bright green, slightly ciliate.

FLOWERS. Staminate aments ½–¾ inch long during winter, becoming 2–2½ inches long, chestnut-brown; pistillate aments about ¾ inch long, green; styles bright red.

FRUIT. Nut nearly as wide as its wing, ovoid or obovoid; strobiles 1–1¼ inches long, cylindric, puberulous or glabrous, long-stalked; scales lobed, ciliate.

TWIGS. At first light green and glandular, becoming dark red-brown; marked by horizontal lenticels. Winter buds: ¼ inch long, ovoid, acute, very resinous, chestnut-brown.

BARK. Thin (¼ inch); smooth; lustrous dark bronze; marked by pale horizontal lenticels, becoming on old trunks 6–8 inches long and ¼ inch wide.

WOOD. Rather light and soft; strong; heartwood light brown; sapwood thick, light-colored; not important; used locally for fencing and fuel.

SILVICAL CHARACTERS. Upper Sonoran and Transition zones; intolerant; shallow root system; reproduction abundant in moist, mineral soil; generally along borders of streams in moist mountain valleys and cañons.

GENERAL. The variety *fecunda* Fern. is recognized in Montana and Washington; this has somewhat larger leaves and strobiles than the species.

* * *

Yukon birch, *Betula* X *eastwoodiae* Sarg., a hybrid of *B. glandulosa* and *B. papyrifera* is a small tree or shrub in northwest Canada.

[125]

BETULACEAE

THE ALDERS

Characteristics of the Genus *Alnus* Mill.

HABIT: Deciduous shrubs or small to medium-sized trees.

LEAVES. Alternate; simple; usually serrate or dentate; pinnately veined; falling without change of color; petioled; stipules fugacious, ovate, acute, scarious.

FLOWERS. Regular; monoecious; apetalous; mostly appearing before or with leaves (rarely opening in autumn); in 1–3 flowered cymes; formed during previous season; staminate in long, pendulous aments, every scale bearing 3–6 flowers, each flower subtended by 3–5 bractlets and composed of 4-parted calyx and 4 (rarely 1–3) stamens; pistillate in erect, stalked, ovoid or oblong aments, appearing below staminate flowers, individual flowers in pairs, composed of a naked ovary surmounted by 2 stigmas and subtended by 2–4 bractlets.

FRUIT. Small, flat, chestnut-brown, wingless or laterally winged nutlet, bearing remnants of style at apex; in persistent, semi-woody strobiles, each scale bearing 2–4 nutlets.

TWIGS. Slender to moderately stout; round; reddish or tinged with red; marked by raised leaf scars and lenticels; pith homogeneous, triangular in cross section. Winter buds: terminal absent; lateral-stalked, 2–3-scaled, usually red; twig lengthening by one of upper lateral buds.

BARK. Astringent; mostly gray; smooth, except at the base of trunks of large trees.

WOOD. Light; soft; straight-grained; diffuse-porous; durable in water; heartwood red-brown; sapwood very thick and whitish.

SILVICAL CHARACTERS. Tolerant to intolerant; rather short-lived; shallow, spreading roots; on moist or wet sites, commonly along streams or on mountain slopes.

GENERAL. This genus contains about 30 species scattered through the cooler portions of the Northern Hemisphere and extending into the mountains of South America; 8 species attaining tree size are native to North America, however only 1 species is of commercial importance, the red alder *Alnus rubra* Bong. native to the Pacific Coast and reported in the Rocky Mountain region in Idaho.

KEY TO THE SPECIES OF ALNUS

I. Peduncles of fruit slender and as long or longer than strobiles and bearing at least one leaf towards the base; wings of nutlet broad; winter buds dark purple; stamens 4; leaves ovate, lobulate, doubly serrate flowers open in spring with leaves.
.....................................1. *Alnus sinuata*, p. 131.

II. Peduncle of fruit stout, shorter than strobile, leafless; winter buds red; flowers open in winter or before leaves in spring.

A. Wing of nutlet broad; strobiles $3/4-1\frac{1}{8}''$ long; leaf margins with narrow underturned edge; stamens 4................
.............................2. *Alnus rubra*, p. 126.

B. Wing of nutlet reduced to narrow border; leaf margins not underturned.

1. Stamens 4; leaves oblong-ovate, mostly rounded at base, lobulate, doubly serrate, not glandular-dotted; winter buds $1/4-1/3''$ long, bright red, puberulous; through region to northern New Mexico ....3. *Alnus tenuifolia*, p. 129.

2. Stamens 1–3; leaves ovate, oval or oblong-lanceolate, cuneate at base, not lobulate, frequently glandular-dotted; winter buds $1/2''$ long, dark red.

a. Leaves ovate or oval, rounded or acute, seldom doubly serrate; winter buds pubescent; west from northern Idaho................4. *Alnus rhombifolia*, p. 133.

b. Leaves oblong-lanceolate, acute, usually doubly serrate; winter buds glabrous; southern New Mexico and Arizona ....5. *Alnus oblongifolia*, p. 135.

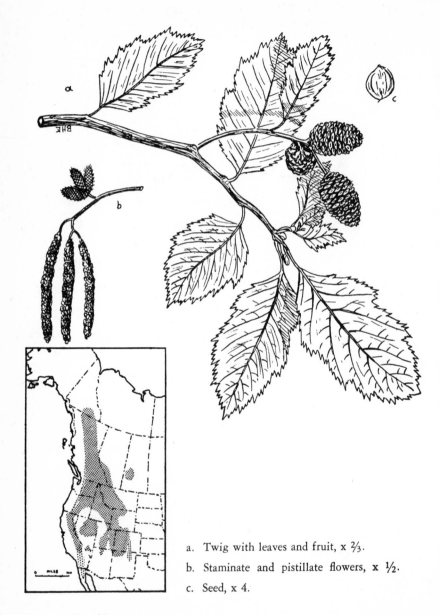

a. Twig with leaves and fruit, x ⅔.

b. Staminate and pistillate flowers, x ½.

c. Seed, x 4.

BETULACEAE

Thinleaf Alder. Mountain Alder
Alnus tenuifolia Nutt.

HABIT. A shrub or small tree occasionally 30 feet high and 6–8 inches in diameter; crown narrow and round-topped with slender, spreading, slightly pendulous branches.

LEAVES. Ovate-oblong; 2–4 inches long and 1½–2½ inches wide; mostly rounded at base; acute or acuminate; slightly, acutely and laciniately lobed; doubly serrate; thin and firm; dark green and glabrous above, pale yellow-green and glabrous or puberulous below with a stout, orange-colored midrib; petioles stout, slightly grooved, orange-colored, ½–1 inch long; stipules ½ inch long, thin, pale-pubescent.

FLOWERS. Staminate aments ¾–1 inch long and light purple during winter, becoming 1½–2 inches long in spring, calyx lobes shorter than the 4 stamens; pistillate aments ¼ inch long, dark red-brown.

FRUIT. Nut nearly circular to slightly obovoid, wing reduced to thin, membranaceous border; strobiles ⅓–½ inch long, obovoid-oblong; scales truncate, much thickened, 3-lobed at apex.

TWIGS. Slender; pubescent, pale brown and marked by few, large orange-colored lenticels at first, becoming glabrous and light brown or gray. Winter buds: ¼–⅓ inch long, bright red, puberulous.

BARK. Thin (½ inch); bright red-brown; broken on surface into closely appressed scales on old trunks.

WOOD. Heartwood light brown; unimportant because of small size.

SILVICAL CHARACTERS. Upper Sonoran to Canadian zones; tolerant when young, becoming intolerant with age; on moist, well-drained sites; banks of mountain streams and cañons; the common alder of the Rocky Mountain region.

GENERAL. Some authors consider this species a synonym of *Alnus incana* (L.) Moench.

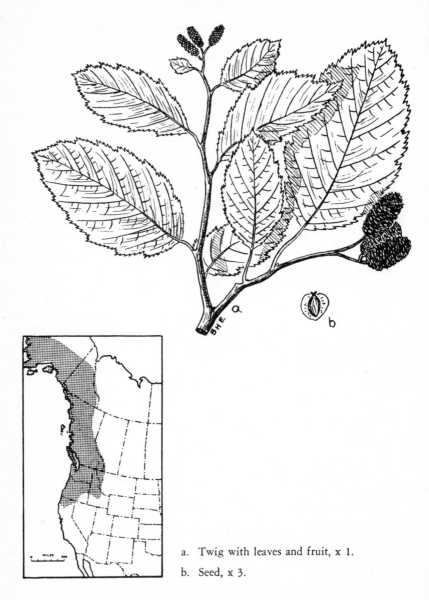

a. Twig with leaves and fruit, x 1.
b. Seed, x 3.

BETULACEAE

SITKA ALDER

Alnus sinuata (Regel) Rydb.

HABIT. A shrub or small tree rarely 40 feet high and 7–8 inches in diameter; crown narrow and open with short, small, horizontal branches; often forming broad thickets.

LEAVES. Ovate; 3–6 inches long and 1½–4 inches wide; acute; usually divided into numerous, short, lateral lobes; sharply and doubly serrate; membranaceous; yellow-green above, pale, lustrous, and glabrous or villose along midrib below; petioles stout, grooved, enlarged at base, ½–¾ inch long; stipules ¼ inch long, puberulous, rounded at apex.

FLOWERS. Staminate aments ½ inch long during winter becoming 4–5 inches long in spring, calyx lobes shorter than the 4 stamens; pistillate aments ⅓ inch long, long-peduncled, in elongated panicles.

FRUIT. Nut oval, about as wide as its wings; strobiles ½–¾ inch long and about ⅓ inch wide; truncate scales thickened at apex; on slender peduncles; in elongated, leafy panicles.

TWIGS. Slender; slightly zigzag; puberulous, glandular and orange-brown at first, becoming smooth, light gray and marked by numerous large, pale lenticels and crowded, elevated leaf scars. Winter buds: ½ inch long, acuminate, dark purple, finely pubescent.

BARK. Thin; blue-gray; bright red inner bark.

WOOD. Heartwood light brown; unimportant because of small size.

SILVICAL CHARACTERS. Transition and Canadian zones; tolerant when young, becoming rather intolerant with age; in moist flats and along stream borders; generally a shrub in the United States and British Columbia, but frequently a tall tree in southeastern Alaska; growing at elevations of more than 3,000 feet.

GENERAL. Some authors include this species in the shrubby species *Alnus crispa* (Ait.) Pursh.

Twig with leaves, flowers and fruit, x 1.

BETULACEAE

WHITE ALDER

Alnus rhombifolia Nutt.

HABIT. A tree frequently 70–80 feet high and 2–3 feet in diameter; trunk tall and straight; crown broad and round-topped with long, slender, pendulous branches.

LEAVES. Ovate, oval, or sometimes orbicular; 2–3 inches long and 1½–2 inches wide; cuneate at base, rounded or acute at apex; finely, coarsely, or doubly serrate; slightly thickened and reflexed on somewhat undulate margins; dark green and lustrous above, light yellow-green and puberulous below, with a stout, yellow midrib; frequently marked with minute, glandular dots; petioles slender, yellow, hairy, flattened and grooved above, ½–¾ inch long; stipules ¼ inch long, puberulous, acute.

FLOWERS. Staminate aments ¾–1 inch long first summer, lengthening through winter and becoming 4–6 inches long in January, deciduous in February before appearance of leaves, calyx shorter than 1–3 stamens; pistillate aments in short, pubescent racemes, emerging from bud in December.

FRUIT. Nut broadly ovoid, narrowly margined; strobiles ⅓–½ inch long, oblong; scales thin, slightly thickened and lobed at apex; remaining closed until tree flowers in following year.

TWIGS. Slender; pubescent and light green at first, becoming glabrous and dark orange-red; marked by small, scattered lenticels. Winter buds: ½ inch long, very slender, dark red, pale-pubescent.

BARK. On old trunks 1 inch thick; dark brown; irregularly furrowed and scaly plated.

WOOD. Light; soft; close-grained; not strong; brittle; heartwood light brown; sapwood thick whitish; little used, but possibly suitable for cabinet work.

SILVICAL CHARACTERS. Transition zone; rather tolerant throughout life; on moist sites; stream banks and cañon bottoms.

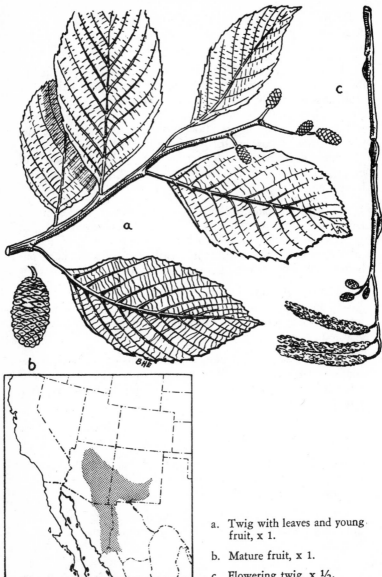

a. Twig with leaves and young fruit, x 1.

b. Mature fruit, x 1.

c. Flowering twig, x ½.

BETULACEAE

Arizona Alder. New Mexican Alder

Alnus oblongifolia Torr.

HABIT. A shrub or small tree rarely more than 20–30 feet high and 8 inches in diameter; crown open and round-topped with long, slender, spreading branches.

LEAVES. Oblong-lanceolate and acute, or rarely obovate and rounded at apex; 2–3 inches long and about 1½ inches wide; cuneate at base; sharply and usually doubly serrate; dark yellow-green and glabrous or puberulous above, pale and glabrous or puberulous along yellow midrib below; more or less thickly covered with black glands; petioles slender, grooved, pubescent, ¾ inch long; stipules ¼ inch long, brown, scarious.

FLOWERS. Staminate aments ½–¾ inch long and light yellow during winter, becoming 2–2½ inches long and orange-brown in spring before leaves appear, calyx shorter than the 2–3 stamens; pistillate aments ⅛–¼ inch long and light brown, stigmas bright red.

FRUIT. Nut broadly ovoid, narrowly margined; strobiles ½–1 inch long; scales thin, truncate, slightly thickened.

TWIGS. Slender; slightly puberulous and orange-red at first, becoming lustrous and dark red-brown or gray; marked by small, conspicuous, pale lenticels and elevated leaf scars. Winter buds: ½ inch long, acute, red, lustrous, glabrous.

BARK. Thin; light brown, tinged with red; smooth.

WOOD. Heartwood light brown; unimportant because of small size.

SILVICAL CHARACTERS. Transition zone; rather intolerant; on moist, well-drained sites; banks of mountain streams and cañons at elevations of 4,000–6,000 feet.

FAGACEAE

The Oaks

Characteristics of the Genus *Quercus* L.

HABIT. Deciduous or evergreen trees or shrubs; with astringent properties; pubescence of fascicled hairs.

LEAVES. Alternate; simple; deciduous or persistent; shape and size often variable on same tree; stipulate.

FLOWERS. Regular; monoecious; vernal; staminate in clustered aments, individual flowers with a 4–7 lobed calyx enclosing 6 (rarely 2–12) stamens; pistillate solitary or in 2 to many-flowered spikes, individual flowers with a 6-lobed calyx surrounding a 3- (rarely 4–5-) celled ovary with 1–2 ovules in each cell, the whole partly enclosed in an involucre.

FRUIT. An acorn; 1-seeded by abortion; maturing in 1–2 years; partially enclosed by scaly cup (modified involucre).

TWIGS. Slender to stout; angled; pith homogeneous, stellate; marked by pale lenticels and semicircular leaf scars. Winter buds: clustered at end of twig; terminal present; with many chestnut-brown scales imbricated in 5 ranks.

BARK. Scaly or dark and furrowed.

WOOD. Heavy; hard; brittle; with prominent rays.

GENERAL. A variable genus containing 75–80 native species which are often difficult to identify. The native oaks have been separated into the white oaks (with leaves rarely bristle-tipped; fruit maturing in 1 year, glabrous on the inner surface of shell and usually sweet to the taste) and the red or black oaks (with leaves commonly bristle-tipped; fruit maturing in 2 years, hairy on inner surface of shell and usually bitter to the taste).

*   *   *

The following species have been reported as occasionally forming small trees in New Mexico or western Texas; *Q. durandii* var. *breviloba* (Torr.) Palmer, *Q. graciliformis* C. H. Muller, *Q. gravesii* Sarg., *Q. havardii* Rydb., *Q. mohriana* Buckl., *Q. pungens* Liebm., and *Q. virginiana* Mill., the Live Oak of the South.

[136]

KEY TO THE ARBORESCENT SPECIES
OF QUERCUS

I. Shell of acorn tomentose within; scales of cup thin; fruit commonly maturing in 2 years (except 3)............Black Oaks.
   A. Leaves deciduous, lobed, bristle-tipped; Texas............
   ....1. *Q. shumardii* var. *texana*, p. 139.
   B. Leaves persistent 1–4 years, not lobed.
      1. Leaves persistent 3–4 years; cup scales covered with dense golden tomentum..............2. *Q. chrysolepis*, p. 141.
      2. Leaves persistent until appearance of new leaves; cup scales pubescent.
         a. Leaves flat, broadly lanceolate, glabrous below except at base of midrib..................3. *Q. emoryi*, p. 143.
         b. Leaves revolute, usually narrowly lanceolate, densely tomentose below..........4. *Q. hypoleucoides*, p. 139.
II. Shell of acorn not tomentose within; cup scales thickened basally, fruit matures in one year.....................White Oaks.
   A. Leaves deciduous, deeply lobed or coarsely serrate.
      1. Leaves deeply lobed.
         a. Acorn cup fringed at top; northeast................
         ....5. *Q. macrocarpa*, p. 151.
         b. Acorn cup not fringed; south and central............
         ....6. *Q. gambellii*, p. 153.
      2. Leaves coarsely and glandularly toothed; Texas and New Mexico ....7. *Q. muehlenbergii*, p. 155.
   B. Leaves persistent until appearance of new leaves, not deeply lobed.
      1. Veins very prominent beneath, slightly impressed above, mucronate or toothed near apex.
         a. Fruit in long-stalked clusters; leaves obovate to suborbicular, concave beneath..........8. *Q. reticulata*, p. 145.
         b. Fruit solitary or paired, short-stalked; leaves obovate to oblanceolate, flat..............9. *Q. arizonica*, p. 149.
      2. Veins not markedly prominent beneath; not impressed and usually prominent above.
         a. Leaves oblong, rounded, glabrous, glaucous, entire; nut enclosed for ⅓ length in fringed cup..............
         ....10. *Q. oblongifolia*, p. 147.
         b. Leaves not with above combination of characters.
            1. Leaves very thick, scabrous, shallow-lobed..........
            ....11. *Q. undulata*, p. 145.
            2. Leaves not crisp or scabrous, flat, glabrous or softhairy.
               a. Leaves lanceolate to narrowly elliptic, usually very small, entire or with few short teeth, nearly glabrous......................12. *Q. toumeyi*, p. 149.
               b. Leaves broadly lanceolate to ovate, hairy below.
                  (1) Leaves entire or with few short teeth, gray-green, lower surface with stellate hairs, upper surface shiny...........13. *Q. grisea*, p. 147.
                  (2) Leaves with many sharp, long teeth, glaucous, dull above, lower surface with resinous pubescence ....14. *Q. turbinella*, p. 153.

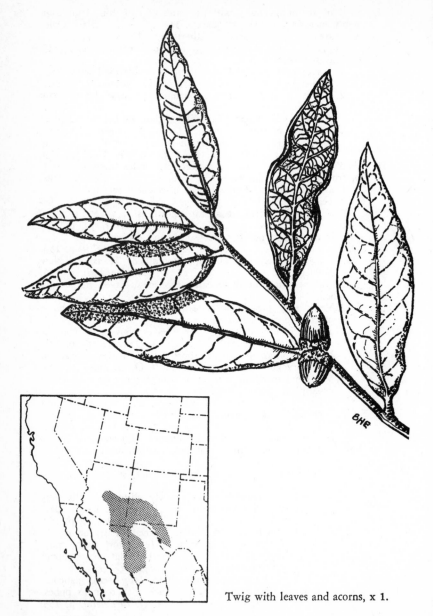

Twig with leaves and acorns, x 1.

FAGACEAE

SILVERLEAF OAK. WHITELEAF OAK

Quercus hypoleucoides A. Camus

HABIT. An evergreen shrub or small tree 20–30 feet high (rarely 60 feet) and 10–15 inches in diameter; narrow, inversely conic, round-topped crown with slender branches.

LEAVES. Lanceolate or oblong-lanceolate to elliptic; occasionally falcate; 2–4 inches long and ½–1 inch wide; acute; entire or with a few coarse teeth near apex; revolute margins; thick and leathery; dark yellow-green and lustrous above, covered below with thick tomentum; turning yellow or brown and falling during the spring after appearance of new leaves; petioles stout, ⅛–¼ inch long, hairy.

FLOWERS. Staminate aments 4–5 inches long, slender, hairy, with 4–5-lobed, hairy calyx; pistillate mosty solitary, with dark red stigmas.

FRUIT. Ovoid; ½–⅔ inch long; acute or rounded at narrow, hoary-pubescent apex; dark green, becoming light chestnut-brown; sessile or peduncled; usually solitary; shell thick and lined with white tomentum; annual, but often maturing in second year; enclosed for about ⅓ its length in turbinate, thick cup, pubescent inside and out.

TWIGS. Stout; rigid; hoary-tomentose at first, becoming glaucous and red-brown to black. Winter buds: ⅛ inch long, ovoid, obtuse, light chestnut-brown.

BARK. Rather thick (¾–1 inch); nearly black; deeply furrowed into broad, thick-scaled ridges.

WOOD. Heavy; hard; very strong; close-grained; heartwood dark brown; sapwood thick, lighter colored.

SILVICAL CHARACTERS. Upper Sonoran and Transition zones; on low, dry, mountain sites; scattered but nowhere abundant through pine forests at elevations of 6,000–7,000 feet.

* * *

Quercus shumardii var. *texana* (Buckl.) Ashe, Texas Oak, occurs in western Texas. It is characterized by deeply lobed, bristle-tipped deciduous leaves.

[139]

a. Twig with leaves, x 1.
b. Different form of leaves, x 1.
c. Acorn, x 1.

FAGACEAE

Canyon Live Oak. Goldencup Oak.
Quercus chrysolepis Liebm.

HABIT. An evergreen shrub or small to medium-sized tree 60–80 feet high and 1–5 feet in diameter; very large, spreading crown, with huge, horizontal branches; forming dense thickets on exposed, mountain slopes.

LEAVES. Oblong-ovate to elliptic; 1–4 inches long and ½–2 inches wide; acute, cuspidate; dimorphous, mostly entire on old trees and dentate or sinuate-dentate on young trees, or the 2 forms appearing together; revolute margins; thick and leathery; bright yellow-green and glabrous above; tawny-tomentose, becoming glabrous and blue-green below; persistent 3–4 years; petioles rarely ½ inch long, yellow.

FLOWERS. Staminate aments 2–4 inches long, slender, tomentose, with 5–7-lobed, yellow and red tipped, pubescent calyx; pistillate with bright red stigmas.

FRUIT. Ellipsoidal or ovoid; ½–2 inches long; acute or rounded at apex; light chestnut-brown; sessile or short-stalked; usually solitary; shell thick and lined with loose tomentum; maturing in second year; enclosed only at base in turbinate or hemispheric cup, pubescent or densely tomentose.

TWIGS. Slender; rigid or flexible; tomentose at first, becoming tomentose to glabrous and brown or gray. Winter buds: ⅛ inch long, ovoid or oval, acute, light chestnut-brown.

BARK. Rather thick (¾–1½ inches); gray-brown, tinged with red; smooth except for small scales.

WOOD. Heavy; hard; very strong; tough; close-grained; heartwood light brown; sapwood thick and darker colored; used to some extent for tools, wagons, etc.

SILVICAL CHARACTERS. Upper Sonoran and Transition zones; tolerant when young; adapted to dry, gravelly soils; in mountain cañons or exposed slopes.

GENERAL. The variety *palmeri* (Engelm.) Sarg., sometimes designated as *Q. wilcoxii* Rydb., growing in Arizona, New Mexico, Utah, and Nevada, differs from the species in being usually shrubby and having rigid, oblong or semiorbicular, spinose-dentate leaves.

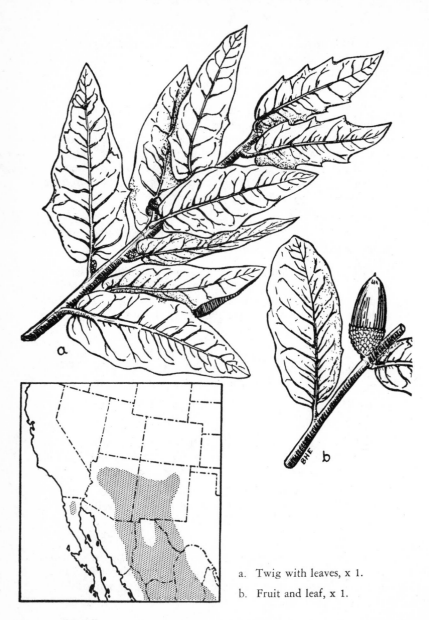

a. Twig with leaves, x 1.

b. Fruit and leaf, x 1.

FAGACEAE

EMORY OAK. BLACK OAK

Quercus emoryi Torr.

HABIT. An evergreen shrub or small tree rarely 40–60 feet high and 2–5 feet in diameter; round-topped, symmetrical crown with stout, rigid, drooping branches.

LEAVES. Oblong-lanceolate; 1–2½ inches long and ½–1 inch wide; acute and mucronate at apex; entire or remotely repand-serrate; thick, rigid, leathery; dark green above, pale below; both surfaces glabrous or puberulous, with tufts of white hairs at base of slender midrib; falling in April with appearance of new leaves; petioles stout, ¼ inch long, pubescent.

FLOWERS. Staminate aments 2–3 inches long, hoary-tomentose, with 5–7-lobed, yellow, hairy calyx, pistillate hairy, styles slightly spreading.

FRUIT. Oblong, oval, or ovoid; ½–¾ inch long; rounded at narrow, pilose apex; light green, becoming dark brown or nearly black; sessile or short-stalked; solitary; shell thin and lined with thick tomentum; maturing in one year; enclosed for ⅓–½ its length in shallow or hemispheric cup, pubescent inside and out.

TWIGS. Slender; rigid; tomentose and bright red at first, becoming glabrous and dark brown. Winter buds: ¼ inch long, ellipsoidal, acute, chestnut-brown, pubescent toward apex.

BARK. Thick (1–2 inches); dark brown or nearly black; deeply furrowed and scaly plated.

WOOD. Heavy; hard; strong; brittle; close-grained; heartwood dark brown or nearly black; sapwood thick, bright brown; unimportant.

SILVICAL CHARACTERS. Upper Sonoran, occasionally extending down into Lower Sonoran zone; on foothill and mountain slopes, at elevations of 4,000–10,000 feet; very abundant, forming a large percentage of forests; growth generally slow and shrubby; coppices freely; acorns are sweet and an important article of human food; evergreen leaves and acorns important winter food for wild and domestic animals.

[143]

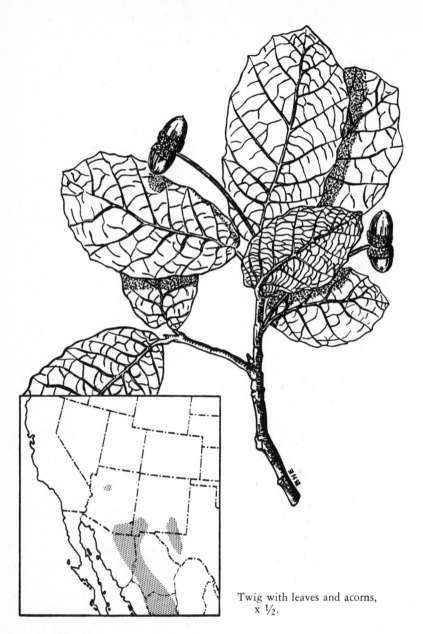

Twig with leaves and acorns,
x ½.

FAGACEAE

NETLEAF OAK

Quercus reticulata Humb. & Bonpl. (*Quercus diversicolor* Trel.)

HABIT. An evergreen shrub or (rarely in the United States) a tree seldom over 40 feet high and 12 inches in diameter; round-topped crown with thick, large branches.

LEAVES. Broadly obovate; 1–5 inches long and ¾–4 inches broad; obtuse and rounded (rarely acute) at apex; entire below and repandly spinose-dentate toward the apex; thick and firm; dark blue and covered with scattered, fascicled hairs above, paler and thickly fulvous-pubescent below; conspicuous reticulate veins; persistent until new leaves form; petioles stout, ¼ inch long.

FLOWERS. Staminate aments about 1–1⅛ inches long, tomentose, with 5–7-lobed, yellow, hairy calyx; pistillate in spikes on long peduncles, tomentose, with dark red styles.

FRUIT. Oblong; ½ inch long; rounded or acute at pilose apex; broad at base; in pairs or many-fruited spikes (rarely solitary); on slender peduncles 2–5 inches long; shell glabrous within; maturing in first year; enclosed for ¼ its length in shallow, dark brown, hairy cup with scales thick-corky on back.

TWIGS. Stout; fulvous-tomentose and light orange at first, becoming more or less pubescent and ash-gray or light brown. Winter buds: ⅛ inch long, ovoid or oval, light red scales ciliate on margin, often surrounded by persistent stipules of upper leaves.

BARK. Thin (¼ inch); dark or light brown; covered by small, closely appressed scales.

WOOD. Very heavy; hard; close-grained; heartwood dark brown; sapwood thick, lighter colored; unimportant.

SILVICAL CHARACTERS. Lower and Upper Sonoran zones, extending into Transition zone; near summits of mountain ranges; at elevations of 7,000–10,000 feet; attaining large size only on the Sierra Madre Mountains of Mexico.

* * *

A related shrubby species, the Wavyleaf Oak, *Quercus undulata* Torr., is a shrub or rarely a small tree from Colorado to Nevada and south to Arizona and Texas. It is characterized by ovate, shallowly lobed, crisp, persistently scabrous leaves and hemispheric acorn cup.

[145]

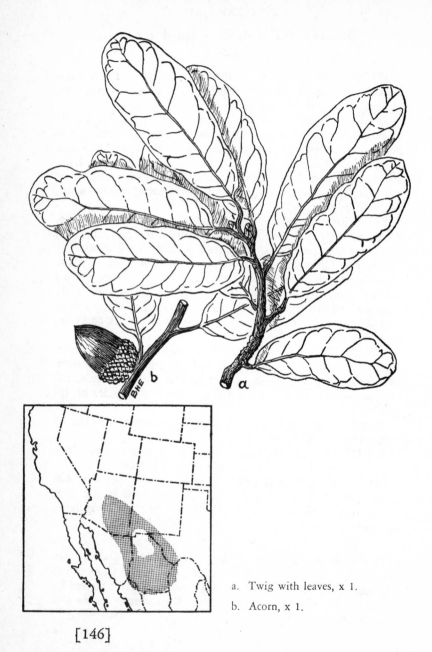

a. Twig with leaves, x 1.

b. Acorn, x 1.

[146]

FAGACEAE

MEXICAN BLUE OAK

Quercus oblongifolia Torr.

HABIT. An evergreen shrub or tree rarely 30 feet high and 18–30 inches in diameter; handsome, symmetrical, round-topped crown with stout, spreading branches.

LEAVES. Ovate or elliptic; 1–2 inches long and ½–¾ inch wide; rounded or acute at apex; entire and sometimes undulate with margins thick and revolute, or rarely coarsely toothed on vigorous shoots; thin and firm; glabrous; blue-green and lustrous above, paler below; conspicuous veins; persistent until appearance of new leaves; petioles stout, ¼ inch long.

FLOWERS. Staminate aments about 1½ inches long, hoary-tomentose, with 5–6-lobed, bright yellow, pilose calyx; pistillate sessile or short-stalked, styles light red.

FRUIT. Ovoid to obovoid; ½–¾ inch long; full and rounded at apex; dark chestnut-brown, becoming lighter; sessile or rarely long-stalked; usually solitary; shell glabrous within; maturing in first year; enclosed for ⅓ its length in cup, yellow-green and pubescent within, hoary-tomentose without, with scales slightly fringed at rim.

TWIGS. Slender; rigid; slightly hairy and reddish at first, soon becoming glabrous and ash-gray. Winter buds: ⅟₁₆–⅛ inch long, oblong, obtuse, chestnut-brown.

BARK. Rather thick (¾–1½ inches); ash-gray; broken into nearly square, platelike scales.

WOOD. Very heavy; hard; strong; brittle; checks badly; difficult to split; heartwood dark brown or nearly black; sapwood thick, brown; unimportant; used for fuel.

SILVICAL CHARACTERS. Upper Sonoran zone; abundant on foothills of Arizona and New Mexico; at elevations of 4,500–6,500 feet; with Emory and Arizona oaks.

* * *

A related species, the Gray Oak, *Quercus grisea* Liebm., is a small to medium-sized tree from western Texas to Arizona. It is difficult to distinguish from *Q. arizonica* and *Q. oblongifolia,* but is characterized by elliptic to ovate gray-green leaves, stellate-pubescent below and deep acorn cup.

a. Acorn, x 1

b. Twig with leaves, x 1.

c. Different leaf forms, x 1.

[148]

FAGACEAE

Arizona White Oak
Quercus arizonica Sarg.

HABIT. Nearly evergreen shrub or tree rarely 40–60 feet high and 3–4 feet in diameter; handsome, large, round-topped crown with massive, contorted, nearly horizontal branches.

LEAVES. Oblong-lanceolate to broadly ovate; 1–4 inches long and ½–2 inches wide; acute or rounded; entire or repandly spinose-dentate above; thickened, revolute margin; thick, firm and rigid; dull, dark, blue-green and glabrous above, paler and densely pubescent below; coarse, reticulate veins; persistent until spring just before appearance of new leaves; petioles stout, ¼–½ inch long, tomentose.

FLOWERS. Staminate aments 2–3 inches long, tomentose, with 4–7-lobed, pale yellow, pubescent calyx; pistillate short-stalked, tomentose.

FRUIT. Oblong, oval, or slightly obovoid; ¾–1 inch long; rounded at puberulous apex; dark chestnut-brown, becoming light brown; sessile or hairy-stalked; shell glabrous within; maturing in first year; enclosed for ½ its length in hairy cup with scales thick-corky and red-tipped.

TWIGS. Stout; fulvous-tomentose and red-brown at first, becoming glabrous and dark red-brown. Winter buds: ¹⁄₁₆ inch long, subglobose, chestnut-brown, ciliate on margins.

BARK. Rather thick (1 inch); pale or ash-gray; furrowed and ridged.

WOOD. Very heavy; hard; strong; close-grained; checks badly; difficult to split; heartwood dark brown or nearly black; sapwood thick, lighter colored; unimportant.

SILVICAL CHARACTERS. Upper Sonoran zone; most common live oak of Southwest; on dry mountain slopes; at elevations of 5,000–10,000 feet; with pinyons and junipers.

* * *

A similar species, the Toumey oak, *Quercus toumeyi* Sarg., of southwestern New Mexico and southeastern Arizona differs from the Arizona white oak in its smaller leaves ½–¾ inch long, ovate to ovate-oblong and puberulous below; and in its smaller nut, ½–⅔ inch long.

[149]

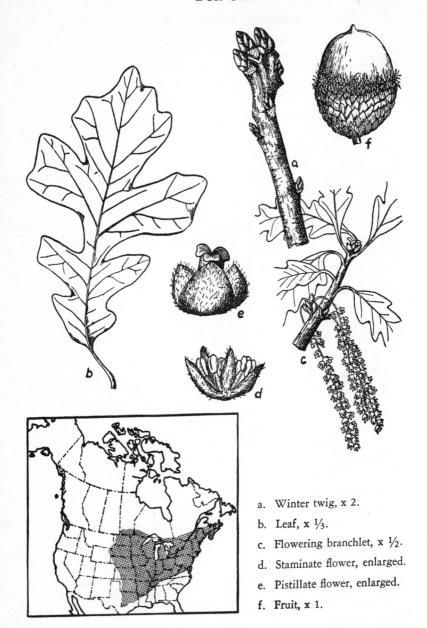

a. Winter twig, x 2.

b. Leaf, x ⅓.

c. Flowering branchlet, x ½.

d. Staminate flower, enlarged.

e. Pistillate flower, enlarged.

f. Fruit, x 1.

FAGACEAE

Bur Oak

Quercus macrocarpa Michx.

HABIT. A shrub or tree in the northeastern portion of the Rocky Mountain region; crown broad with large, spreading branches.

LEAVES. Obovate to oblong; 6–12 inches long and 3–6 inches wide; rounded or acute apex; wedge-shaped at base; crenately 5–9-lobed, usually cut nearly to midrib by two, opposite, central sinuses; lobes often crenately lobed; thick and firm; dark green and lustrous above, pale green or silver-white and soft-pubescent below; deciduous in autumn; petioles stout, 1/3–1 inch long.

FLOWERS. Staminate aments 4–6 inches long, slender, with 4–6-lobed, yellow-green, pubescent calyx; pistillate sessile or stalked, tomentose, with bright red styles.

FRUIT. Variable in size or shape; ellipsoidal to broadovoid; 3/5 inch long in region (sometimes 2 inches long in South); rounded at obtuse or depressed hairy apex; brown; sessile or long-stalked; usually solitary; shell glabrous within; maturing in first year; enclosed for 1/3 to all of its length in tomentose, short-fringed cup; edible.

TWIGS. Stout; yellow-brown and pubescent at first, becoming ash-gray to brown and glabrous; sometimes developing corky wings. Winter buds: 1/8–1/4 inch long, broadly ovoid, red-brown, pubescent.

BARK. Thick (1–2 inches); gray-brown; deeply furrowed and ridged.

WOOD. Heavy; hard; strong; tough; close-grained; durable; heartwood dark to light brown; sapwood thin, lighter; important.

SILVICAL CHARACTERS. Transition zone; moist, rich bottom-lands to low, dry hills in Northwest; extending farthest Northwest of eastern oaks; common and attaining large size in Crook County, Wyoming.

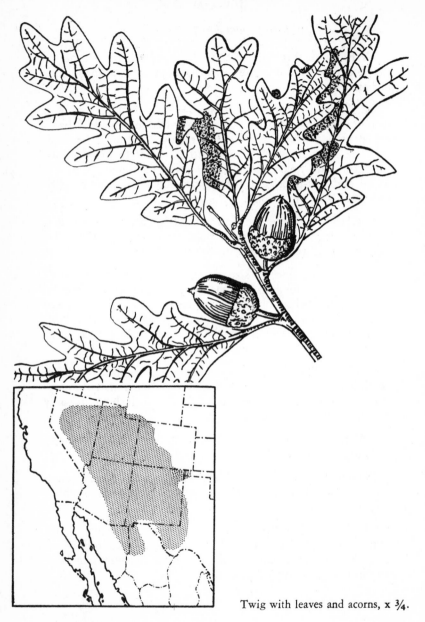

Twig with leaves and acorns, x ¾.

FAGACEAE

GAMBEL OAK. ROCKY MOUNTAIN WHITE OAK

Quercus gambelii Nutt. (*Quercus utahensis* Rydb.)
(*Quercus leptophylla* Rydb.) (*Quercus novomexicana* Rydb.)

HABIT. A shrub or small tree 25–35 feet high and 6–10 inches in diameter; narrow, open crown with thick, erect branches.

LEAVES. Oblong-obovate; 2½–7 inches long and 1½–3½ inches wide; rounded at apex; divided, often nearly to midrib, into 3–5 pairs of lateral lobes; thick and firm; dark green and nearly glabrous above, pale and soft-pubescent below; deciduous in autumn; petioles stout; ⅖–1 inch long, tomentose becoming glabrous.

FLOWERS. Staminate aments 2–2½ inches long, hairy, with scarious calyx; pistillate usually solitary, tomentose.

FRUIT. Ovoid; ⅗–¾ inch long; broad and rounded at ends; sessile or short-stalked; usually solitary; shell glabrous within; maturing in first year; enclosed for about ½ its length in thick, hemispheric, pubescent cup, with scales thickened on back.

TWIGS. Stout; red-brown and pubescent at first, becoming orange-brown. Winter buds: ⅛–¼ inch long, brown, hairy.

BARK. Thin; gray-brown; rough and superficially scaly.

WOOD. Heavy; hard; close-grained; lumber used locally.

SILVICAL CHARACTERS. Upper Sonoran and Transition zones; dry foothills and cañon walls; the only abundant deciduous oak tree in the low Rocky Mountain forests.

GENERAL. This is a large and variable species and attempts have been made to divide it into numerous species and varieties. Botanists have had difficulty in distinguishing between those forms and they are not considered distinct in this book.

* * *

Quercus turbinella Greene, Shrub Live Oak, is a shrubby form, rarely becoming a small tree, that extends from California to New Mexico and north into Colorado. It is characterized by persistent, small, ovate leaves with many sharp teeth and a resinous pubescence on the lower surface.

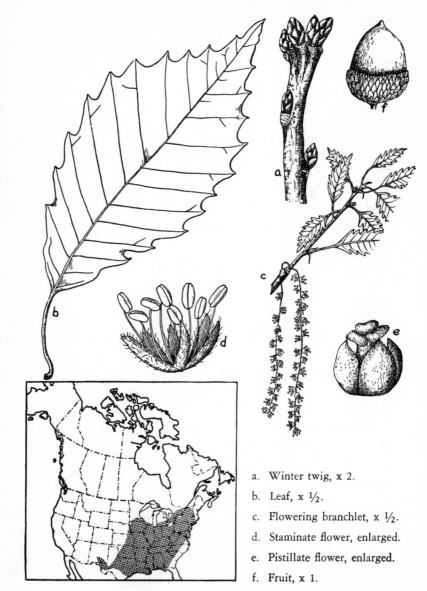

a. Winter twig, x 2.

b. Leaf, x ½.

c. Flowering branchlet, x ½.

d. Staminate flower, enlarged.

e. Pistillate flower, enlarged.

f. Fruit, x 1.

FAGACEAE

CHINQUAPIN OAK. CHESTNUT OAK

Quercus muehlenbergii Engelm.

HABIT. A small tree 20–30 feet high in the Rocky Mountain region, but much larger farther east; narrow crown.

LEAVES. Oblong-lanceolate to broad-obovate; 4–7 inches long and 1–4 inches wide; acute or acuminate at apex; coarsely serrate with large, glandular-tipped teeth; thick and firm; light yellow-green and glabrous above, pale and short-pubescent below; deciduous; petioles slender, 3/4–1½ inches long.

FLOWERS. Staminate aments 3–4 inches long, pilose, with 5–6-lobed, light yellow, hairy calyx; pistillate solitary or spiked, tomentose, with bright red styles.

FRUIT. Broad-ovoid; ½–1 inch long; narrowed and rounded at apex; light chestnut-brown; sessile or short-stalked; solitary or paired; shell glabrous within; maturing in first year; enclosed for about ½ its length in thin, tomentose cup.

TWIGS. Slender; orange-brown to gray; glabrous. Winter buds: 1/8–1/4 inch long, ovoid, acute, chestnut-brown.

BARK. Thin (rarely over ½ inch); ash-gray; more or less rough and scaly.

WOOD. Heavy; very hard; strong; durable; close-grained; heartwood light brown; sapwood thin, light-colored; used for cooperage, fencing, ties, etc.

SILVICAL CHARACTERS. Upper Sonoran and lower part of Transition zones; intolerant; moist to dry sites.

GENERAL. The western variety of this species, Bray's oak, *Q. muehlenbergii* var. *brayi* (Small) Sarg., becomes a large tree in New Mexico and western Texas. This is differentiated by larger acorns (1¼ inches long) and deeper cups up to 1 inch in diameter.

* * *

GIANT CHINQUAPIN. GOLDEN CHINQUAPIN

Castanopsis chrysophylla A.DC.

A Pacific Coast tree which barely enters this region in western Nevada. While resembling the oaks, to which it is closely related, it can be readily identified by the spiny bur covering the nut and by the persistent leaves golden-scaly below.

[155]

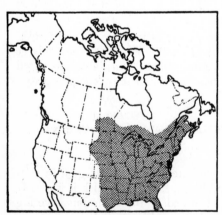

a. Winter twig, x 2.

b. Leaf, x ½.

c. Flowering branchlet, x ½.

d. Flower, enlarged.

e. Fruit, x 2.

[156]

ULMACEAE

American Elm. White Elm

Ulmus americana L.

HABIT. A handsome tree sometimes 100–120 feet high and 6–11 feet in diameter; trunk sometimes single, usually divided near the ground into several erect limbs; symmetrical, vase-shaped crown.

LEAVES. Alternate; simple; obovate-oblong to elliptical; 4–6 inches long and 1–3 inches wide; acuminate; unequal and oblique at base; margins coarsely doubly serrate; dark green and glabrous or scabrous above, pale and pubescent or rarely glabrous below; turning clear yellow in autumn; deciduous; petioles ¼ inch long, stout; stipules linear, ½–2 inches long, fugacious.

FLOWERS. Regular; perfect; small; in 3–4-flowered, short-stalked fascicles; on long, slender, drooping pedicels; appearing before leaves; calyx 7–9-lobed, green, puberulous and ciliate; corolla absent; stamens 5–6, anthers bright red; ovary usually 1-celled by abortion, 1-ovuled, flattened, light green, ciliate, with 2-lobed style.

FRUIT. Flattened, ovoid to obovoid-oblong samara ½ inch long; seed cavity encircled by thin, membranaceous, notched wing; ciliate on margins.

TWIGS. Slender; round; light green and pubescent at first, becoming red-brown, glabrous and marked by pale lenticels and large, raised leaf scars. Winter buds: terminal absent; lateral ⅛ inch long, scaly, ovoid, acute, brown.

BARK. Thick (1–1½ inches); ash-gray; interspersed with light-colored, corky layers; diamond-shaped ridges common.

WOOD. Heavy; hard; strong; tough; coarse-grained; ring-porous; heartwood light brown; sapwood thick, lighter colored; important for specialty uses.

SILVICAL CHARACTERS. Upper Sonoran and Transition zones; moderately tolerant; shallow-rooted; adapted to variety of sites; seriously threatened by Dutch Elm disease.

GENERAL. The American elm, rock elm (*U. thomasii* Sarg.), slippery elm (*U. rubra* Muhl.), and Siberian elm (*U. pumila* L.) are commonly planted as ornamental trees in this region.

ULMACEAE

The Hackberries

Characteristics of the Genus *Celtis* L.

HABIT. Shrubs or trees often planted for shade or ornamentals; irregularly pinnate branching.

LEAVES. Alternate; simple; lanceolate to ovate; acute or acuminate at apex; often oblique at base; serrate or entire margins; membranaceous or subcoriaceous; deciduous; mostly long petiolate; stipules thin, caducous, fugacious, enclosing leaf in bud.

FLOWERS. Regular; polygamo-monoecious or rarely monoecious; minute; the staminate in fascicles toward the base of twig; above these the pistillate or perfect, solitary or in few-flowered fascicles; pedicellate; appearing soon after the unfolding of the leaves; calyx 4–5-lobed, green-yellow, deciduous; corolla absent; stamens as many as calyx lobes and opposite them; ovary 1-celled, ovoid, sessile, green and lustrous.

FRUIT. Subglobose or ovoid drupe; tipped with remnants of style; thick firm skin; thin, pulpy flesh; nutlet bony, thick-walled, reticulate-pitted; ripening in autumn and often remaining long after leaves fall. Seed: filling cavity in nutlet.

TWIGS. Round; unarmed or spinose. Winter buds: terminal absent; lateral small, scaly; branchlets prolonged by an upper lateral bud.

BARK. Usually gray and smooth, sometimes with conspicuous, corky, warty excrescences.

WOOD. Rather heavy; fairly hard; not strong; odorless; ring-porous; moderately important; often sold as elm.

GENERAL. This genus consists of about 70 species scattered through the north temperate and tropical regions; five species and several varieties have been listed for the United States; native species often disfigured by gall-making insects distorting the buds and producing broomlike clusters of branchlets; this genus is in a confused state and needs revision; distributions have not been accurately determined.

[158]

KEY TO THE SPECIES OF CELTIS

I. Fruit dark purple, on pedicels somewhat longer than petioles of leaf; leaves sharply serrate with numerous teeth, veinlets not conspicuous on lower surface; scattered through eastern parts of region ....1. *Celtis occidentalis,* p. 161.

II. Fruit orange-red to yellow; leaves entire or sparingly toothed.

   A. Fruit on pedicels shorter or only slightly longer than petioles of leaf, dark orange-red; leaves oval to lanceolate, entire or rarely sparingly toothed; veinlets not conspicuous; Texas and southern New Mexico............................
    ....2. *Celtus laevigata* var. *texana,* p. 163.

   B. Fruit on pedicels much longer than petioles of leaf, orange-red or yellow; leaves broadly ovate, entire to coarsely serrate; veinlets conspicuous on lower surface; scattered through region ....3. *Celtis reticulata,* p. 165.

HACKBERRY

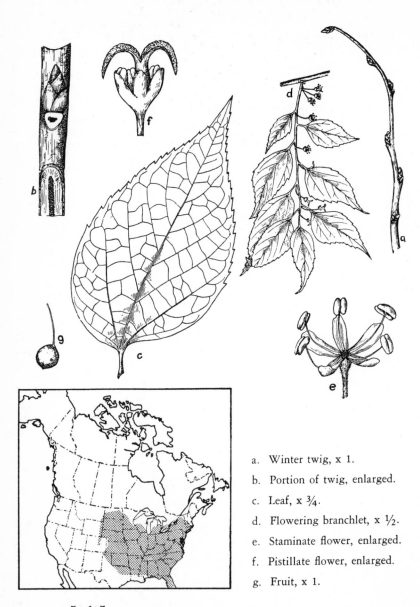

a. Winter twig, x 1.

b. Portion of twig, enlarged.

c. Leaf, x ¾.

d. Flowering branchlet, x ½.

e. Staminate flower, enlarged.

f. Pistillate flower, enlarged.

g. Fruit, x 1.

[160]

ULMACEAE

HACKBERRY

Celtis occidentalis L.

(*Celtis occidentalis* var. *crassifolia* Gray)

HABIT. Occasionally shrubby, but usually a rather large tree 100–120 feet high and 1–2 feet in diameter; crown rounded and of large, spreading, often pendulous branches.

LEAVES. Ovate to ovate-lanceolate; 2½–4 inches long and 1½–2 inches wide in Rocky Mountain region; long-acuminate apex; obliquely rounded base; coarsely serrate or rarely almost entire; rather thin; light, dull green and rough above, slightly paler and pilose along veins below; turning light yellow in autumn; petioles ¼–½ inch long, villose-pubescent or rarely glabrous.

FLOWERS. On drooping pedicels; calyx with 5 linear, acute, thin, scarious lobes more or less laciniately cut, often hairy-tufted at apex; receptacle hoary-tomentose.

FRUIT. ⅓ inch in diameter; subglobose, ovoid, or obovoid; dark purple; on stems ½–¾ inch long; thick, tough skin; dark orange-colored flesh; oblong, pointed, light brown, slightly rugose nutlet. Seed: pale brown.

TWIGS. Slender; ridged; light brown, becoming darker; pubescent or glabrous; marked by pale, oblong lenticels; pith finely chambered at nodes. Winter buds: ¼ inch long, ovoid, pointed, pubescent, chestnut-brown.

BARK. Rather thick (1–1½ inches); dark brown; smooth, or more or less roughened by irregular wartlike excrescences or by long ridges.

WOOD. Heavy; rather soft; not strong; coarse-grained; heartwood clear, light yellow; sapwood thick, lighter colored; of little use in the west.

SILVICAL CHARACTERS. Upper Sonoran and lower portions of Transition zone; moderately tolerant; rapid growing; the largest and most handsome member of the genus; frequently planted in west because of drought resistance; adapted to variety of sites, doing best on moist, rich soils, and stunted and scraggly on poor, dry sites.

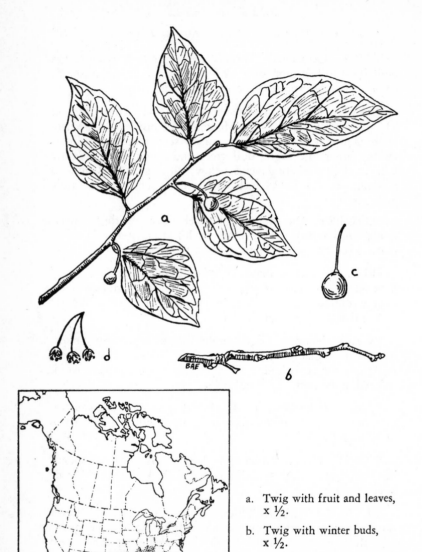

a. Twig with fruit and leaves,
   x ½.

b. Twig with winter buds,
   x ½.

c. Fruit, x 1.

d. Staminate flowers, x 1.

[162]

ULMACEAE

Texas Sugarberry. Hackberry
Celtis laevigata var. *texana* (Scheele) Sarg.

HABIT. A shrub or small tree rarely over 25 feet high and 12 inches in diameter; crown broad with spreading or pendulous branches; often growing in clusters.

LEAVES. Ovate to lanceolate; 1½–3 inches long and ¾–1½ inches wide; acuminate apex; unsymmetrically rounded or cordate at base; entire or sparingly and irregularly serrate; often subcoriaceous; dark green and smooth or granulate above, paler and glabrous or hairy along veins below; veinlets not conspicuous; petioles ⅕–¼ inch long, slender, pale-pubescent.

FLOWERS. On slender, glabrous pedicels; calyx divided into 5, ovate-lanceolate, glabrous or puberulous, scarious lobes hairy-tufted at apex.

FRUIT. ¼ inch long; subglobose or short-oblong; dark orange-red; on glabrous or puberulous pedicels slightly longer than petioles; nutlet slightly rugose.

TWIGS. Slender; red and glabrous or gray-brown and pubescent; marked by pale, oblong lenticels and narrow, elevated leaf scars. Winter buds: 1/16–⅛ inch long, ovoid, pointed, puberulous, chestnut-brown.

BARK. Rather thin (⅓–⅔ inch); pale or grayish; rough; not often covered with wartlike excrescences.

WOOD. Heavy; soft; not strong; close-grained; heartwood light yellow; sapwood thick and lighter colored; unimportant.

SILVICAL CHARACTERS. Upper Sonoran zone; site varies from moist to rocky bluffs and dry hillsides; southern New Mexico and east.

GENERAL. The species proper, *Celtis laevigata* Willd., is distributed through the southeastern portions of the United States, extending west to eastern Texas. The distribution shown includes both the species and its variety.

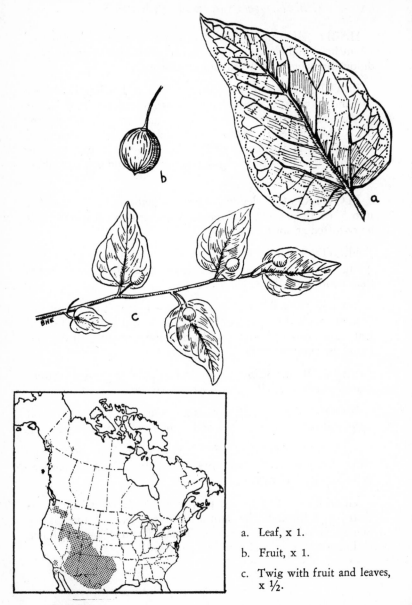

[164]

a. Leaf, x 1.

b. Fruit, x 1.

c. Twig with fruit and leaves, x ½.

ULMACEAE

Netleaf Hackberry

Celtis reticulata Torr.

[*Celtis laevigata* var. *brevipes* (S. Wats.) Sarg.]

HABIT. A shrub or small tree rarely 30 feet high and 6–12 inches in diameter; crown open and irregular with stout, ascending branches.

LEAVES. Broadly ovate; 1¼–3 inches long and ¾–1½ inches wide; acute or acuminate apex; obliquely rounded at base; entire margins or with a few broad teeth; thick; dark green and rough or smooth above, yellow-green, somewhat hairy, and with conspicuous reticulate veinlets below; petioles ⅛–¼ inch long, stout, more or less densely pubescent.

FLOWERS. On slender, pubescent pedicels; calyx divided into 5, linear, acute, scarious lobes laciniately cut at apex; receptacle hoary-tomentose.

FRUIT. ¼ inch in diameter; subglobose to ellipsoidal; lustrous; orange-red or yellow; on pubescent pedicels, ⅓–½ inch long.

TWIGS. Slender; green and pubescent or tomentose at first, becoming red-brown and pubescent or glabrous; marked by small, pale lenticels.

BARK. Thick; ash-gray; rough with prominent, short, projecting ridges.

WOOD. Rather heavy; soft; not strong; heartwood clear, light yellow; sapwood thick, lighter colored; unimportant.

SILVICAL CHARACTERS. Upper Sonoran zone; in mountain ravines and on dry, rocky hillsides and cañon slopes.

* * *

A closely related form has been considered by some authors to be a separate species, *Celtis douglasii* Planch. This was distinguished by the following characters: Leaves rough above, pale below, and coarsely serrate; fruit light orange-brown, with pedicels often 3–4 times as long as leaf petioles; distribution is in the Upper Sonoran zone from Arizona (south slope of Grand Cañon), western Texas and Colorado (eastern foothills) into Utah, Idaho, California, Oregon, Washington, and British Columbia.

[165]

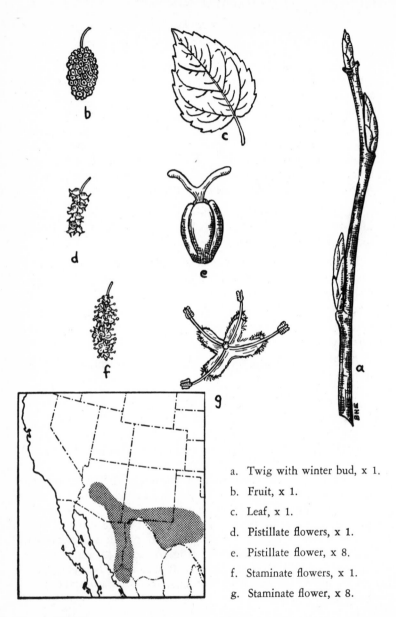

a. Twig with winter bud, x 1.

b. Fruit, x 1.

c. Leaf, x 1.

d. Pistillate flowers, x 1.

e. Pistillate flower, x 8.

f. Staminate flowers, x 1.

g. Staminate flower, x 8.

[166]

MORACEAE

Texas Mulberry. Mexican Mulberry

Morus microphylla Buckl.

HABIT. A shrub or small tree 15–20 feet high and 12–14 inches in diameter; crown scraggly and irregular.

LEAVES. Alternate; simple; ovate; 1–2 inches long; entire or shallowly 3-lobed; acute or acuminate; margins coarsely serrate; thin and firm; dark green and often roughened by tubercles above, paler and glabrous or pubescent below; deciduous; petioles slender, hairy, ⅓ inch long; stipules white, tomentose, ½ inch long, linear-lanceolate, acute, enclosing, leaf in the bud.

FLOWERS. Regular; dioecious (rarely monoecious); minute; staminate in many-flowered spikes; pistillate in few-flowered spikes; calyx 4-lobed, dark green, hairy; corolla absent; stamens 4, anthers bright yellow; ovary 2-celled (one of cells smaller and disappearing), ovoid, flat, included within calyx, green and glabrous.

FRUIT. Drupaceous, enclosed in thickened, berry-like calyx and united into a compound fruit (syncarp); ½ inch long; subglobose or short ovoid; red, becoming nearly black; sweet and palatable; drupe ⅙ inch long, ovoid, with thin-walled brown nutlet. Seed: ovoid, pointed, pale yellow.

TWIGS. Slender; round; unarmed; pubescent, becoming glabrous; orange-red; marked by small lenticels and elevated, nearly orbicular leaf scars. Winter buds: scaly, terminal absent, branchlets prolonged by upper axillary bud, ovoid, acute, lustrous, chestnut-brown.

BARK. Thin (rarely ½ inch); light gray, tinged with red; furrowed and scaly.

WOOD. Heavy; hard; close-grained; ring-porous; heartwood dark orange or brown; sapwood thick, light-colored; unimportant.

SILVICAL CHARACTERS. Upper Sonoran zone; intolerant; fibrous roots; dry hills and mountain cañons; possibly not distinct from the Mexican species, *Morus celtidifolia* H.B.K.

* * *

The eastern Red Mulberry, *Morus rubra* L., and the Asiatic White Mulberry, *Morus alba* L. are commonly planted as ornamentals in this region.

[167]

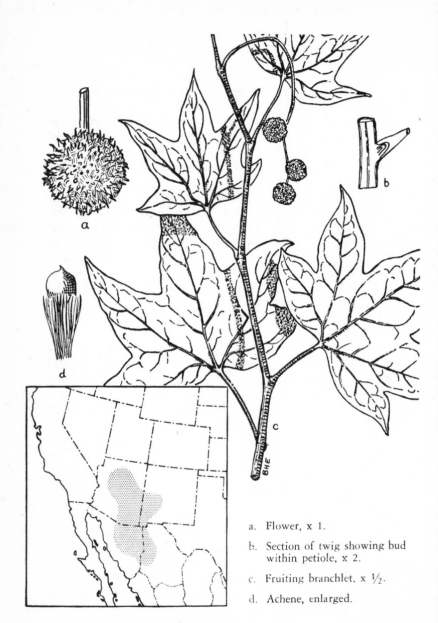

a. Flower, x 1.

b. Section of twig showing bud within petiole, x 2.

c. Fruiting branchlet, x ½.

d. Achene, enlarged.

PLATANACEAE

Platanus wrightii S. Wats.

HABIT. A tree often 60–80 feet high and 4–5 feet in diameter; trunk erect or divided and more or less reclining; crown broad and open with large, contorted branches.

LEAVES. Alternate; simple; broadly ovate; 6–8 inches long and broad; deeply divided into 3–7, acute lobes; entire or dentate margins; thin and firm; light green and glabrous above, pale pubescent below; deciduous; petioles 1½–3 inches long, enlarged at base and enclosing buds; stipules membranaceous, united into tube surrounding twig.

FLOWERS. Regular; monoecious; minute; in dense, racemose heads; on hoary-tomentose peduncles; the staminate red on axillary peduncles, the pistillate light green on terminal peduncles; calyx 3–6-sepaled; corolla 3–6-petaled; stamens as many as sepals and opposite them; ovaries as many as sepals, superior, surrounded at base by pale hairs persistent around the fruit; ovules 1 or rarely 2.

FRUIT. Numerous, elongated achenes; in 1–4 globose heads; in slender, glabrous, pendulous racemes; surmounted by persistent styles; 1-seeded; light yellow-brown; coriaceous. Seed: light chestnut-brown.

TWIGS. Slender; round; zigzag; ash-gray or brown; tomentose at first, becoming glabrous; marked by minute, scattered lenticels; pith conspicuous. Winter buds: terminal absent; lateral ⅛ inch long, smooth, lustrous, 3-scaled, nearly covered at base by narrow leaf scar.

BARK. At base of old trunks thick (3–4 inches), furrowed and ridged; on young trunks thin, cream-white, tinged with green, exfoliating in large, thin, brittle plates.

WOOD. Heavy; hard; not strong; cross-grained; diffuse-porous; with broad rays; heartwood light brown, tinged with red; sapwood thick, lighter colored; used locally for fabrication products.

SILVICAL CHARACTERS. Upper Sonoran zone; intolerant; reproduction scanty; in moist sites on banks of streams in mountain cañons.

GENERAL. This tree is very similar to and perhaps not distinct from the California sycamore, *P. racemosa* Nutt.

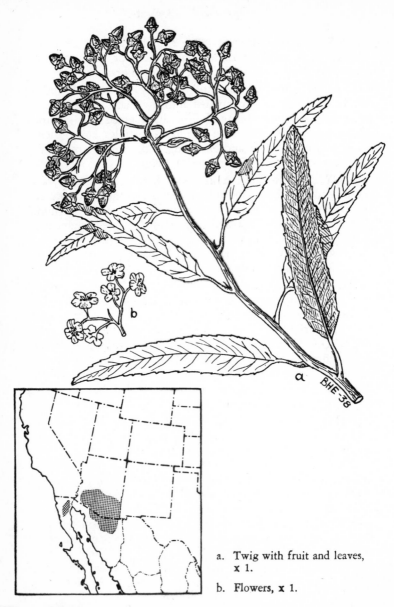

a. Twig with fruit and leaves, x 1.

b. Flowers, x 1.

ROSACEAE

Torrey Vauquelinia

Vauquelinia californica (Torr.) Sarg.

HABIT. A shrub or rarely a small tree 18–20 feet high and 5–6 inches in diameter; trunk slender, often hollow; branches upright, stiff, and crooked.

LEAVES. Alternate or rarely opposite; simple; oblong to narrowly lanceolate; 1½–3 inches long and ¼–½ inch wide; acuminate or rarely rounded at apex; remotely serrate with minute, glandular teeth; coriaceous; bright yellow-green; glabrous above, tomentose below; persistent through winter; long-petiolate; stipules minute, acute, deciduous.

FLOWERS. Regular; perfect; small; in terminal, leafy, hoary-tomentose panicles 2–3 inches across; on slender, hairy, bracted pedicels; calyx short, obconic, leathery, persistent; corolla white, ¼ inch in diameter, of persistent, oblong, reflexed petals; stamens 15–25, in 3–4 rows, persistent filaments; 5 carpels united below into 5-celled, hairy ovary.

FRUIT. Woody, ovoid, 5-celled, tomentose capsule; subtended by remnants of flower; adherent below and splitting down the back at maturity; long persistent on branches. Seed: $\frac{1}{12}$ inch long, 2 in each cell, winged.

TWIGS. Slender; round; bright red-brown, becoming light brown or gray; tomentose; marked by large, elevated leaf scars. Winter buds: axillary, minute, acuminate, red-brown, pubescent.

BARK. Thin ($\frac{1}{16}$ inch); dark red-brown; broken on surface into small, square, persistent, platelike scales.

WOOD. Very hard and heavy; close-grained; diffuse-porous; heartwood dark brown, streaked with red; sapwood thick, lighter colored; unimportant.

SILVICAL CHARACTERS. Transition zone; intolerant; on grassy slopes or in rocky gulches of mountain ranges; reaching tree size at altitudes of about 5,000 feet in the Santa Catalina Mountains of Arizona.

* * *

V. angustifolia Rydb., a similar shrub or small tree has been reported from southern parts of western Texas, New Mexico and Arizona.

[171]

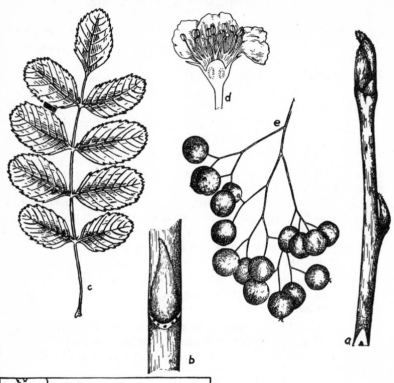

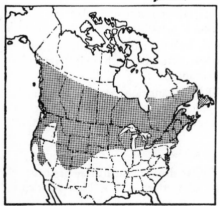

a. Winter twig, x 1.

b. Portion of twig, enlarged.

c. Leaf, x ½.

d. Vertical section of flower, enlarged.

e. Portion of a fruiting cyme, x 1.

ROSACEAE

SITKA MOUNTAIN-ASH

Sorbus sitchensis Roem. [*Sorbus americana* var. *sitchensis*
(Roem.) Sudw.]

HABIT. A shrub or rarely a small tree, seldom 30 feet high
and 12 inches in diameter; crown round-topped, handsome;
with spreading, slender branches.

LEAVES. Alternate; pinnately compound; 4–6 inches long;
with 7–13 mostly sessile leaflets; oblong-oval to ovate-lanceolate; 2–4 inches long and ½–1 inch wide; apex rounded, usually short-pointed; sharply serrate; glabrous; blue-green above,
pale below; deciduous; petioles stout, usually red, 1½–2 inches
long; stipules foliaceous, free from petiole.

FLOWERS. Regular; perfect; small; in broad, flat cymes
3–4 inches across; on short, stout pedicels; appearing after
leaves; calyx tube urn-shaped, puberulous, persistent; corolla
cream-white, ¼ inch in diameter; stamens usually 20 in 3
rows; 2–5, usually 3, carpels, partly united and half-superior or
wholly united and inferior; ovules 2 in each cell.

FRUIT. Berry-like pome; subglobose; ¼–½ inch in diameter; bright orange-red; thin, acid flesh; papery carpels.
Seed: 2, or 1 by abortion, in each cell, ⅛ inch long, ovoid,
brown.

TWIGS. Stout; round; red-brown and pubescent, becoming dark brown and glabrous; marked by large leaf
scars and oblong lenticels. Winter buds: terminal ¼–¾ inch
long, acute, dark red, pilose, with gummy exudation.

BARK. Thin (⅛ inch); light gray; smooth or slightly
roughened by scales; inner bark fragrant.

WOOD. Light; soft; weak; close-grained; diffuse-porous;
heartwood pale brown; sapwood thick and lighter colored.

SILVICAL CHARACTERS. Transition and Canadian
zones; intolerant; slow-growing; abundant seeder; fibrous
roots; prefers moist, rich sites on borders of streams, but
grows well on rocky hillsides; often cultivated.

GENERAL. The taxonomy within this genus is so confused
that it is impossible to show accurate distributions; the map
includes the eastern *Sorbus americana* Marsh and the shrubby
Western Mountain-ash *Sorbus occidentalis* (S. Wats.) Greene.
European Mountain-ash, *Sorbus aucuparia* L., is a frequently
planted ornamental that has become widely naturalized.

[173]

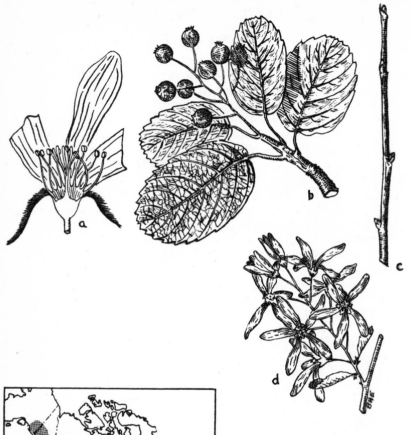

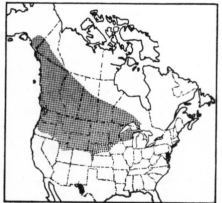

a. Diagram of flower, x 2.

b. Twig with leaves and fruit, x 1.

c. Twig with winter buds, x 1.

d. Flower raceme, x 1.

ROSACEAE

Saskatoon Serviceberry. Western Shadbush

Amelanchier alnifolia Nutt.

HABIT. A shrub or rarely a small tree 25–40 feet high and 8–14 inches in diameter; crown open and oblong.

LEAVES. Alternate; simple; oblong-ovate to oval or ovate; $1\frac{1}{2}$–$2\frac{1}{2}$ inches long and 1–$1\frac{1}{2}$ inches wide; rounded or rarely acute at apex; coarsely serrate only above the middle; thick or thin; dark green and glabrous above, pale below; deciduous; petioles slender, $\frac{1}{2}$-1 inch long; stipules rose color, linear, elongated.

FLOWERS. Regular; perfect; in erect, crowded racemes; appearing with leaves; calyx tube campanulate, persistent on fruit; corolla white, $\frac{1}{2}$–$\frac{3}{4}$ inch long, of 5, oblong-obovate, clawed petals; stamens usually 20 in 3 rows, filaments persistent on fruit; ovary 5-celled with each cell divided by partition, densely tomentose at summit; ovules 2 in each cell, erect.

FRUIT. Berry-like pome; short oblong or ovoid; $\frac{1}{4}$–$\frac{1}{2}$ inch in diameter; dark blue; more or less covered with glaucous bloom; flesh sweet and succulent; open at summit. Seed: 10 or often 5 by abortion, dark chestnut-brown.

TWIGS. Slender; round; becoming glabrous and red-brown to dark gray-brown. Winter buds: terminal $\frac{1}{6}$–$\frac{1}{4}$ inch long, ovoid to ellipsoidal, acute or acuminate, chestnut-brown.

BARK. Thin ($\frac{1}{8}$ inch); light brown, tinged with red; smooth or slightly furrowed.

WOOD. Heavy; hard; close-grained; diffuse-porous; heartwood light brown; sapwood thick, lighter colored; unimportant.

SILVICAL CHARACTERS. Upper Sonoran to Canadian zones; tolerant when young; abundant seeder; deep fibrous roots capable of sprouting repeatedly; moist valleys, prairies, and borders of streams to dry mountain slopes.

GENERAL. A highly variable species. Other similar shrubby western forms that sometimes become small trees are Pacific Serviceberry, *A. florida* Lindl., ranging from Alaska to northwestern California; and Utah Serviceberry, *A. utahensis* Koehne, ranging from southeastern Wyoming to southern Montana to southeastern Oregon and south to Baja California and western Texas. The Eastern Serviceberry, *A. arborea* (Michx.) Fern. is reported from eastern Wyoming.

ROSACEAE

THE HAWTHORNS

Characteristics of the Genus *Crataegus* L.

HABIT. Deciduous shrubs or small trees; usually spiny; crown generally rounded and widespreading.

LEAVES. Alternate; simple; deciduous; usually serrate and often more or less lobed; membranaceous to coriaceous; stipules persistent until autumn or early deciduous, small to leaflike, often bright-colored; petiolate.

FLOWERS. Regular; perfect, in few- or many-flowered terminal corymbs; pedicellate; calyx 5-lobed, tubular, persistent on fruit or deciduous; corolla 5-petaled, white, inserted on edge of disk lining calyx-tube; stamens 5–25; ovary inferior, of 1–5 carpels connate at base, with 2 ovules in each cell; styles as many as carpels.

FRUIT. Small, variously colored pome with 1–5 bony, 1-seeded nutlets; flesh usually dry and mealy; generally open or concave at apex.

TWIGS. Round; rigid; more or less zigzag; generally armed with stiff, sharp thorns; marked by oblong lenticels and small leaf scars. Winter buds: small, globose, scaly, lustrous, brown.

BARK. Dark red to gray; scaly or shallowly furrowed.

WOOD. Heavy; hard; tough; close-grained; diffuse-porous; heartwood red-brown; sapwood thick, light-colored; unimportant; used for tool handles, canes, and turned articles.

SILVICAL CHARACTERS. Intolerant; reproduction aggressive; growth slow.

GENERAL. An extremely large and complex genus containing several hundred species, the identification of which presents great difficulties even to the specialist; the number of stamens, which is variable but usually within constant limits, and the color of the anthers appear to be the most satisfactory characters for the identification of species. Some 10 species have been listed as occurring in the Rocky Mountain region; of these, *C. douglasii* is the most important and is described individually; the other species are keyed out.

KEY TO THE SPECIES OF CRATAEGUS

I. Mature fruit black.
  A. Spines numerous, mostly over 1″ long.
    1. Leaves broad obovate to ovate, incisely lobed; stamens 1–8; Wyoming..............1. *C. erythropoda* Ashe.
    2. Leaves narrow rhombic to oval, scarcely lobed; stamens 20; Colorado...................2. *C. saligna* Greene.
  B. Spines few, mostly under 1″ long.
    1. Leaves broad obovate to ovate, incisely lobed, lustrous above; north from northern Nevada and Wyoming......
    ....3. *C. douglasii* Lindl.
    2. Leaves lanceolate to narrow oblong-obovate, scarcely lobed, dull above; south from southern Idaho and Wyoming....
    ....4. *C. rivularis* Nutt.
II. Mature fruit red.
  A. Southwestern.
    1. Leaves concave-cuneate at base, coarsely serrate with gland-tipped teeth; west Texas................5. *C. tracyi* Ashe.
    2. Leaves truncate at base, finely serrate or doubly serrate with eglandular teeth; central and southern New Mexico
    ....6. *C. wootoniana* Eggles.
  B. Central and northern.
    1. Teeth of leaves not glandular; fruit villous, dark red; nutlets deeply pitted; eastern foothills of Rockies and east...
    ....7. *C. succulenta* Schrad.
    2. Teeth of leaves glandular; fruit not villous; nutlets not pitted.
      a. Leaves suborbicular; eastern Colorado and Wyoming and east.....................8. *C. chrysocarpa* Ashe.
      b. Leaves ovate, oval or obovate, more or less cuneate at base.
        (1) Fruit scarlet; leaves ¾–2¼″ long; North Dakota, Idaho, Oregon, British Columbia...............
        ....9. *C. columbiana* Howell.
        (2) Fruit red; leaves 2–3½″ long; northwestern Montana..................10. *C. williamsii* Eggles.

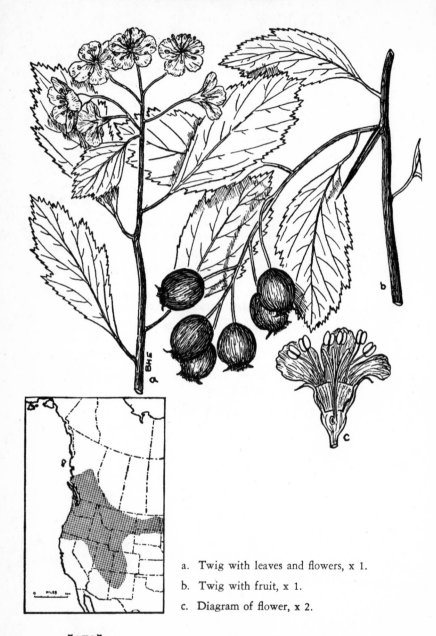

a. Twig with leaves and flowers, x 1.
b. Twig with fruit, x 1.
c. Diagram of flower, x 2.

[178]

ROSACEAE

Black Hawthorn. Western Thornapple

Crataegus douglasii Lindl. (*Crataegus brevispina*) Hel.

HABIT. A shrub or small tree rarely 35 feet high or 20 inches in diameter; compact, round-topped crown with spreading and ascending branches.

LEAVES. Broad obovate to ovate; 1–2 inches long and $\frac{1}{2}$–$1\frac{1}{2}$ inches wide; often incisely lobed toward acute apex; base cuneate, entire; coarsely serrate above middle with glandular teeth; thin; glabrous and lustrous dark green above, paler below; petioles slender, $\frac{1}{2}$–$\frac{3}{4}$ inch long, wing margined above, villose becoming glabrous.

FLOWERS. In broad, glabrous corymbs; on long, slender, glabrous pedicels; with linear caducous bracts; calyx tube obconic, glabrous, lobes bright red at apex; corolla $\frac{1}{2}$ inch in diameter; stamens 10 or rarely 5 by abortion, anthers pale rose color; styles 2–5, surrounded at base by tufts of long pale hairs.

FRUIT. About $\frac{1}{2}$ inch in diameter; short-oblong; black and lustrous; on slender pedicels; in compact, many-fruited, drooping clusters; calyx persistent; flesh sweet and succulent. Seed: nutlets usually 5, about $\frac{1}{4}$ inch long.

TWIGS. Slender; glabrous; bright red or orange-red; lustrous; unarmed or with straight, blunt spines $\frac{1}{3}$–1 inch long. Winter buds: terminal usually present, $\frac{1}{8}$ inch, globose, scaly, lustrous, brown.

SILVICAL CHARACTERS. Upper Sonoran to Canadian zones; intolerant; banks of mountain streams or in rich bottomlands; at elevations of 900–5,500 feet; often forming dense thickets.

GENERAL. A closely related form is here considered a distinct species, *C. rivularis* Nutt. This more southern form differs from the species in its narrower, thinner leaves, dull blue-green above, not lobed, and finely serrate; and in its slender, less numerous spines. The map shows both distributions.

[179]

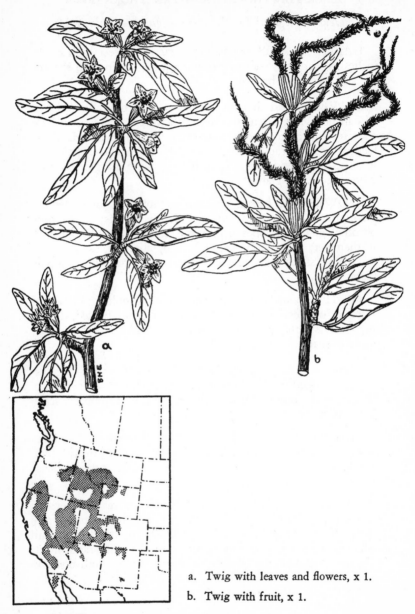

a. Twig with leaves and flowers, x 1.

b. Twig with fruit, x 1.

ROSACEAE

CURLLEAF MOUNTAIN-MAHOGANY

Cercocarpus ledifolius Nutt.

HABIT. A shrub or small tree rarely 40 feet high and 30 inches in diameter; trunk short and crooked; crown round and compact with stout, more or less crooked, spreading branches.

LEAVES. Alternate; simple; narrow-lanceolate, lance-elliptic, or oblanceolate; ½–1 inch long and ⅓–⅔ inch wide; acute at ends; entire; coriaceous; thick, revolute margins; dark green, lustrous and glabrous above, pale and tomentulose below; resinous; persistent for 2 years; short-petiolate; stipules triangular, minute, deciduous.

FLOWERS. Regular; perfect; solitary; inconspicuous; sessile in axils of leaves; calyx tube long, hoary-tomentose, whitish; corolla absent; stamens 15–30, in 2–3 rows, free, anthers hairy; ovary inferior, composed of 1 carpel and ovule.

FRUIT. Linear-oblong, coriaceous achene ¼ inch long, enclosed in persistent calyx tube ½ inch long; chestnut-brown; covered with long hairs; tipped with persistent, hairy, elongated style 2–3 inches long. Seed: solitary, linear, acute.

TWIGS. Stout; round; rigid; red-brown and pubescent at first, becoming dark brown or silver-gray and glabrous; often covered with glaucous bloom; conspicuously marked for many years by elevated, crowded, narrow leaf scars; spurlike lateral branches. Winter buds: minute, scaly, pubescent.

BARK. Thick on old trunks (1 inch); red-brown; hard; firm; furrowed and scaly.

WOOD. Exceedingly heavy and hard; brittle; close-grained; diffuse-porous; warping badly; heartwood clear red or dark brown; sapwood rather thin, yellow; unimportant.

SILVICAL CHARACTERS. Upper Sonoran to lower parts of Canadian zones; intolerant; rather long-lived; slow-growing; between 2,000–5,000 feet in the north, and up to 9,000 feet in the south; on dry, gravelly, wind-swept slopes.

GENERAL. The high mountain form, growing chiefly in the southern Rocky Mountains, has been designated as *C. ledifolius* var. *intricatus* (Wat.) Jones; this is a small shrub with very small, narrow, curved leaves and smaller fruit.

[181]

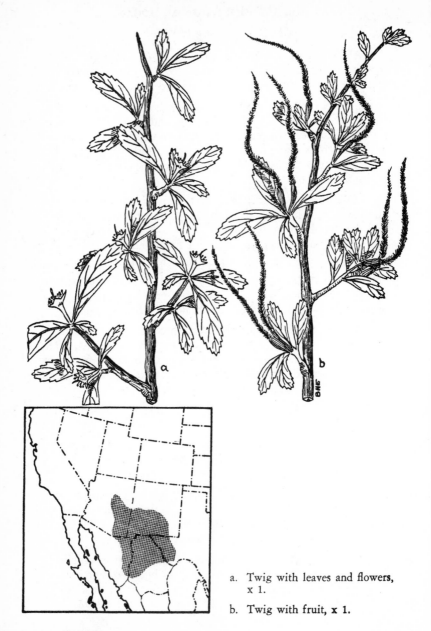

a. Twig with leaves and flowers, x 1.

b. Twig with fruit, **x 1**.

ROSACEAE

HAIRY MOUNTAIN-MAHOGANY

Cercocarpus breviflorus A. Gray

[Cercocarpus paucidentatus (S. Wat.) Britt.]

HABIT. A shrub or small tree 20–25 feet high and 6–8 inches in diameter; crown narrow, open, or irregular.

LEAVES. Alternate; simple; oblong-obovate to narrow-elliptic; ½–1 inch long and ¼–½ inch wide; acute or rounded at apex; entire, or dentate toward apex with few, small teeth; thick; revolute, often undulate margins; gray-green and hairy or nearly glabrous above, pale and tomentulose below; persistent; short-petiolate; stipules, tomentose, deciduous.

FLOWERS. Regular; perfect; inconspicuous; solitary, in pairs, or in 3-flowered clusters; nearly sessile in axils of crowded leaves; calyx tube slender, densely white-hairy; corolla absent; stamens 15–30, in 2–3 rows, free, anthers hairy; ovary inferior, composed of 1 carpel with solitary ovule.

FRUIT. Linear-oblong, coriaceous achene included in persistent, red-brown calyx tube; ¼ inch long; covered with long white hairs; tipped with persistent, hairy, elongated style 1–1½ inches long. Seed: solitary, linear, acute, erect.

TWIGS. Slender; round; rigid; bright red-brown and hairy at first, ultimately becoming ash-gray or red-gray and glabrous; marked by large, scattered, pale lenticels; spurlike lateral branches. Winter buds: minute, pubescent, scaly.

BARK. Thin (⅛ inch); light red-brown, shallow furrows, and scaly.

WOOD. Exceedingly heavy and hard; brittle; close-grained; diffuse-porous; warping badly; heartwood red-brown; sapwood lighter; unimportant; used for fuel.

SILVICAL CHARACTERS. Upper Sonoran zone; intolerant; at elevations of about 5,000 feet; on dry ridges of mountains; in pure and oak forests.

* * *

Birchleaf cercocarpus, *C. betuloides* Nutt. is a shrubby species occasionally forming a small tree with oval finely toothed leaves. Its range is central Arizona and from western Oregon through California and into Baja California.

[183]

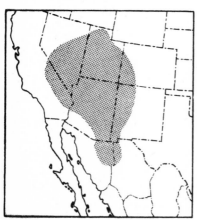

a. Twig with leaves, flowers, and fruit, x 1.

b. Achene, x 1½.

c. Leaf, x 3.

ROSACEAE

CLIFFROSE. QUININEBUSH

Cowania mexicana D. Don. (*Cowania stansburiana* Torr.)

(*Cowania davidsonii* Rydb.)

HABIT. A spreading shrub or rarely a small tree 20–25 feet high and 6–8 inches in diameter; crown narrow with short, stiff, spreading branches.

LEAVES. Alternate; simple; 3-(rarely 5-) lobed above the middle; ⅓–½ inch long; lobes linear, entire, or slightly divided; rounded at apex; revolute at margins; coriaceous; dark green above, hoary-tomentose below; glandular-dotted on upper surface; short-petioled; stipules adnate to base of petiole, ciliate on margins, acute, persistent; tardily deciduous or persistent until spring; on vigorous shoots occasionally linear and entire.

FLOWERS. Perfect; regular; showy solitary at ends of lateral branchlets; appearing in early spring; calyx tube turbinate, persistent, hoary-tomentose, and covered with rigid, glandular hairs, attenuate into short pedicel; corolla 5-petaled, pale yellow or nearly white, 1 inch in diameter, larger than calyx; stamens numerous, in 2 rows, persistent; carpels 5–12, inserted at base of calyx tube, free, villose, 1-celled and 1-ovuled.

FRUIT. 5–12, 1-celled, ellipsoidal achenes; about ¼ inch long; included in tube of calyx; tipped with persistent, white-hairy styles; often 2 inches long; coriaceous. Seed: linear-obovoid, erect, filling cavity of carpel.

TWIGS. Slender; round; rigid and rather brittle; red and glandular, becoming dark red-brown and glabrous.

BARK. Thin; pale gray; shreddy.

WOOD. Diffuse-porous; unimportant.

SILVICAL CHARACTERS. Upper Sonoran zone; intolerant; dry rocky foothill slopes and mesas; between altitudes of 4,000–8,000 feet, extending to the lower limits of the yellow pine belt; common and of largest size near southern rim of Grand Cañon and on lower slopes of San Francisco Mountains, Arizona; an important browse species, although herbage is bitter.

ROSACEAE

The Cherries and Plums

Characteristics of the Genus *Prunus* L.

HABIT. Shrubs or usually small trees, only a few species reaching sizes of commercial importance.

LEAVES. Alternate; simple; deciduous or persistent; usually serrate, rarely entire; stipules free from petiole, early deciduous; petiolate.

FLOWERS. Regular; perfect or rarely dioecious; solitary or in terminal or axillary racemes, corymbs, or umbels; appearing from separate buds with, before, or after leaves; calyx 5-lobed, tubular; corolla 5-petaled, usually white, deciduous, stamens usually 15–20; ovary inserted in bottom of calyx tube, inferior or superior, 1-celled, 2-ovuled.

FRUIT. Thin dry, or thick fleshy, 1-seeded drupe; stone bony, smooth or rugose; indehiscent; important as food in several species. Seed: filling cavity of nut, suspended, thin-coated, pale brown.

TWIGS. Slender or stout; round; astringent; red to brown; marked by lenticels and usually by small, elevated, horizontal leaf scars. Winter buds: terminal usually present, lateral nearly equal in size, scales imbricated and the inner accrescent and often colored.

BARK. Astringent; gray to dark brown; plated or scaly.

WOOD. From light to heavy and hard; close-grained; diffuse-porous; durable; heartwood light or dark brown, often reddish; sapwood lighter colored; a few species are important timber trees.

GENERAL. About 30 species of Prunus are native to the United States, 24 of these being arborescent at times. In the Rocky Mountain region there are 8 unimportant tree species and 5 others which never reach tree size, namely: *P. besseyi* Bailey, *P. corumbulosa* Rydb., *P. havardii* Mason, *P. minutiflora* Engelm. and *P. pumila* L. Many species are cultivated for their edible fruits or showy flowers and a few for their edible seeds. Some which have become naturalized locally are *P. avium* L., Sweet Cherry; *P. cerasus* L., Sour Cherry; *P. domestica* L., Plum; and *P. persica* Batsch, Peach.

[186]

KEY TO THE SPECIES OF PRUNUS

I. Fruit pubescent, with thin, dry flesh; leaves fascicled, entire or with crenulate, glandless teeth. Almonds. Shrubby.
  A. Leaves oblanceolate, acute; petals orbicular; southern Nevada, Arizona, and Utah............1. *Prunus fasiculata*, p. 189.
  B. Leaves spatulate, mostly obtuse; petals spatulate; central Nevada ....2. *Prunus andersonii*, p. 189.
II. Fruit glabrous, with pulpy flesh; leaves alternate, with gland-tipped teeth.
  A. Fruit more than 1/2" in diameter, grooved; flowers in 2–5-flowered, sessile, axillary umbels, calyx tube bright red without; eastern foothills and northeastern Utah. Plum........
    ....3. *Prunus americana*, p. 189.
  B. Fruit less than 1/2" in diameter, not grooved; calyx tube green without. Cherries.
    1. Flowers in 2–12-flowered axillary umbels or corymbs.
      a. Leaves mostly oblong-lanceolate, acuminate or rarely acute at apex; flowers in 2–5-flowered umbels or corymbs; fruit sour-fleshed; northern and eastern........
      ....4. *Prunus pensylvanica*, p. 191.
      b. Leaves oblong-obovate, usually obtuse or rarely acute at apex; flowers in 6–12-flowered corymbs; fruit with intensely bitter flesh; northern, western, and in New Mexico ....5. *Prunus emarginata*, p. 193.
    2. Flowers in many-flowered, terminal racemes.
      a. Calyx lobes deciduous from fruit.
        (1) Leaves glabrous below...........................
        6. *Prunus virginiana* var. *melanocarpa*, p. 195.
        (2) Leaves pubescent below...........................
        ....7. *Prunus virginiana* var. *demissa*, p. 195.
      b. Calyx lobes persistent under fruit; fruit black........
      ....8. *Prunus serotina* var. *rufula*, p. 197.

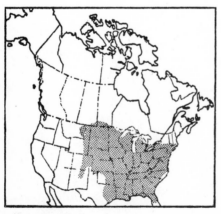

a. Winter twig, x 1.

b. Portion of twig, enlarged.

c. Leaf, x ½.

d. Flowering branchlet, x ½.

e. Vertical section of flower, x 1.

f. Fruiting branchlet, x ½.

ROSACEAE

American Plum

Prunus americana Marsh.

HABIT. A shrub or small tree 25–30 feet high and rarely 12 inches in diameter; trunk short, usually dividing near the ground; crown broad, with many spreading branches; usually spreading by shoots from the roots into dense thickets.

LEAVES. Oval to slightly oblong-oval, or sometimes obovate; acuminate at apex; sharply and often doubly serrate; thick and firm; dark green above, pale and glabrous below; 3–4 inches long and 1½–1¾ inches wide; petiole slender, ½–¾ inch long.

FLOWERS. In 2–5-flowered umbels; on slender, glabrous pedicels ½–⅔ inch long; appearing before or with leaves; ill-scented; calyx tube narrow, bright red without, green and pubescent within; corolla white, 1 inch in diameter.

FRUIT. Subglobose; about 1 inch in diameter; red and often spotted at maturity; thick-skinned; nearly free from bloom; flesh bright yellow, juicy, acid; used for jellies; stone oval, rounded at apex, ¾–1 inch long.

TWIGS. Slender; glabrous; bright green at first, becoming orange-brown and marked by minute, circular, raised lenticels; sometimes spiny-tipped. Winter buds: terminal absent, lateral ⅛–¼ inch long, acute, chestnut-brown.

BARK. Up to ½ inch thick; dark brown, tinged with red; outer layer forming persistent plates.

WOOD. Heavy; hard; close-grained; strong; heartwood dark brown, tinged with red; sapwood thin, lighter colored.

SILVICAL CHARACTERS. Upper Sonoran and Transition zones; intolerant; on moist bottomlands to banks of intermittent streams on dry uplands and mountain slopes.

* * *

The Desert-almond, *Prunus fasciculata* Gray. (*Emplectocladus fasciculatus* Torr.), a thorny, densely branched shrub or small tree, extends from southern Nevada and Utah through Arizona into southern and lower California, and is also reported in west Texas. It is characterized by dioecious flowers; pubescent, thin-fleshed fruit; and fascicled, entire or nearly entire leaves. The similar, shrubby Nevada Wild Almond, *P. andersonii* Gray, of central Nevada, occasionally becomes a small tree.

[189]

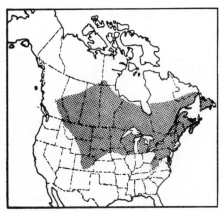

a. Winter twig, x 1.

b. Portion of twig, enlarged.

c. Leaf, x ½.

d. Flowering branchlet, x ½.

e. Flower, enlarged.

f. Fruit, x 1.

ROSACEAE

Pin Cherry. Wild Red Cherry

Prunus pensylvanica L.

HABIT. A shrub or small tree rarely 30–40 feet high and 18–20 inches in diameter; short trunk; crown narrow, rounded or flat-topped, with slender, horizontal branches.

LEAVES. Obovate to oblong-lanceolate; acuminate or acute at apex; sharply and coarsely serrate, with incurved teeth; glabrous; bright green and lustrous above, paler below; 3–4 inches long and 1–2 inches broad; turning bright yellow in autumn; petiole slender, glabrous or pilose.

FLOWERS. In 2–5-flowered, sessile umbels; on slender pedicels nearly 1 inch long; appearing when leaves half grown; calyx tube glabrous, marked by conspicuous, orange band in mouth of throat; corolla cream-white; ½ inch in diameter.

FRUIT. Globose; ¼–⅓ inch in diameter; on slender pedicels; light red; thick-skinned; flesh thin, quite sour; occasionally made into jelly; stone oblong, thin-walled, pointed, 3⁄16 inch long, ridged.

TWIGS. Slender; round; puberulous and light red at first, becoming glabrous and bright to dull red; marked by orange-colored, raised lenticels; bark easily separable from green inner bark; lateral branchlets short, spurlike. Winter buds: terminal ⅛ inch long, acute, ovoid, bright red-brown.

BARK. Thin (⅓–½ inch); red-brown, marked by orange-colored bands of lenticels; smooth or scaly.

WOOD. Light; soft; close-grained; heartwood light brown; sapwood thin, yellow; unimportant.

SILVICAL CHARACTERS. Transition to Canadian zones; intolerant; fast-growing; short-lived; the abundant reproduction often completely taking over burned areas.

GENERAL. The variety *Prunus pensylvanica* var. *saximontana* Rehd. which was included in the 1927 check list is properly a shrub and does not reach tree size.

[191]

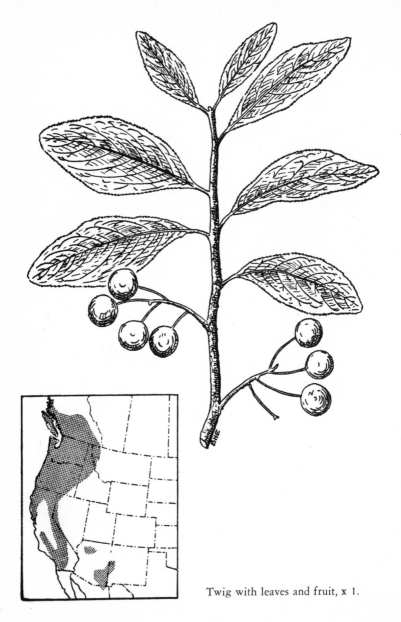

Twig with leaves and fruit, x 1.

ROSACEAE

Bitter Cherry

Prunus emarginata (Doug.) D. Dietr.

HABIT. A low shrub or a small tree 35–40 feet high and 6–14 inches in diameter; trunk straight, clean; crown symmetrical and oblong with slender, rather upright branches.

LEAVES. Oblong-obovate to oblanceolate; rounded and usually obtuse at apex; glandular at base; serrate with subulate, glandular teeth; dark green above, paler and glabrous or pubescent below; 1–3 inches long and $\frac{1}{3}$–$1\frac{1}{2}$ inches wide; petioles usually pubescent, $\frac{1}{8}$–$\frac{1}{4}$ inch long.

FLOWERS. In 6–12-flowered, glabrous or pubescent corymbs; on slender pedicels; appearing when leaves are half grown; calyx tube glabrous or pubescent, bright orange in the throat; corolla white tinged with green, $\frac{1}{3}$–$\frac{1}{2}$ inch in diameter.

FRUIT. Globose; $\frac{1}{4}$–$\frac{1}{2}$ inch in diameter; on slender pedicels; in long-stalked corymbs; bright red, becoming almost black; more or less translucent; thick-skinned; flesh thin, extremely bitter, astringent; stone ovoid, turgid, $\frac{1}{8}$ inch long, pointed, pitted and grooved walls.

TWIGS. Slender; round; flexible; pubescent and greenish at first, becoming glabrous, bright red, and marked conspicuously by large, pale lenticels; short, lateral branchlets. Winter buds: terminal $\frac{1}{8}$ inch long, acute, chestnut-brown.

BARK. Thin ($\frac{1}{4}$ inch); dark brown; smooth, marked by horizontal, light gray bands and by rows of oblong, orange-colored lenticels; very bitter.

WOOD. Rather light; soft; close-grained; brittle; rots quickly in contact with earth; heartwood dull brown, streaked with green; sapwood thick and lighter colored; unimportant.

SILVICAL CHARACTERS. Upper Sonoran to Canadian zones; intolerant; short-lived; abundant seeder; in moist sites near banks of streams and less commonly on dry hillsides; frequently forms dense thickets at higher elevations; altitudinal range from sea level to 8,000 feet.

GENERAL. The form with large leaves pubescent below, which occurs within the range of the species, has been designated as *Prunus emarginata* var. *villosa* Sudw. by some authors.

a. Twig with winter buds, x 1.

b. Twig with leaves and fruit, x ⅔.

c. Diagram of flower, x 3.

ROSACEAE
Western Chokecherry
Prunus virginiana L.
[*Prunus virginiana* var. *demissa* (Nutt.) Torr.]

HABIT. A shrub or rarely a small tree 20–50 feet high and 6–8 inches in diameter; trunk slender, often crooked; crown spreading with small, erect or horizontal branches; often forming dense thickets.

LEAVES. Oval, oblong, or obovate; abruptly acute at apex; usually cordate at base; sharply and often doubly serrate with spreading, sharp teeth; thick; glabrous, dark green and lustrous above, pale and pubescent below; 2–4 inches long and 1–2 inches wide; turning bright yellow before falling; petiole slender, ½–1 inch long, biglandular near apex.

FLOWERS. In many-flowered, erect or nodding racemes 3–6 inches long, on slender pedicels; opening from April to June; calyx tube cup-shaped, globose; corolla white, ⅓–½ inch in diameter, petals orbicular and contracted below into claw.

FRUIT. Globose; ¼–⅓ inch in diameter; in dense, cylindrical racemes; lustrous, bright red, becoming scarlet or nearly black; thick-skinned; flesh dark, juicy, astringent; stone oblong-ovoid, broadly ridged on one suture.

TWIGS. Slender; round; glabrous; red-brown or orange-brown; lustrous, marked by pale lenticels. Winter buds: terminal ⅛–¼ inch long, acute or obtuse, pale chestnut-brown.

BARK. Thin (⅛ inch); red-brown; slightly furrowed and scaly; strongly and disagreeably scented.

WOOD. Heavy; hard; close-grained; brittle; heartwood light brown; sapwood thick and whitish; unimportant.

SILVICAL CHARACTERS. Upper Sonoran to Canadian zones; intolerant; short-lived; abundant seeder with aggressive reproduction; mountain slopes, stream borders and dry hills.

GENERAL. The Black Chokecherry, *Prunus virginiana* var. *melanocarpa* (A. Nels.) Sarg., also extending through the Rocky Mountain region, differs from the form *demissa* in having thicker leaves glabrous below and darker, often less astringent fruit. The Common Chokecherry *Prunus virginiana* L. is found through most of the United States east of the Rocky Mountain region.

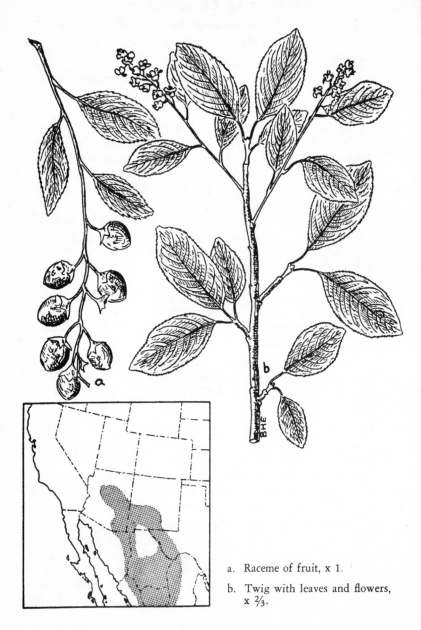

a. Raceme of fruit, x 1.

b. Twig with leaves and flowers, x ⅔.

ROSACEAE

SOUTHWESTERN BLACK CHERRY

Prunus serotina var. *rufula* (Woot & Standl.) McVaugh

[*Prunus virens* (Woot & Standl.) Shreve]

HABIT. A shrub or small tree 25–30 feet high and 18–20 inches in diameter; small, drooping or widespreading branches.

LEAVES. Elliptic, ovate, or rarely slightly obovate; acute or rounded at apex; finely crenately serrate; glabrous; light green and lustrous above, paler below; 1½–2 inches long and ¾–1 inch wide; petiole slender, glabrous, ¼–½ inch long, without glands.

FLOWERS. In many-flowered, glabrous or puberulous, erect or spreading racemes 3–6 inches long; on slender, glabrous pedicels; appearing when leaves nearly full grown; calyx tube saucer-shaped, glabrous, persistent under fruit; corolla white, ¼ inch in diameter, petals broad-ovoid.

FRUIT. Subglobose or short-oblong; ¼–½ inch in diameter; in erect or spreading racemes; purple-black and lustrous; flesh thin, juicy, acrid; stone obovoid, compressed, ¼ inch in diameter.

TWIGS. Slender; round; glabrous; pendulous; red-brown to gray-brown; marked by small, pale lenticels. Winter buds: terminal 1/16–⅛ inch long, acute or acuminate, red-brown, slightly villose.

BARK. Thin (up to ¼ inch) red-brown to nearly black; marked by narrow, oblong, horizontal lenticels; smooth or furrowed and scaly on base of old trunks.

WOOD. Rather light; hard; strong; close-grained; heartwood light brown; sapwood yellowish.

SILVICAL CHARACTERS. Upper Sonoran zone; intolerant; cañons and mountain slopes; widely and generally distributed at altitudes of 5,000–8,000 feet, but nowhere abundant.

GENERAL. This species passes into the variety *rufula* Sarg., in the Gila river valley in Arizona; it differs from the species in the rusty brown pubescence on the twigs, lower side of the midrib of the leaves and petiole.

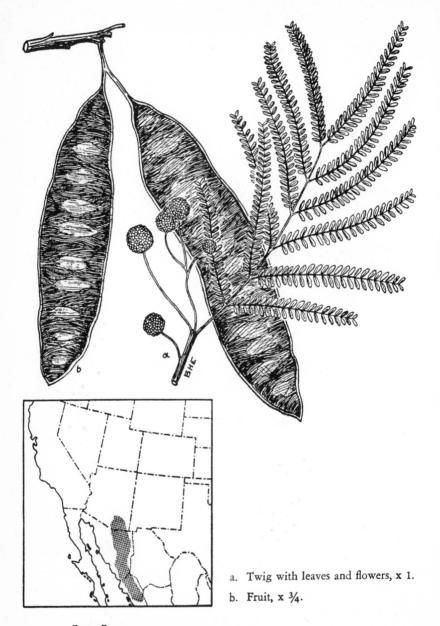

a. Twig with leaves and flowers, x 1.

b. Fruit, x ¾.

LEGUMINOSAE

LITTLELEAF LYSILOMA

Lysiloma microphylla Benth.

(*Lysiloma thornberi* Britt. & Rose.) (*Lysiloma watsoni* Rose)

HABIT. A rare shrub or small tree rarely more than 9 feet high and 3½ inches in diameter.

LEAVES. Alternate; doubly compound with 15–45 pairs of leaflets on each of 4–8 pairs of pinnae; rachis densely pilose; petiole ½–¾ inch long, bearing large conic gland; stipules large, membranaceous; leaflets linear-oblong, ⅙–⅓ inch long, papery, obtuse, pubescent on both surfaces; persistent.

FLOWERS. Nearly regular; perfect, minute; dense globose heads; calyx campanulate, 5-toothed; corolla funnel-form, deeply 5-lobed, green-white; stamens 12–30, long, exserted, filaments united into tube; ovary sessile, contracted into slender style with minute stigma.

FRUIT. Linear-oblong, straight, compressed legume 5–8 inches long and ¾–1 inch broad; glabrous; acute; submembranaceous. Seed: ⅓ inch long, oblong-oval, compressed.

TWIGS. Slender; round; unarmed; densely hairy; covered with small wartlike excrescences. Winter buds: minute.

WOOD. Heavy; hard; not strong; tough; close-grained; unimportant.

SILVICAL CHARACTERS. Lower and Upper Sonoran zones; reported only from the south slopes of the Rincon Mountains in the United States.

* * *

LITTLELEAF LEADTREE

Leucaena retusa Benth.

A shrub or small tree rarely 25 feet high and 6–8 inches in diameter which enters this region only in the rocky hillsides of southern New Mexico and southwestern Texas. While resembling Lysiloma in leaves and flowers (except that it has but 10 stamens), it can be distinguished by its fruit 6–10 inches long and ⅓–½ inch wide, which is on a peduncle 3–5 inches long. *Leucaena greggii* S. Wats., Gregg's Leadtree, is a similar Texas species.

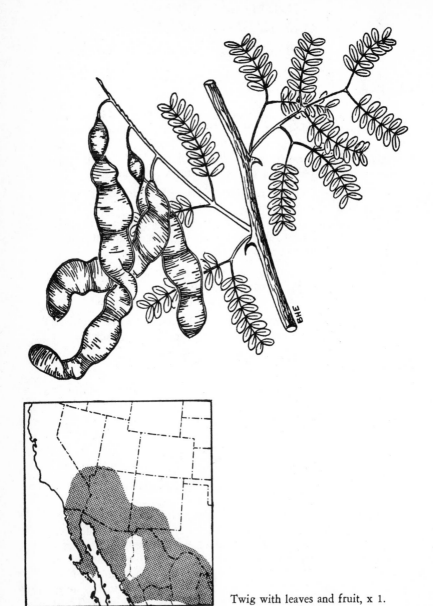

Twig with leaves and fruit, x 1.

LEGUMINOSAE

Catclaw Acacia. Paradise Flower

Acacia greggii Gray.

HABIT. A shrub or small tree rarely 30 feet high and 10–12 inches in diameter; trunk short; crown irregular.

LEAVES. Alternate; evenly doubly pinnate; 1–3 pairs of pinnae, each with 4–5 pairs of obovate, obtuse, thick, pubescent leaflets $\frac{1}{16}$–$\frac{1}{4}$ inch long; persistent; petiole short, glandular near middle; stipules linear, caducous.

FLOWERS. Nearly regular; perfect or polygamous; fragrant; in dense, pubescent spikes; calyx 5-lobed, puberulous; corolla 5-petaled, bright yellow, $\frac{1}{8}$ inch long; stamens numerous, exserted, $\frac{1}{4}$ inch long; ovary stalked and hairy.

FRUIT. Linear-oblong, flat, much-curved and contorted, indehiscent, light brown legume 2–6 inches long and $\frac{1}{2}$–$\frac{3}{4}$ inch wide; contracted between the seeds; valves thin and membranaceous. Seed: compressed, dark brown, lustrous, $\frac{1}{4}$ inch long.

TWIGS. Slender, angled; puberulous or glabrous; pale brown; armed with stout, broad, recurved, infrastipular spines $\frac{1}{4}$ inch long, giving tree its common name.

BARK. Thin ($\frac{1}{8}$ inch); furrowed and scaly; light gray-brown; astringent.

WOOD. Very heavy; hard; strong; close-grained; durable; ring-porous; heartwood red-brown; sapwood thin, light yellow.

SILVICAL CHARACTERS. Lower Sonoran zone; intolerant; vigorous reproducer; thrives in driest and poorest soils; on dry mesas, plains, and in low cañons.

* * *

Seven other species of *Acacia* may reach tree size in the southwest:
1. *A. amentacea* DC., with long spines, yellow flowers in spikes, and a flattened arcuate legume; southwestern Texas. 2. *A. angustissima* Kuntze, with no spines, white flowers in capitate heads, and flat legume; New Mexico and Texas. 3. *A. constricta* var. *paucispina* Woot., with long spines, yellow flowers in capitate heads, and a terete legume; Texas to Arizona. 4. *A. farnesiana* (L) Willd., with spines, yellow flowers in capitate heads, and a terete legume; Texas. 5. *A. millefolia* S. Wats., with slender or no spines, cream-colored flowers in racemes, and a very flat pod; rare in southern Arizona and Mexico. 6. *A. tortuosa* Willd., like No. 4 but with longer pod (3–5") ; Texas. 7. *A. wrightii* Benth., yellow flowers in spikes; short spines; Texas.

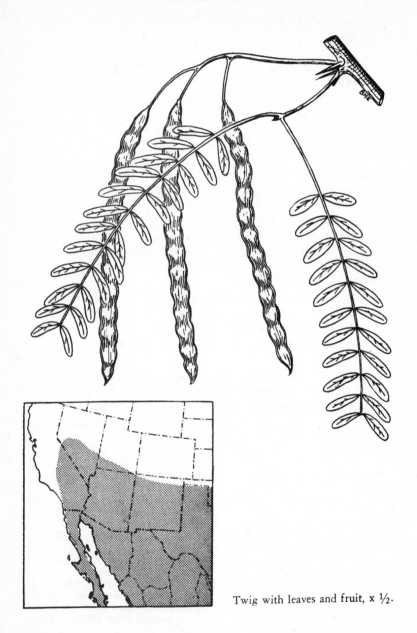

Twig with leaves and fruit, x ½.

LEGUMINOSAE
Mesquite

Prosopis juliflora (Swartz) DC.

(*Prosopis chilensis* (Mol.) Stuntz.)

HABIT. A shrub or small tree rarely 20 feet high and 6–8 inches in diameter; trunk short; crown loose and straggling with numerous, irregularly arranged, crooked branches.

LEAVES. Alternate; evenly, doubly (rarely 3–4-) pinnate; pinnae with 12–30 linear to linear-oblong, small, deciduous, glabrous leaflets ½–2 inches long; petioles glandular and spine-tipped; stipules membranaceous, deciduous.

FLOWERS. Nearly regular; perfect; fragrant; minute; in axillary, pedunculate spikes 1½–4 inches long; calyx 5-toothed, glabrous, deciduous, corolla green-white, 5-petaled; stamens 10, twice as long as corolla, free; ovary villose.

FRUIT. Linear, flat to subterete, indehiscent, yellowish, straight or falcate legume 4–9 inches long and ¼–½ inch wide; constricted and pulpy between the 10–20 seeds; edible. Seed: oblong, compressed, light brown, ¼ inch long.

TWIGS. Slender; round; smooth; mostly zigzag; pale yellow-green first year, becoming darker; usually armed with sharp, supra-axillary, persistent spines ½–2 inches long. Winter buds: terminal absent; lateral small, obtuse, dark brown.

BARK. Thick; dark red-brown; furrowed and scaly.

WOOD. Very heavy; hard; close-grained; not strong; very durable; ring-porous; heartwood dark brown or red; sapwood clear yellow, thin; used for posts, fuel, etc.

SILVICAL CHARACTERS. Lower and Upper Sonoran zones; intolerant; long-lived; adapted to desert sites by huge taproot descending 40–50 feet; abundant seeder; aggressive; confined to areas below 6,000 feet in elevation.

GENERAL. This variable species ranges from the United States to South America; in this region are three tree varieties: *glandulosa* (Torr.) Cock., with larger leaflets (¼–2 inches long) and usually glabrous, found in New Mexico and east; *torreyana* Benson, with smaller glabrous leaflets from Calif. and Nevada to Texas; and *velutina* (Woot.) Sarg., with smaller leaflets (¼–½ inch long) and hairy throughout, found from southern Arizona to Texas.

[203]

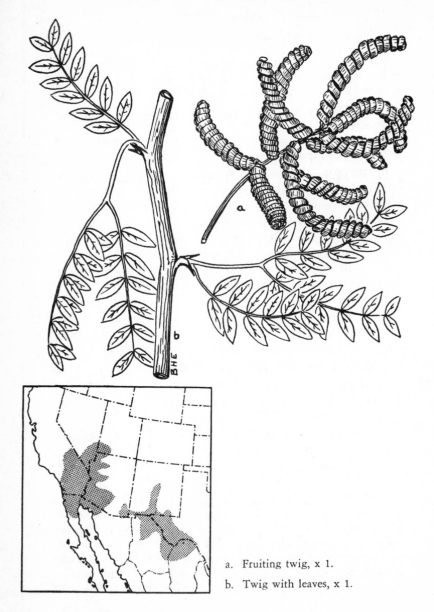

a. Fruiting twig, x 1.
b. Twig with leaves, x 1.

LEGUMINOSAE

Fremont Screwbean. Screwbean Mesquite
Prosopis pubescens Benth. (*Prosopis odorata* Torr. & Frem.)

HABIT. A shrub or small tree 15–30 feet high and 3–12 inches in diameter; trunk short; crown open.

LEAVES. Alternate; evenly, doubly (rarely 3–4-) pinnate; pinnae with 10–16, oblong or falcate, small, deciduous, acute, pubescent leaflets ⅓–⅔ inches long; petioles glandular at apex and base, spine-tipped; stipules spinescent, deciduous.

FLOWERS. Nearly regular; perfect; fragrant; minute; in cylindric spikes 2–3 inches long; calyx obscurely 5-lobed, pubescent, deciduous; corolla green-white, 5-petaled, tomentose; stamens 10, slightly exserted, free; ovary hoary-tomentose.

FRUIT. Linear, thick, indehiscent, pale yellow legume 1–2 inches long; twisted by 12–20 turns into a narrow, straight spiral; pulpy within, between the 10–20 seeds; valued as fodder. Seed: obovate, pale brown, 1/16 inch long.

TWIGS. Slender; round; slightly zigzag; glabrous and light red-brown; armed with sharp, persistent spines ⅓–½ inch long. Winter buds: terminal absent; lateral small, obtuse, dark brown.

BARK. Thick; light brown, tinged with red; separating into long, persistent, thin, shaggy strips.

WOOD. Very heavy; hard; close-grained; not strong; very durable; ring-porous; heartwood light brown; sapwood thin, light-colored; contains much tannin; used for fuel and fencing.

SILVICAL CHARACTERS. Lower Sonoran zone; intolerant; long-lived; adapted to desert sites by deep taproot system; abundant seeder; in desert river bottoms, water holes and cañons; confined to areas below 5,000 feet in elevation.

* * *

Bird-of-paradise Flower
Poinciana gilliesii Hook. (*Caesalpinia gilliesii* Wall.)

An ill-scented shrub or small tree naturalized in southern Texas, New Mexico, and Arizona. Characterized by large bipinnate leaves with very numerous small leaflets; large, perfect, nearly regular, yellow flowers, with long-exserted, red stamens and pistil. Commonly planted as ornamental and frequently escaping.

[205]

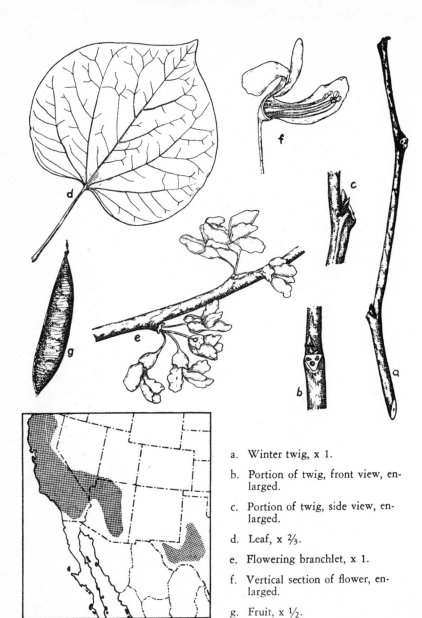

a. Winter twig, x 1.

b. Portion of twig, front view, enlarged.

c. Portion of twig, side view, enlarged.

d. Leaf, x ⅔.

e. Flowering branchlet, x 1.

f. Vertical section of flower, enlarged.

g. Fruit, x ½.

LEGUMINOSAE

CALIFORNIA REDBUD. MOUNTAIN REDBUD
Cercis occidentalis Torr.

HABIT. Usually a shrub, but not infrequently a small tree up to 25 feet high and 13 inches in diameter; frequently planted as an ornamental.

LEAVES. Alternate; simple; broad ovate to reniform; 2–3 inches in diameter; apex obtuse; base cordate; margins entire; glabrous; deciduous; petioles long, slender; stipules small, membranaceous, caducous.

FLOWERS. Irregular (subpapilionaceous); perfect; in simple fascicles; appearing before the leaves; calyx short, top-shaped, purple, 5-toothed, persistent; corolla 5-petaled, rose-colored; stamens 10, free, inserted in 2 rows on margin of thin disk, persistent; ovary short-stalked; ovules numerous in 2 ranks.

FRUIT. Stalked, flat, oblong, russet-brown legume 2–3 inches long; tipped with remnant of style. Seed: ¼ inch long, ovoid or oblong, compressed, red-brown.

TWIGS. Slender; round; unarmed; marked by numerous pale lenticels and elevated leaf scars. Winter buds: terminal absent; axillary small, scaly, obtuse, chestnut-brown.

BARK. Thin; gray; smooth or becoming scaly on old trunks.

WOOD. Heavy; hard; not strong; ring-porous; heartwood dark yellow-brown; sapwood white, thin; unimportant.

SILVICAL CHARACTERS. Upper Sonoran zone; rather tolerant; reproduction vigorous; in dry, gravelly soils; along mountain streams or on dry hills and cañons; has been reported in tree form from Bright Angel Trail in the Grand Cañon in Arizona and from California. The simliar Texas Redbud, *C. canadensis,* var. *texensis* (S. Wats.) Hop. is included on the map.

* * *

SIBERIAN PEA TREE
Caragana arborescens Lam.

This introduced form has been extensively planted in portions of the region for shelterbelts and as an ornamental. It is characterized by even pinnate leaves with 8–12 leaflets; and papilionaceous, yellow flowers, ½–¾ inch long, in fascicles of 1–4.

[207]

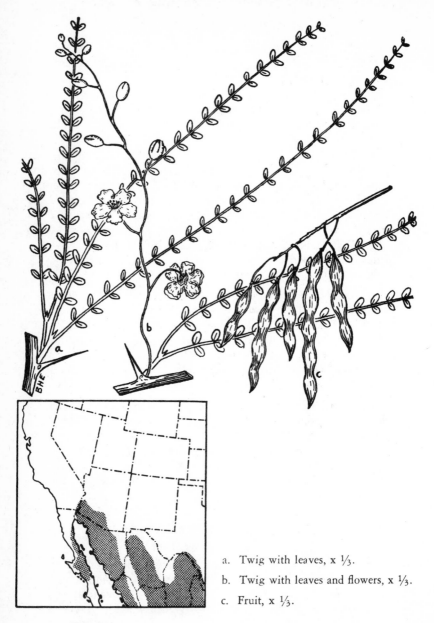

a. Twig with leaves, x ⅓.
b. Twig with leaves and flowers, x ⅓.
c. Fruit, x ⅓.

LEGUMINOSAE

Jerusalem-thorn. Horsebean

Parkinsonia aculeata L.

HABIT. A graceful, striking shrub or small tree 15–30 feet high and 4–12 inches in diameter; trunk short; crown broad and graceful with slender, spreading, pendulous branches.

LEAVES. Alternate; obscurely doubly pinnate; light green; mostly glabrous; short-petiolate; persistent; of 2 forms; primary leaves on young branches with 2–4 pinnae and a rachis which develops into a stout spine appearing forked by spiny stipules; secondary leaves fascicled from axils of primary leaves, with pinnae 6–18 inches long, each bearing 25–30 pairs of ovate or obovate leaflets 1/16–1/8 inch long.

FLOWERS. Nearly regular; perfect; in slender, erect racemes 5–6 inches long; on slender, jointed pedicels 1/3–1/2 inch long; fragrant; calyx 5-lobed, deciduous; corolla 5-petaled, bright yellow, the upper marked on inside with conspicuous red spots, imbricated in bud, 1 inch in diameter; stamens 10, shorter than petals; ovules numerous.

FRUIT. Linear, torulose, long-tapering, brown legume 2–10 inches long; contracted between the remote 1–8 seeds; hanging on pedicels 1/2–3/4 inch long; in racemes. Seed: nearly terete, 1/3 inch long.

TWIGS. Round; slender; slightly zigzag; with spines, and themselves spinelike; puberulous and yellow-green at first, becoming glabrous and gray or orange-colored. Winter buds: terminal absent; lateral minute.

BARK. Thin (1/8 inch); smooth or broken into small, persistent, platelike scales; brown, tinged with red.

WOOD. Heavy; hard; close-grained; ring-porous; heartwood light brown; sapwood very thick and yellowish; unimportant.

SILVICAL CHARACTERS. Lower Sonoran zone; intolerant; in low, moist, hot sites; cultivated for ornamental hedge and fodder; resistant to alkaline conditions; free from pests; naturalized from Florida to California.

[209]

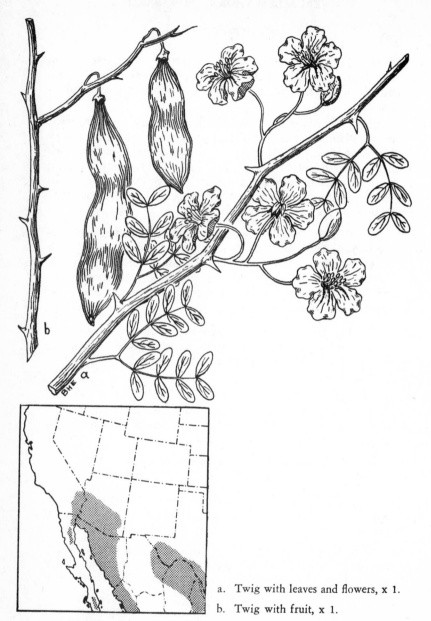

a. Twig with leaves and flowers, x 1.

b. Twig with fruit, x 1.

LEGUMINOSAE

BLUE PALOVERDE. GREENBARKED ACACIA

Cercidium floridum Benth. [*Cercidium torreyanum*
(Wat.) Sarg.]

HABIT. A thorny shrub or small tree 15–30 feet high and
10–20 inches in diameter; trunk short, often inclined; wide,
irregular, open crown with stout, tortuous branches.

LEAVES. Alternate; doubly and evenly pinnate with 2–3
pairs of oblong, obtuse, glaucous leaflets $\frac{1}{12}$–$\frac{1}{6}$ inch long on
each of 2 pinnae; few and totaling less area than green twigs;
falling soon, but frequently bearing a second crop during the
rainy season of July and August.

FLOWERS. Nearly regular; perfect; in conspicuous 4–5-
flowered, axillary racemes; on slender pedicels $\frac{3}{4}$–1 inch long;
calyx 5-lobed, reflexed; corolla of 5, clawed, bright yellow
petals, $\frac{3}{4}$ inch in diameter; stamens 10, free, exserted.

FRUIT. Oblong, compressed or somewhat turgid legume
3–4 inches long and $\frac{1}{4}$–$\frac{1}{3}$ inch wide; straight or somewhat
contracted between the 2–8 seeds. Seed: ovoid, compressed.

TWIGS. Stout; rounded; slightly zigzag; glabrous and glaucous; light yellow or pale olive-green; armed with thin, straight
or curved spines $\frac{1}{4}$ inch long. Winter buds: minute.

BARK. Thin ($\frac{1}{8}$ inch); smooth and pale olive-green on
young trunks, becoming furrowed, scaly, and red-brown.

WOOD. Rather heavy; soft; weak; close-grained; ring-
porous; heartwood light brown; sapwood clear, light yellow,
rather thick; unimportant; used as fuel.

SILVICAL CHARACTERS. Lower Sonoran zone; intolerant; abundant seeder; typical of arid, desert sinks, cañons, and
depressions; in sandy or gravelly soil.

* * *

Two other species of Cercidium reach tree size:
1. *C. microphyllum* (Torr.) R. & J. (*Parkinsonia microphylla* Torr.),
the Yellow Paloverde, a desert species reaching tree size only in Mar-
icopa County, Arizona, although a shrub in California and northern
Mexico. This species has leaves with 4–6 pairs of leaflets, each $\frac{1}{8}$
inch long, twigs terminating in spines, and a 1–2-seeded legume.
2. *C. macrum* Johnst. (*floridum* of auth.), (*C. texanum* A. Gray)
the Border Paloverde, of Southern Texas and adjacent Mexico. This
species has leaflets $\frac{1}{16}$ inch long, slightly glandular and dull green,
and a 2–3-seeded legume.
The distribution map includes *C. floridum* and *C. microphyllum* in
Arizona and California, and *C. macrum* in Texas.

[211]

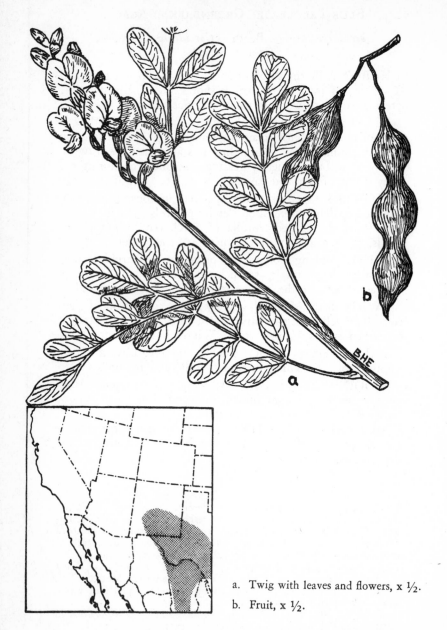

a. Twig with leaves and flowers, x ½.

b. Fruit, x ½.

LEGUMINOSAE

MESCALBEAN. FRIJOLITO

Sophora secundiflora (Ortega) Lag. (*Broussonetia secundiflora* Ortega)

HABIT. A shrub or rarely a small tree 20–35 feet high and 6–8 inches in diameter; crown narrow with numerous upright branches; commonly thicket-forming.

LEAVES. Alternate; unequally pinnate with 7–9 oblong-elliptic, coriaceous, glabrous, entire, thick-margined leaflets 1–2½ inches long and ½–1½ inches wide; rounded at apex; lustrous and yellow-green above, paler below; persistent; stout, puberulous petiole.

FLOWERS. Irregular (papilionaceous); perfect; fragrant; appearing with leaves; in conspicuous 1-sided, canescent, terminal racemes; on stout pedicels; calyx campanulate, 2 upper teeth larger; corolla 1 inch long, of 5, clawed, violet-blue or rarely white, petals, the standard broad, erect; stamens 10, mostly free or slightly diadelphous at base; ovary coated with long, silky, white hairs; ovules numerous.

FRUIT. Oblong, terete, indehiscent legume 1–7 inches long and ½ inch broad; thick, woody valves; much contracted between seeds; covered with dense, hoary tomentum; tipped with remnant of style. Seed: short-oblong, rounded, ½ inch long, bright scarlet, contain sophorin and are very poisonous.

TWIGS. Slender; round; unarmed; tomentose at first, becoming glabrous and pale orange-brown. Winter buds: terminal absent; lateral minute, scaly.

BARK. Thin, red-brown.

WOOD. Very heavy; hard; close-grained; ring-porous; heartwood orange, streaked with red; sapwood thick, bright yellow; unimportant.

SILVICAL CHARACTERS. Lower Sonoran zone; intolerant; fibrous roots; moist sites; borders of streams, and seacoasts; rarely more than a shrub in the Rocky Mountain region.

[213]

a. Twig with leaves and fruit,
   x ½.

b. Flower raceme, x ½.

c. Fruit, x 2.

LEGUMINOSAE

KIDNEYWOOD. EYSENHARDTIA

Eysenhardtia polystachya (Ortega) Sarg. (*Eysenhardtia orthocarpa* S. Wat.) (*Viborquia polystachya* Ortega)

HABIT. Commonly a low, rigid shrub, reaching tree size only near the summit of the Santa Catalina Mountains in Arizona, where it becomes 18–25 feet high.

LEAVES. Alternate; equally pinnate with 10–23 pairs of oval, rounded or slightly emarginate, thin, short-petioluled leaflets ½–⅔ inch long and ⅛–¼ inch wide; pale, gray-green and glabrous above; pubescent and conspicuously brown-glandular below; thickened, revolute margins; minute, deciduous stipules; pubescent, grooved rachis; deciduous.

FLOWERS. Slightly irregular; perfect; in axillary, pubescent spikes; on slender, pubescent pedicels; opening in May; calyx campanulate, pubescent, glandular, persistent; corolla subpapilionaceous, white, ½ inch long, erect, free, with 5 petals nearly equal in size and shape; stamens 10, diadelphous; ovary superior, 1-celled, oblique, ovules 2–3, rarely 4.

FRUIT. Small (½ inch long), pendent, compressed, oblong, straight or slightly falcate legume; usually with single seed (rarely 2) near apex. Seed: oblong-reniform, compressed, light red-brown, ¼ inch long.

TWIGS. Slender; round; unarmed; at first gray-pubescent, later glabrous, red-brown and roughened by numerous, glandular excrescences. Winter buds: minute.

BARK. Thin (¹⁄₁₆ inch), light gray, broken into large, platelike scales, exfoliating on the surface into thin layers.

WOOD. Heavy; hard; close-grained; ring-porous; heartwood light red-brown; sapwood thin, clear yellow; not important; known for its fluorescent properties.

SILVICAL CHARACTERS. Lower and Upper Sonoran zones; intolerant; on arid slopes and dry ridges; in gravelly soil; valuable browse plant.

GENERAL. *Eysenhardtia angustifolia* Pennell is a small, much-branched tree included on the map in western Texas.

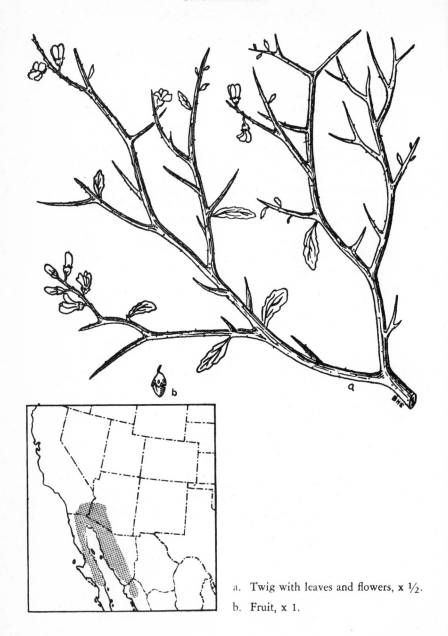

a. Twig with leaves and flowers, x ½.
b. Fruit, x 1.

LEGUMINOSAE

SMOKETHORN. INDIGO BUSH

Dalea spinosa A. Gray. [*Parosela spinosa* (Gray) Heller.]

HABIT. Usually a spiny shrub, but occasionally a small tree 18–20 feet high and 8–12 inches in diameter.

LEAVES. Alternate, simple and few on young trees; minute or absent on old trees; cuneate or linear-oblong; subsessile; hoary-pubescent; glandular-dotted; entire or remotely serrate; falling early, causing plant usually to appear leafless.

FLOWERS. Irregular (papilionaceous); perfect; in axillary racemes 1–1½ inches long; on short pedicels; calyx 5-lobed, 10-ribbed, ciliate; corolla papilionaceous, indigo blue, ½ inch long, standard cordate and reflexed; stamens 10, diadelphous; ovary superior, pubescent, glandular-dotted; ovules 4–6.

FRUIT. Ovoid, pubescent, glandular-dotted, beaked, 1-seeded legume; twice as long as enclosing calyx; membranaceous. Seed: kidney-shaped, pale brown, often mottled, ⅛ inch long.

TWIGS. Reduced to slender, sharp spines; at first with dense, white pubescence, and bearing minute triangular bracts; becoming glabrous and pale brown in third year; marked by lenticels; bark exfoliates showing pale green inner bark.

BARK. Thin (¼ inch), dark gray-brown, furrowed and roughened by persistent scales.

WOOD. Moderately soft; light; coarse-grained; ring-porous; heartwood walnut-brown; sapwood thick and nearly white; fuel.

SILVICAL CHARACTERS. Lower Sonoran zone; intolerant; reproduction sparse and species nowhere abundant; adapted to very dry, desert plains in rocky or gravelly soil.

* * *

SOUTHWESTERN CORALBEAN
Erythrina flabelliformis Kearney

A Mexican shrub or small tree extending into southern Arizona and New Mexico. Characterized by spiny branches; alternate, pinnately compound leaves, with 3 broad leaflets, each 1½–3 inches long; showy flowers in dense racemes, with a red, narrow standard 1½–2 inches long; and a linear legume sometimes 12 inches long, with 2 to many, large, red seeds.

[217]

a. Flower, opened, x 1.

b. Legume, x 1.

c. Flowering branchlet, x ⅓.

LEGUMINOSAE
New Mexican Locust
Robinia neomexicana A. Gray.

HABIT. A prickly shrub or small tree 20–25 feet high and 6–8 inches in diameter.

LEAVES. Alternate; unequally pinnate, with 15–21 ultimately glabrous, short-petioluled, elliptic-oblong, entire, round-tipped, mucronate leaflets 1½ inches long; deciduous; rachis stout and pubescent; stipules papery and becoming spines.

FLOWERS. Irregular (papilionaceous); perfect; in short, pendulous, many-flowered, glandular-hispid racemes; on long, slender, glandular-hispid pedicels; calyx campanulate, 5-lobed; corolla pale rose to nearly white, 1 inch long, with broad standard hardly longer than wings; stamens 10, diadelphous; ovary superior, 1-celled; ovules numerous.

FRUIT. Glandular-hispid, compressed legume; 3–4 inches long and about ⅓ inch wide; thin-valved; many-seeded. Seed: oblong-oblique, dark brown, thin-coated, 1/16 inch long.

TWIGS. Slender; spiny; mostly round or slightly angled; zigzag; at first covered with glandular hairs, becoming smooth, red-brown, and marked by small scattered lenticels. Winter buds: terminal absent; lateral minute, naked, subpetiolar, depressed-globose, 3–4 superposed together.

BARK. Thin; slightly furrowed; light brown; the surface separating into small, platelike scales.

WOOD. Very heavy; hard; strong; close-grained; ring-porous; heartwood yellow, streaked with brown; sapwood thin, light yellow; unimportant; fence posts, stakes, etc.

SILVICAL CHARACTERS. Transition zones; intolerant; on dry hills or banks of mountain streams.

GENERAL. Some authors consider the tree form to be a variety *luxurians* Dieck.

* * *

R. *rusbyi* W. & S., a shrub or rarely a small tree with glabrous fruit, is found in southern New Mexico. The eastern black locust, R. *pseudoacacia* L. has proved hardy when planted as far north as Idaho. It differs from New Mexican locust in having glabrous leaves, flowers, and fruits.

[219]

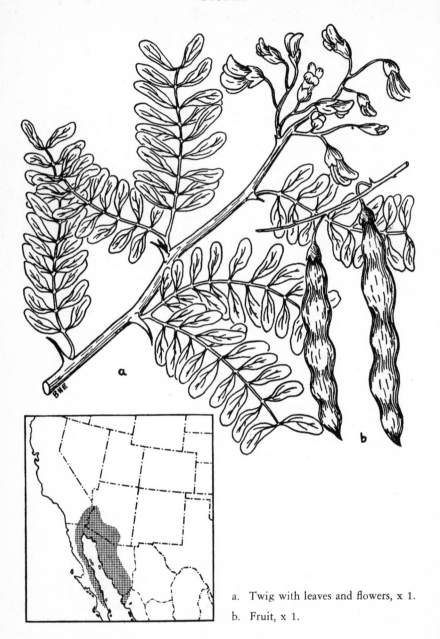

a. Twig with leaves and flowers, x 1.

b. Fruit, x 1.

LEGUMINOSAE
Tesota. Ironwood
Olneya tesota A. Gray.

HABIT. A beautiful, spiny shrub or small, bushy tree sometimes 25–30 feet high and 8–18 inches in diameter.

LEAVES. Alternate; equally or unequally pinnate with 10–15 hoary-canescent, short-petioluled, oblong or obovate, entire, obtuse and often mucronate leaflets ½–¾ inch long; persistent until new leaves appear; stipules absent.

FLOWERS. Irregular (papilionaceous); perfect; in short, axillary, few-flowered, hoary-canescent racemes; calyx hoary-canescent; 6-lobed; corolla papilionaceous, purplish, ½ inch long, with orbicular standard appendaged at base; stamens 10, diadelphous; ovary superior, 1-celled, pilose; ovules numerous.

FRUIT. Oblique, compressed, glandular-haired legume 2–2½ inches long; light brown; thick and leathery; 1–5-seeded. Seed: broad ovoid, flattened, bright chestnut-brown, edible.

TWIGS. Slender; hoary-canescent at first, becoming smooth and brown; armed with stout, sharp, paired spines.

BARK. Thin, scaly, red-brown, peeling off in long strips.

WOOD. Exceedingly heavy; hard; strong; heartwood chocolate-brown streaked with red; sapwood thin, clear yellow; unimportant; used locally for canes, small articles, and fuel.

SILVICAL CHARACTERS. Lower Sonoran zone; intolerant; thrives in hot, desert regions, sides of depressions, and dry water courses; a monotypic genus; attacked by mistletoe.

* * *

ZYGOPHYLLACEAE
Texas Porlieria. Soapbush

Porlieria angustifolia (Engelm.) A. Gray.
(*Guaiacum angustifolium* Engelm.)

A shrub or small tree entering this region in southwestern Texas. Characterized by persistent, opposite, pinnately compound leaves with 8–16, entire, smooth leaflets; stipules persistent; flowers perfect, regular, purple, ½–¾ inch in diameter, sweet-scented; fruit an obcordate, 2-lobed capsule containing 2 large, yellow seeds. Wood very durable, hard and heavy; used for fence posts. An important honey plant.

[221]

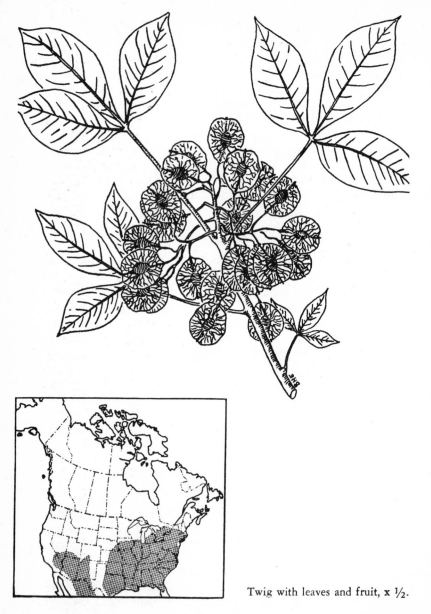

Twig with leaves and fruit, **x** ½.

RUTACEAE
Narrowleaf Hoptree. Wafer-ash
Ptelea angustifolia Benth.

HABIT. An unarmed shrub or small tree 20–25 feet high and 6–8 inches in diameter; crown round-topped with small branches.

LEAVES. Alternate or rarely opposite; compound with 3 (rarely 5) subsessile, ovate to oblong leaflets; acuminate at apex; entire or crenulate-serrate margins; becoming glabrous and rather leathery; dark green above, pale and dotted with transparent glands below; deciduous; long-petioled; without stipules.

FLOWERS. Regular; polygamous; in terminal cymes or compound umbels; on pubescent pedicels; calyx 4–5-parted, pubescent; corolla green-white; 4–5-petaled; stamens 3–4; ovary superior, 2–3-celled, compressed, puberulous; ovules, 2 in each cell.

FRUIT. Dehiscent samara; 2–3-celled; broad, thin, almost orbicular wing, nearly 1 inch across; in drooping clusters on slender pedicels; persisting on branches through winter. Seed: ⅓ inch long, oblong, acute, dark red-brown.

TWIGS. Slender; round; pubescent at first, becoming glabrous, dark brown, lustrous and marked by wartlike excrescences and conspicuous leaf scars. Winter buds: terminal absent; lateral small, depressed, nearly round, pale-colored, tomentose.

BARK. Smooth; thin; bitter; ill-scented; dark brown on old trunks; that of the roots sometimes used as a tonic.

WOOD. Rather heavy; hard; close-grained; ring-porous; heartwood yellow-brown; sapwood thin; unimportant.

SILVICAL CHARACTERS. Lower Sonoran and Transition zones; in the Southwest found mostly on dry hills and cañons. This western form is not separated from the eastern *P. trifoliata* L. by some authors. Both distributions are shown on the map. Pale Hoptree, *P. pallida* Greene, is a shrubby form in Arizona and New Mexico.

* * *

SIMAROUBACEAE
Ailanthus. Tree of Heaven
Ailanthus altissima (Mill.) Swingle.
(*Ailanthus glandulosa* Desf.)

A large, fast-growing tree introduced from China and naturalized over much of the country. Characterized by alternate, pinnately compound leaves, 1–3 feet long, the leaflets glandular-toothed at base; fruit of clustered samaras; and thick-pithed twigs. Coppices freely and is aggressively spontaneous.

[223]

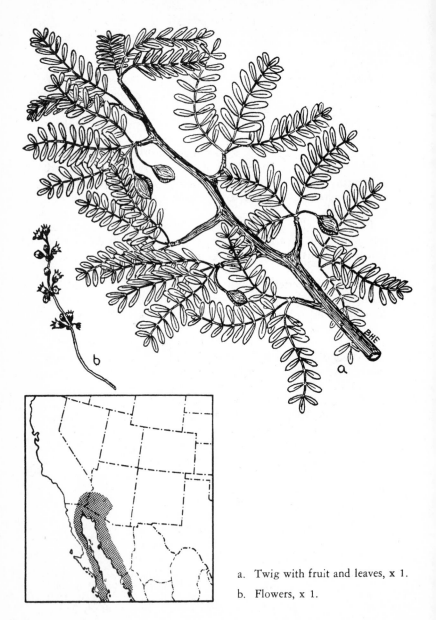

a. Twig with fruit and leaves, x 1.
b. Flowers, x 1.

BURSERACEAE

ELEPHANTTREE. BURSERA

Bursera microphylla A. Gray (*Elaphrium mircophyllum* Rose.)

HABIT. A low shrub or small tree 10–12 feet high and 4–8 inches in diameter; trunk rapidly tapering; crown wide.

LEAVES. Alternate; unequally pinnately compound; 1–1¼ inches long with usually 10–20 pairs of leaflets; deciduous; leaflets opposite, ¼ inch long, oblong or oblong-obovate, sessile, rounded at apex, entire or subserrate, thin.

FLOWERS. Regular; polygamous, small (⅙ inch long); calyx minute; corolla 5-petaled, white, 3–4 times longer than calyx, stamens 10, shorter than petals; ovary superior, 3-celled with 2 ovules in each cell; styles united; stigma 3-lobed.

FRUIT. Capsule-like drupe; ¼ inch long; ellipsoid or slightly obovoid; red; glabrous; splitting into 3 valves; drooping on thickened pedicels; flesh leathery; nutlets 1–3, usually solitary, ovoid, acute, thin-walled, 3-angled, gray.

TWIGS. Slender; glabrous; red; roughened during first year by crowded leaf scars.

BARK. Thin (½ inch); pale yellow, separating into membranaceous, red-brown scales; the outer layer thin and firm, the inner layer corky; resinous.

WOOD. Hard; close-grained; pale yellow; diffuse-porous; resinous; unimportant.

SILVICAL CHARACTERS. Upper and Lower Sonoran zones; in sterile, rocky soil; on dry plains and low mountains.

* * *

A similar species, the fragrant Bursera, *Bursera fagaroides* (H.B.K.) Engler, is a shrub or small tree found in the Arizona desert.

* * *

EUPHORBIACEAE

Two members of this family rarely become trees in southern Arizona: *Sapium biloculare* (S. Wats.) Pax., with alternate, simple, glabrous, narrow-oblong leaves, 1–3 inches long; milky, poisonous juice; and a 2-celled capsular fruit, ½ inch long. Castor-bean, *Ricinus communis* L., with alternate, simple palmately lobed leaves, often 12 inches long; and a large, 3-seeded, capsular fruit containing the important castor-beans is naturalized through the southern states.

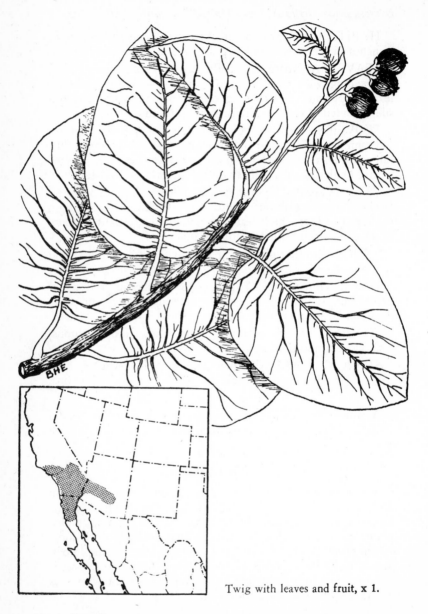

Twig with leaves and fruit, x 1.

ANACARDIACEAE

SUGAR SUMAC

Rhus ovata S. Wats.

HABIT. A shrub or small tree rarely 30 feet high; trunk short, stocky; crown open, irregular.

LEAVES. Alternate; simple (rarely 3-foliate); ovate-elliptic to broadly ovate; 2–3½ inches long; apex acute; margins entire, revolute; thick and leathery; lustrous yellow-green; glabrous; deciduous; tending to fold along midrib; petioles stout, ½ inch long, purplish, glabrous; stipules absent.

FLOWERS. Regular; dioecious or rarely polygamous; minute; in large, dense, terminal compound spikes; bracts ovate, ciliate; calyx 5-lobed; corolla 5-petaled, pink or white; stamens 5, alternate to petals and inserted with them on disk; ovary superior, 1-celled, 1-ovuled.

FRUIT. Drupaceous; globose; ⅓ inch in diameter; covered by sweet, waxy exudate; pubescent; thin, dry outer coat enclosing bony seed.

TWIGS. Stout; round; chocolate-brown and puberulent, soon becoming glabrous; pith terete, not large. Winter buds: small, ovate, hairy, gray-brown.

BARK. Thin; generally smooth; gray-brown.

SILVICAL CHARACTERS. Lower and Upper Sonoran zones; intolerant; on dry, rocky hillsides and ridges; coppices rapidly after burning; important for soil protection and wildlife cover.

GENERAL. *Rhus kearneyi* Barkl., a related form, is a small evergreen tree in southwestern Arizona. *Rhus lanceolata* (Gray) Britton. is a small tree entering this region in New Mexico and Chisos Mountains of western Texas. *Rhus glabra* L., distributed over most of the United States, has been reported as a small tree, but not from the Rocky Mountain region. *Rhus microphylla* Engelm., reported as a small tree, occurs in Mexico and Texas to New Mexico and Arizona. *Rhus choriophylla* W. & S. is a shrub or small tree ranging from west Texas to southeastern Arizona.

* * *

The Texas Pistache, *Pistacia texana* Swingle (*Pistacia mexicana* H.B.K.), a shrub or tree of western Texas and Mexico, is characterized by alternate, pinnately compound, persistent leaves with 9–19, spatulate, small leaflets; dioecious flowers; and a small, red-brown drupe.

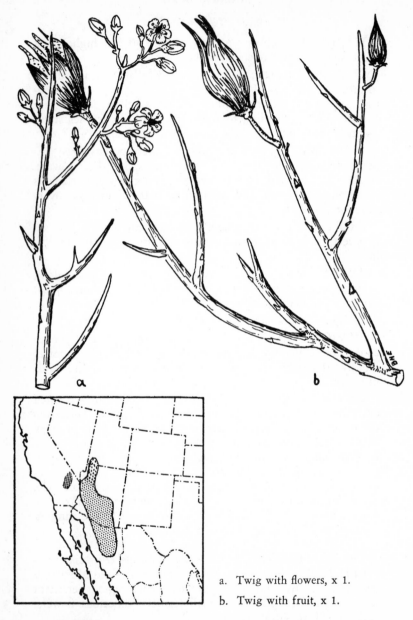

a. Twig with flowers, x 1.
b. Twig with fruit, x 1.

CELASTRACEAE

CANOTIA. MOHAVETHORN

Canotia holacantha Torr.

HABIT. An odd, leafless shrub or small shrublike tree 20–30 feet high and rarely 12 inches in diameter; trunk short and stocky; branches rushlike.

FLOWERS. Regular, perfect, small ($\frac{1}{8}$–$\frac{1}{4}$ inch in diameter); in 3–7-flowered fascicles; calyx 5-lobed, persistent, minute; corolla 5-petaled, white, reflexed, deciduous; stamens 5, opposite lobes of calyx, filaments shorter than petals, persistent on fruit; ovary 5-celled, papillose-glandular; ovules 6 in each cell, in 2 ranks.

FRUIT. Dry, woody, ovoid, acuminate capsule 1 inch long; crowned with subulate, persistent style; 5-valved, splitting open at top. Seed: solitary or paired; about $\frac{3}{4}$ inch long; flattened; seed coat subcoriacious, papillate, produced below into a subfalcate, membranaceous wing.

TWIGS. Slender, rushlike, round, alternate, glabrous, rigid, and spine-tipped; pale green and carrying on photosynthetic functions; characteristic, black, triangular, cushion-like processes located at base of each twig and flower cluster.

BARK. Light brown and deeply furrowed.

WOOD. Heavy; hard; close-grained; light brown; diffuse-porous; unimportant.

SILVICAL CHARACTERS. Lower Sonoran zone; this monotypic genus has been placed in 3 other families; grows on dry, mountain slopes and mesas between 2,000–4,000 feet; often in pure stands; the loss of leaves apparently aids the plant in enduring the hot, dry climate.

* * *

WAHOO. BURNING BUSH

Euonymus atropurpureus Jacq.

A shrub reported from Montana, this eastern species reaches tree size in Arkansas and eastern Texas. It can be distinguished by its opposite, petioled leaves; 4-parted flowers; and fleshy, capsular fruit enclosed in a thin scarlet aril. The western Wahoo, *E. occidentalis* Nutt. enters this region in western Nevada.

[229]

ACERACEAE

The Maples

Characteristics of the Genus *Acer* L.

HABIT. Deciduous trees or shrubs, with handsome foliage, usually assuming brilliant colors in autumn.

LEAVES. Opposite; simple or compound; deciduous; petioled; without stipules; simple leaves palmately 3–7-lobed; compound leaves pinnate, with 3–7 leaflets.

FLOWERS. Regular; polygamous, dioecious, or rarely perfect; small; borne either in lateral fascicles from separate flower buds and appearing before the leaves, or in lateral and terminal racemes, panicles, or corymbs and appearing with or after the leaves; calyx colored, generally 5-parted; corolla usually 5-petaled or absent; stamens 4–12, usually 7–8; ovary 2-celled, 2-lobed, compressed, with 2 styles; ovules 2 in each cell, ascending.

FRUIT. Double samara united at base (key); each nutlike carpel laterally compressed and produced into large, obovate wing. Seed: usually solitary by abortion, ovoid, compressed.

TWIGS. Slender to moderately stout; round; pith homogeneous, round; marked at base by bud scales with ringlike scars; leaf scars more or less U-shaped, with 3 (rarely 5–7) bundle scars. Winter buds: with valvate or imbricated scales, inner scales accrescent, terminal buds larger than lateral.

BARK. Astringent and variable.

WOOD. Variable from soft to heavy and hard; diffuse-porous; pores all small and not crowded; rays distinct on cross section without lens; widely used for interior finish, etc., sap of some species manufactured into sugar.

SILVICAL CHARACTERS. Mostly tolerant; fibrous root systems; widely used for ornamental and shade trees.

GENERAL. This genus contains over 600 species of trees widely scattered through the Northern Hemisphere with one species extending into Sumatra and Java. In the United States there are 13 native species, 4 of these reaching tree size in the Rocky Mountain region.

KEY TO THE SPECIES OF ACER

I. Leaves compound; winter buds enclosed by tomentose scales; twigs encircled by crescent-shaped leaf scars.................
....1. *Acer negundo.*
  A. Entire or dentate leaflets; slender, bluish, glabrous twigs; Idaho and Montana to Colorado.....var. *violaceum,* p. 233.
  B. Serrate leaflets; moderately stout, greenish, puberulous twigs
.................................var. *interius,* p. 233.

II. Leaves simple (rarely compound in glabrum); winter buds not enclosed by tomentose scales; twigs not encircled by leaf scars.
  A. Leaves sharply and doubly serrate; flowers with petals.
    1. Leaves with deep, narrow sinuses, lobes not toothed to base; south and central........2. *Acer glabrum,* p. 237.
    2. Leaves with shallow, open sinuses, lobes toothed to base; northwestern.....3. *Acer glabrum* var. *douglasii,* p. 237.
  B. Leaves with entire margins; flowers without petals.......
......................4. *Acer grandidentatum,* p. 235.

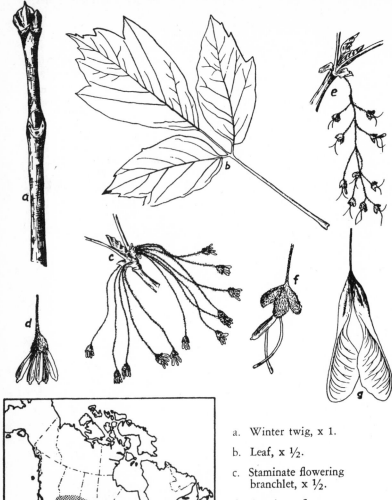

a. Winter twig, x 1.

b. Leaf, x ½.

c. Staminate flowering
   branchlet, x ½.

d. Staminate flower, en-
   larged.

e. Pistillate flowering
   branchlet, x ½.

f. Pistillate flower, enlarged.

g. Fruit, x 1.

ACERACEAE

BOXELDER

Acer negundo L.

HABIT. A small tree, rarely 75 feet high and 4 feet in diameter; trunk usually irregular and dividing near ground into several, stout, widespreading branches.

LEAVES. Compound, 3 (rarely 5–7) leaflets; petiole long, slender, puberulous; leaflets ovate to lanceolate, 3–4 inches long and 1½–4 inches wide, glabrous, acuminate, coarsely serrate and sometimes 3-lobed at base.

FLOWERS. Dioecious; minute; the male fascicled; the female in drooping racemes; appearing with leaves or a little before them; calyx 5-lobed, hairy, yellow-green; corolla absent; stamens 4–6, with slender, exserted, hairy filaments; ovary hairy, partly enclosed by calyx.

FRUIT. Pendent; 1–2 inches long; glabrous; ripening in autumn; in drooping racemes 6–8 inches long. Seed: narrowed at the ends, smooth, bright red-brown, ½ inch long.

TWIGS. Moderately stout; greenish; pubescent, or rarely nearly glabrous; marked by conspicuous bud scale scars and crescent-shaped leaf scars which surround the twig. Winter buds: acute, ⅛–¼ inch long, tomentose.

BARK. Thin (¼–½ inch); pale gray or light brown; deeply divided by furrows into broad, rounded ridges.

WOOD. Light, soft, close-grained, weak; heartwood cream-white to yellow-brown, often streaked; sapwood thick; used occasionally for cheap furniture, woodenware, etc.

SILVICAL CHARACTERS. Upper Sonoran and Transition zones; moderately tolerant; shallow-rooted, except on deep soils; hardy to extremes of climate; rapid grower but short-lived and usually of poor form; reproduction by sprout and seed plentiful.

GENERAL. This species contains several intergrading varieties or races which differ chiefly in hairiness, shape and thickness of leaflets. Western forms include the variety *interius* (Britt.) Sarg., in the high mountains of Arizona and New Mexico, characterized by thicker and more hairy leaves; and the variety *violaceum* Jaeg. & Beisnn., from Idaho and Montana to Colorado, characterized by entire or dentate leaflets and bluish twigs.

[233]

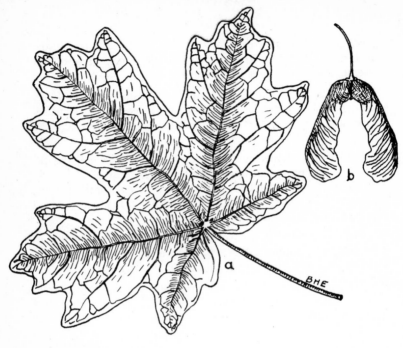

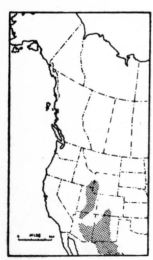

a. Leaf, x 1.

b. Fruit, x 1.

ACERACEAE

BIGTOOTH MAPLE

Acer grandidentatum Nutt.

(*Acer brachypterum* Woot. & Standl.)

HABIT. A tree 30–40 feet high and 8–10 inches in diameter; branches stout and usually erect.

LEAVES. Simple; 3–5-lobed by broad, shallow sinuses; distinctly lobulate; 2–5 inches in diameter; dark green and lustrous above, pale and usually pubescent below; petioles stout, glabrous; turning yellow and scarlet before falling.

FLOWERS. Polygamous, small (¼ inch); in short-stalked corymbs; calyx yellow, villose, often persistent under fruit; corolla absent; stamens 7–8; ovary usually glabrous.

FRUIT. Spreading or erect wings, ½–1 inch long; glabrous or sparingly hairy; often rose-colored in summer, green at maturity. Seed: smooth, light red-brown, about ¼ inch long.

TWIGS. Slender, glabrous, bright red; nearly encircled by narrow leaf scars with conspicuous bands of long hair in their axils. Winter buds: terminal acute, $\frac{1}{16}$ inch long, bright red-brown, with puberulous-ciliate outer scales.

BARK. Thin, dark brown, separating on surface into plate-like scales.

WOOD. Heavy; hard; close-grained; heartwood light brown to nearly white; sapwood thick and white.

SILVICAL CHARACTERS. Upper Sonoran to Canadian zones; rather tolerant; shallow root system; on moist sites along mountain streams and on sides of cañons usually at altitudes of 5,000–8,000 feet.

GENERAL. A small tree entering this region only in the San Luis Mountains of southwestern New Mexico was designated as a separate species in the 1927 Check List *Acer brachypterum* Woot. & Standl., but is here considered a synonym. This form was distinguished from the bigtooth maple by the slightly lobed or nearly entire leaves, glabrous leaf scars, smooth, pale bark on young trees, and shorter wing of the fruit (⅜–¾ inch long).

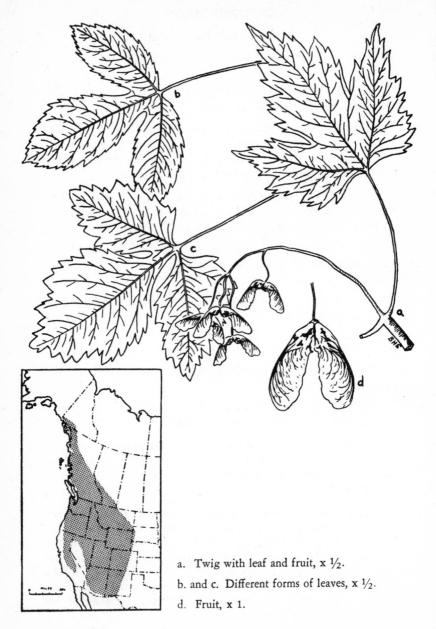

a. Twig with leaf and fruit, x ½.

b. and c. Different forms of leaves, x ½.

d. Fruit, x 1.

ACERACEAE

Rocky Mountain Maple

Acer glabrum Torr.

HABIT. A shrub or small tree rarely 20–30 feet high and 6–12 inches in diameter; narrow crown with small branches.

LEAVES. Mostly 3–5-lobed and simple, but sometimes divided into 3 leaflets; rounded in outline; 3–5 inches in diameter; sharply and doubly serrate; glabrous; thin; dark green above, paler below; petioles glabrous, stout, grooved, 1–6 inches long, often bright red.

FLOWERS. Mostly dioecious; small (⅛ inch long); in loose, glabrous, few-flowered, racemose corymbs, on slender drooping peduncles from the end of 2-leaved branches; calyx oblong, obtuse, petal-like; petals yellow-green; stamens 7–8, with glabrous, unequal filaments; ovary glabrous.

FRUIT. Slightly spreading or nearly erect, broad wings, ¾–⅞ inch long; glabrous; often rose-colored in summer. Seed: ovoid, bright chestnut-brown, about ¼ inch long.

TWIGS. Slender; glabrous; pale green-brown at first, becoming bright red-brown; conspicuously marked by encircling bud scale scars and crescent-shaped leaf scars. Winter buds: acute, ⅛–¼ inch long, bright red or rarely yellow scales tomentose on the inner surface.

BARK. Thin, smooth, dark red-brown.

WOOD. Heavy; hard; close-grained; heartwood light brown or nearly white; sapwood white and very thick.

SILVICAL CHARACTERS. Upper Sonoran to Canadian zones; rather intolerant; in moist locations along stream banks or cañon sides; at elevations of 5,000–6,000 feet in the north to 8,000–9,000 feet in the south.

GENERAL. A variable species including several different forms which have been treated as separate species by some authors. The northwestern form, *Acer glabrum* var. *douglassii* (Hook) Dipp. (*Acer douglasii* Hook.), typically differs in having leaves with shallow, open sinuses and lobes toothed all the way to the base, and fruit with more erect and broader wings. This form extends north and west from northwestern Wyoming.

[237]

a. Leaf, x ⅔.

b. Floral stalk, x ⅔.

c. Fruit, x 1.

SAPINDACEAE

WESTERN SOAPBERRY. CHINABERRY
Sapindus drummondi Hook. & Arn.

HABIT. A shrub or small tree rarely 40–50 feet high and 1½–2 feet in diameter; branches round, usually erect.

LEAVES. Alternate; pinnately compound with 4–9 pairs of alternate, obliquely lanceolate, acuminate, short-petioled leaflets, each 2–3 inches long and ½–⅔ inch wide; margins entire; glabrous above and pubescent beneath; pale yellow-green; deciduous; rachis slender, grooved, puberulous, without wings; stipules absent.

FLOWERS. Regular; polygamo-dioecious; minute; in many-flowered clusters 6–9 inches long; calyx of 4–5 acute sepals; corolla of 4–5 white petals, contracted into a claw hairy on inner surface, furnished with deeply cleft scale at base; stamens 8–10, filaments hairy; ovary superior, 2–4-celled; ovules solitary and ascending in each cell.

FRUIT. Drupaceous, ripening into a leathery, 1–3-celled and seeded berry; ½ inch in diameter; glabrous; yellow, turning black in drying; persistent on branches until spring; formerly used as soap. Seed: solitary in each carpel; obovoid; dark brown; with a smooth, bony coat.

TWIGS. Moderately stout; round; at first pubescent and pale yellow-green, becoming puberulous, gray, and marked by large, obcordate leaf scars and numerous small lenticels; pith rather large, pale, continuous. Winter buds: terminal absent; lateral small, globose, often superposed in pairs.

BARK. Thin (⅓–½ inch); red-brown; furrowed into long, superficially scaly plates; bitter and astringent.

WOOD. Heavy; hard; strong; close-grained; ring-porous; similar to ash in appearance; heartwood light brown, tinged with yellow; sapwood thick and whitish; used for baskets, boxes, crates, furniture, and pack saddle frames.

SILVICAL CHARACTERS. Lower and Upper Sonoran zones; intolerant; roots fleshy; growth rapid; on moist clay soils or dry limestone uplands; in mountain valleys and cañons up to the woodland type and seldom over 6,000 feet in elevation; contains large quantities of saponin, a severe poison.

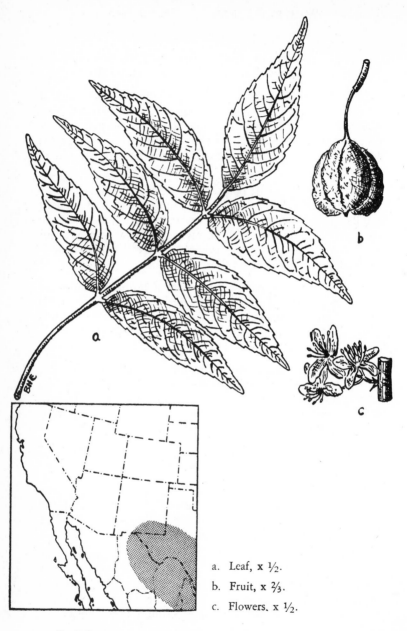

a. Leaf, x ½.
b. Fruit, x ⅔.
c. Flowers, x ½.

SAPINDACEAE

Mexican-buckeye. Spanish-buckeye

Ungnadia speciosa Endl.

HABIT. A shrub, or rarely a small tree 25–30 feet high and 6–8 inches in diameter; numerous, small, upright branches.

LEAVES. Alternate; odd-pinnately compound; 6–12 inches long with petiole 2–6 inches long; leaflets 5–7 (rarely 3); ovate-lanceolate, 3–5 inches long; acuminate; crenulate-serrate; rather coriaceous; dark green and lustrous above, pale, and at first tomentose below; deciduous; stipules absent.

FLOWERS. Irregular; polygamous; in small, crowded, pubescent fascicles or corymbs 1½–2 inches long; appearing just before or with leaves; calyx 5-lobed, campanulate, deciduous; corolla 4–5-lobed, one inch across, bright rose color; stamens 7–10, exserted; ovary superior, hairy, 3-celled.

FRUIT. Loculicidally 3-valved capsule; coriaceous; broad ovoid; 2 inches wide; stalked; crowned with remnant of style; wrinkled; dark red-brown; empty pods persistent. Seed: solitary; subglobose; ½–⅝ inch in diameter; seed coat coriaceous, shiny, nearly black, reputed to be poisonous.

TWIGS. Slender, round, and slightly zigzag; finely hairy at first, becoming glabrous and marked by lenticels and conspicuous leaf scars; pale brown. Winter buds: terminal absent; lateral small (⅛ inch in diameter), obtuse, subglobose, scaly.

BARK. Thin (¼ inch or less); light gray; numerous, reticulated furrows.

WOOD. Heavy; rather soft; brittle; close-grained; heartwood red, tinged with brown; sapwood light; unimportant.

SILVICAL CHARACTERS. Upper Sonoran zone; a monotypic genus; mountain cañons, limestone hillsides, and along streams.

* * *

MALVACEAE

Arizona Tree Cotton

Gossypium thurberi Tod. (*Thurberia thespesioides* Gray)

A shrub or tree 18–20 feet high in southern Arizona and adjacent Mexico, characterized by simple, alternate, lobed leaves and a capsular fruit, the seed covered with long cotton.

[241]

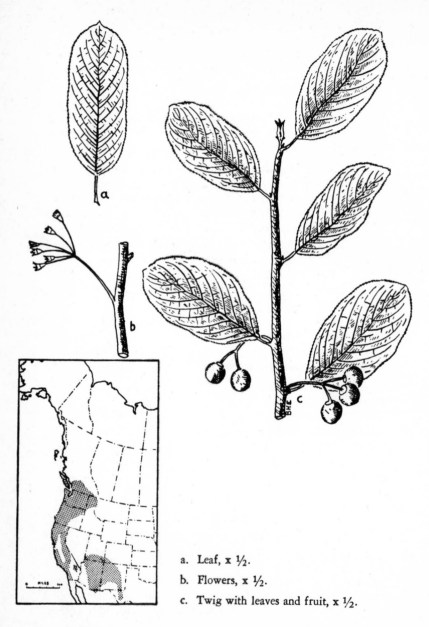

a. Leaf, x ½.

b. Flowers, x ½.

c. Twig with leaves and fruit, x ½.

RHAMNACEAE
Cascara Buckthorn
Rhamnus purshiana DC.

HABIT. A shrub or tree 20–40 feet high and 6–20 inches in diameter; wide, open crown with numerous, stout branches.

LEAVES. Alternate, or rarely obliquely opposite; simple; broad-elliptic; $1\frac{1}{2}$–7 inches long and $1\frac{1}{2}$–2 inches wide; apex obtuse or bluntly pointed; base rounded; undulate margins finely serrate or nearly entire; thin; villous below and on veins above; deciduous; turning pale yellow before falling; petioles stout, hairy, $\frac{1}{2}$–1 inch long; stipules minute, deciduous.

FLOWERS. Regular; perfect; small; in axillary peduncled cymes; long-pedicelled; calyx campanulate, 5-lobed; corolla greenish, minute, 5-lobed, folded around short stamens; stamens 5, alternate to calyx lobes; ovary superior, 2–4-celled; ovules solitary, erect.

FRUIT. Drupaceous; subglobose; $\frac{1}{3}$–$\frac{1}{2}$ inch in diameter; black; bearing remnants of style; flesh thin and juicy; with 2–3 obovoid, 1-seeded nutlets with a thin gray or yellow-green shell. Seed: erect, obtuse, yellow-brown.

TWIGS. Slender; round; pubescent, usually becoming glabrous; yellow-green or red-brown; marked by elevated, oval, horizontal leaf scars. Winter buds: terminal absent; lateral small, naked, hoary-tomentose.

BARK. Thin ($\frac{1}{4}$ inch); gray to dark brown, often tinged with red; scaly; important because of laxative properties.

WOOD. Rather light; soft; not strong; ring-porous; heartwood brown, tinged with red; sapwood thin and light-colored; used rarely for turnery, furniture, and fuel.

SILVICAL CHARACTERS. Upper Sonoran and Transition zones; moderately tolerant; prolific seeder and coppices freely; no taproot; hardy tree with few enemies; rich bottomlands to dry hillsides; usually in coniferous forests.

GENERAL. Buckthorn enters this region in Montana and Idaho. A related form, *R. betulaefolia* Greene, is shown on the map in Utah, Arizona, Nevada, Colorado, New Mexico, and Texas. California Buckthorn, *R. californica* var. *ursina* (Greene) McMinn, is characterized by persistent, leathery leaves densely hairy beneath. It is found in the mountains from southwestern New Mexico through Arizona into southern Nevada.

[243]

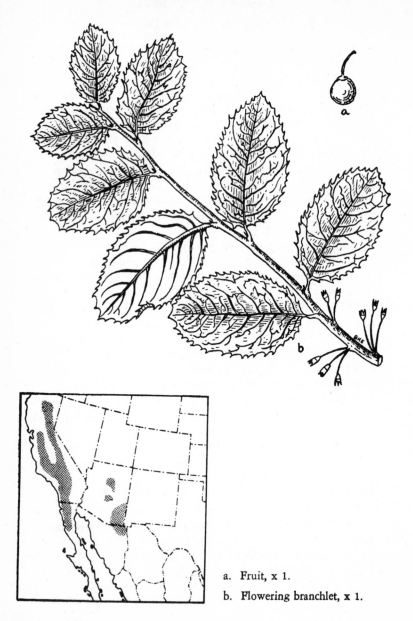

a. Fruit, x 1.

b. Flowering branchlet, x 1.

RHAMNACEAE

HOLLYLEAF BUCKTHORN

Rhamnus crocea var. *ilicifolia* (Kell.) Greene.

HABIT. A shrub or small evergreen tree rarely 25 feet high and 6–8 inches in diameter; crown rounded; branches stout.

LEAVES. Alternate or obliquely opposite; simple; oval or orbicular; 1–1½ inches long and ¾–1 inch wide; apex rounded; margin spinulose-dentate; thin and leathery; glabrous; yellow-green and lustrous above, often golden below; persistent; petioles short and stout; stipules minute, acuminate.

FLOWERS. Regular; polygamo-dioecious; in small clusters from axils of leaves; calyx about ⅛ inch long, 4- (or rarely 5-) lobed; petals absent; stamens short, as many as calyx lobes and alternate to them; ovary superior, 2–4-celled.

FRUIT. Drupaceous; obovoid; ¼ inch in diameter; red; flesh thin and dry; with 2–3 nutlets. Seed: ⅛ inch long, hard, erect, broadly ovoid, pointed, grooved, chestnut-brown.

TWIGS. Slender; round; rigid and often spinescent; red-brown; glabrous. Winter buds: terminal absent; lateral 1⁄16 inch long, scaly, obtuse, scales hairy-fringed.

BARK. Thin (1⁄16–⅛ inch); dark gray; slightly roughened by minute tubercles; acrid and bitter.

WOOD. Moderately heavy and hard; brittle; fine-grained; ring-porous; heartwood light yellow-brown; unimportant.

SILVICAL CHARACTERS. Upper Sonoran zone; prolific seeder; on hot, dry hillsides, cañons, and mountain slopes; in pure groups or scattered with chaparral and shrubby trees.

* * *

BLUEWOOD. LOGWOOD

Condalia obovata Hook.

This velvety-pubescent shrub or small tree is one of the common chaparral species of western Texas, commonly forming dense thickets. It is characterized by small (½–¾ inch long), entire, alternate or fascicled leaves; small axillary flowers; and a deep red, subglobose drupe ⅕ inch in diameter.

a. Flowering branchlet, x 1.

b. Fruit, x 1.

STERCULIACEAE
California Fremontia. Flannelbush
Fremontodendron californicum (Torr.) Cov.
(Fremontia californica Torr.)

HABIT. A shrub or small tree 20–30 feet high and 12–14 inches in diameter; crown open with stout branches.

LEAVES. Alternate, simple; broadly ovate; 1½ inches in diameter; usually 3-lobed; thick; stellate rusty-pubescent below; persistent 2 years; petioles stout, ½–⅔ inch long.

FLOWERS. Regular; perfect; solitary; on spurlike branches; calyx campanulate, deeply 5-lobed, yellow, 1 inch long; corolla absent; stamens 5, filaments united; ovary 5-celled; styles elongated; ovules numerous.

FRUIT. Ovoid, acuminate, 4-valved capsule; 1 inch long; densely woolly dehiscent; inner surface villose-pubescent. Seed: oval, small (about 3⁄16 inch long), very dark brown.

TWIGS. Stout; round; stellate rusty-pubescent at first, becoming glabrous and light red-brown. Winter buds: naked.

BARK. Thin (rarely over ¼ inch thick); furrowed; dark red-brown; inner bark mucilaginous and used locally for poultices.

WOOD. Heavy; hard; close-grained; ring-porous; heartwood red-brown; sapwood thick and whitish; not used commercially.

SILVICAL CHARACTERS. Upper Sonoran and Transition zones; intermediate in tolerance; usually an abundant seeder; on very poor, dry, rocky foothills and lower mountain slopes; often forming dense, extensive thickets; a monotypic genus.

* * *

TAMARICACEAE
Tamarix. Tamarisk
Tamarix pentandra Pall.

A large shrub or small tree introduced from Europe but more or less naturalized in the south and central parts of the region. Characterized by alternate, scalelike, feathery, sparse leaves (resembling those of conifers); showy, pink flowers; and 3–5-valved, capsular fruit containing many, minute seeds. *Tamarix aphylla* (L.) Karst., known as Athel, is an introduced shrub or tree widely planted through the Southwest.

ALLTHORN

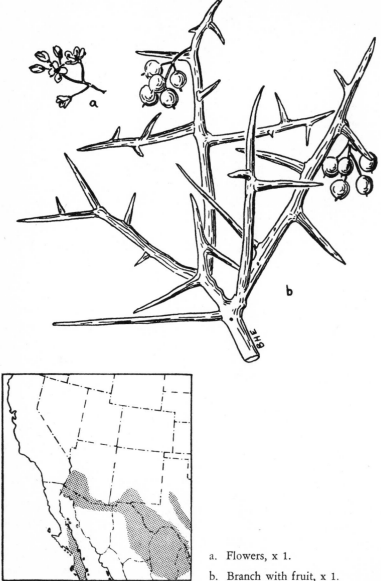

a. Flowers, x 1.
b. Branch with fruit, x 1.

[248]

KOEBERLINACEAE

ALLTHORN. CORONO DE CRISTO

Koeberlinia spinosa Zucc.

HABIT. A shrub forming extensive, impenetrable thickets, or a small bushy tree rarely 20–25 feet high and 12 inches in diameter; trunk short, thorny, crooked; often appearing to bear neither leaf, flower, nor fruit.

LEAVES. Alternate; simple; early deciduous, the tree usually leafless; scalelike and minute (not over ⅛ inch long); narrow obovate; rounded at apex.

FLOWERS. Regular; perfect; small (¼ inch in diameter); in short umbel-like racemes; on short peduncles; calyx of 3–5 minute, deciduous sepals; petals 4, green-white, much longer than sepals; stamens 8, as long as, or shorter than petals; ovary 2-celled, contracted at base into a short stalk and above into a simple style with terminal stigma; ovules numerous.

FRUIT. Small (³⁄₁₆–¼ inch), subglobose, 2-celled, black berry; tipped with remnants of pointed style; flesh thin and succulent; cells 1–2-seeded. Seed: vertical, coiled and shell-shaped; seed coat brittle and wrinkled.

TWIGS. Stout; glabrous; terminating in sharp, rigid spine; pale green in color. Winter buds: minute and inconspicuous on spinelike twigs.

BARK. Thin, red-brown, scaly.

WOOD. Very hard; heavy (sp. gr. 1.12); close-grained; diffuse-porous; heartwood dark brown, somewhat streaked with orange; sapwood thin, yellow, or nearly white; rich in oil; used occasionally for canes, handles, and turned articles.

SILVICAL CHARACTERS. Lower Sonoran zone; on dry, gravelly plains, mesas, and foothills; a monotypic botanical curiosity. The variety *tenuispina* K. & P. becomes a small tree in southwestern Arizona.

* * *

Closely resembling *Koeberlinia* in leaves (present only on seedlings) and twigs and also known as Corono de Cristo or Crucifixion-thorn is *Holacantha emoryi* Gray; this belongs to the *Simaroubaceae* family and is a much-branched shrub or small tree which is native to southern Arizona, California, and Mexico; it differs in its dioecious, 7- or 8-petaled flowers and fruit of 6–8 small, nutlike drupes.

[249]

CACTACEAE

Characteristics of the Cactus Family

HABIT. Shrubs or seldom trees, rarely 50–60 feet high and 2 feet in diameter; stems commonly columnar, fluted, succulent, and branched; numerous spines springing from cushions of small bristles (areolae).

LEAVES. Alternate; simple; mostly reduced to spines or scales or absent; photosynthetic processes taking place in the green parts of the fleshy stems.

FLOWERS. Regular; perfect; usually single; large and showy; calyx of numerous sepals forming a tube, those of inner series petal-like; corolla showy, of numerous petals; stamens many, inserted on calyx tube; ovary inferior, 1-celled, with several parietal placentae and numerous horizontal ovules, styles united into one, stigmas as many as placentae.

FRUIT. 1-celled, fleshy (rarely dry) berry, often edible. Seed: numerous and small.

WOOD. An internal, woody frame or skeleton, made up of a cylinder or a meshed network of strands.

BUDS. Modified into pulvini or cushions which are usually depressions often consisting of a complex series of spines, wool, glands, and growing points.

SILVICAL CHARACTERS. Very intolerant; although seed generally produced abundantly, natural reproduction by seed is rather scanty because of unfavorable environment; vegetative reproduction common; typical of very dry desert areas where they are often the only woody plants.

GENERAL. This family contains about 120 genera and 1,200 species; there are 2 genera and 5 species reaching tree size in the United States in southern California, Arizona and New Mexico. Two species, *Cereus schottii* Engelm. and *Cereus thurberi* Engelm., of southern Arizona and Mexico have columnar branches 20 to 25 feet high but cannot be considered trees as they do not have a definite trunk.

KEY TO THE ARBORESCENT SPECIES
OF CACTACEAE

I. Branches and stems columnar, ribbed, not tuberculate, continuous; areoles (growing centers) without glochids (minute bristles); leaves spinelike; tube of flower elongated; seeds dark-colored; spines not barbed; a tree often 50–60 feet high; the state flower of Arizona....................................
   1. *Cereus giganteus,* Engelm. [*Carnegiea gigantea* (Engelm.) B. & R.]; Saguaro.

II. Branches and stems slender, columnar, tuberculate, conspicuously jointed; areoles with both glochids and spines; leaves small and fleshy on young parts; tube of flower short; seed light-colored; spines retrorsely barbed; small plants not over 15 feet high.....
.... *Opuntia.*
  A. Tubercles of branches broad, full and rounded below areolae; flowers pink or purple; fruit sparingly spiny or without spines.
    1. Flowers pink; fruit green, proliferous (one growing from another), usually spineless; joints pale olive-green, readily detached, freely falling, their tubercles broad and ovoid; spines yellow...... 2. *Opuntia fulgida* Engelm.; Cholla.
    2. Flowers purple; fruit yellow, rarely proliferous, spiny; joints green or purple, not readily detached, persistent, their tubercles elongated; spines white to red-brown.....
    ....3. *Opuntia spinosior* (Engelm.) Toumey; Tasajo.
  B. Tubercles of branches narrow, high and flattened laterally. Flowers purple, or green tinted with red or yellow.
    1. Fruit smooth or but slightly tuberculate, spiny, green; branch tubercles ⅔″ long; spines 5–11, ⅛″ long or less, dark red-brown; flowers green, tinted with red or yellow ....4. *Opuntia versicolor* Engelm.; Cholla.
    2. Fruit manifestly tuberculate, naked, yellow; branch tubercles ¾–1″ long; spines 8–30, ¾–1¼″ long, brown, flowers purple...
     5. *Opuntia imbricata* (Haw.) DC (*Opuntia arborescens* Engelm.); Cane Cactus.

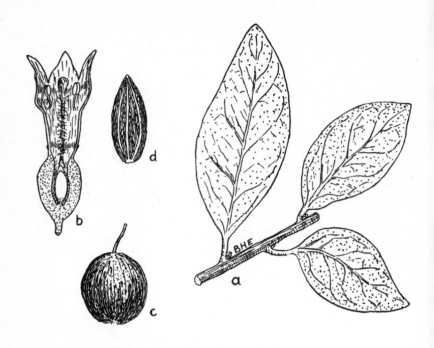

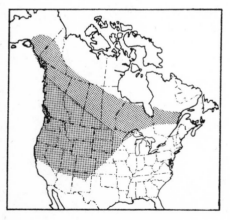

a. Twig with leaves and flower, x 1.

b. Section through flower, x 2.

c. Fruit, x 2.

d. Stone, x 2.

ELAEAGNACEAE

SILVER BUFFALOBERRY. SILVERBERRY

Shepherdia argentea (Pursh.) Nutt. (*Elaeagnus utilis* A. Nels.)

HABIT. A bushy, silvery shrub or small tree rarely 15–16 feet high, stoloniferous and thicket-forming.

LEAVES. Alternate; simple; elliptic to oblong; 1–3 inches long and $1/3$–1 inch wide; rounded or acute at apex; margin entire; densely silvery-scurfy on both faces; thick; deciduous; petioles stout, $1/4$ inch long.

FLOWERS. Regular; polygamous; 1–3 in axil of each leaf; appearing after leaves; calyx tube silvery without, $1/4$ inch long, 4-lobed; corolla lacking, stamens 4, short, attached near calyx throat; ovary enveloped in receptacle.

FRUIT. Drupe; globose to oval; $1/3$–$1/2$ inch long; silvery; flesh mealy; the stone with about 8 longitudinal ridges.

TWIGS. Rather slender; round; rusty-brown and covered with scurfy scales; leaf scars minute. Winter buds: $1/8$–$1/4$ inch long, oblong, scales scurfy.

BARK. Thin; dull gray; smooth or slightly furrowed.

WOOD. Light; soft; weak; coarse-grained; heartwood dark brown; fairly durable; unimportant.

SILVICAL CHARACTERS. Upper Sonoran to Alpine zones; along streams or on moist to dry hillsides.

* * *

RUSSIAN-OLIVE

Elaeagnus angustifolia L.

An introduced shrub or small tree which has become established in parts of the region. Hardy, very drought and alkaline resistant and much planted as a dry area ornamental and for windbreaks. Characterized by lanceolate, silvery-scurfy leaves; silvery and often spiny branches; and yellow, silvery-scurfy, drupaceous fruit, $1/2$ inch in diameter.

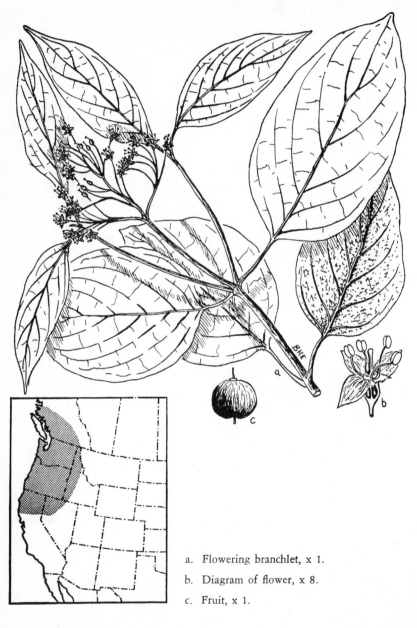

a. Flowering branchlet, x 1.

b. Diagram of flower, x 8.

c. Fruit, x 1.

CORNACEAE

Western Dogwood. Western Cornel

Cornus occidentalis Cov. (*Cornus pubescens* Nutt.)

(*Cornus californica* var. *pubescens* Macbr.)

HABIT. Usually a shrub, but not infrequently a small tree 20 feet high.

LEAVES. Opposite; simple; elliptic to ovate; 1½–4 inches long; apex short acuminate to obtuse; margins entire; thick and firm; slightly pubescent above; glaucous and pubescent below; deciduous; petioles slender, ½–1 inch long.

FLOWERS. Regular; perfect; small; in dense cymes 2 inches broad; calyx tube minutely 4-toothed; corolla yellow-white, 4-petaled, oblong-ovate, inserted on margin of disk; stamens 4, alternate to petals, filaments exserted; ovary 2-celled and 2-ovuled, inferior; style exserted with capitate stigma.

FRUIT. Drupaceous; white; ovoid or oblong; flesh thin and succulent; stone bony, 2-celled, much broader than long.

TWIGS. Slender; round; purple; glabrous or sparingly pubescent; pith large, round, light-colored. Winter buds: terminal present, ¼ inch long, covered by 2 valvate scales; axillary buds appressed.

BARK. Thin; brown; smooth or scaly on old trunks; astringent.

WOOD. Heavy; hard; strong; diffuse-porous; heartwood pale brown; sapwood cream-white, thick; unimportant.

SILVICAL CHARACTERS. Upper Sonoran and Transition zones; moderately tolerant; often common on bottomlands, stream banks, and other moist alluvial soils at altitudes of from 2,500–6,500 feet.

GENERAL. About 16 shrubby species of *Cornus* are native to the western United States; the Pacific flowering dogwood, *Cornus nuttallii* Aud., becomes a good-sized tree; it has been reported in the Rocky Mountains in the valleys of northwestern Idaho; the red-osier dogwood or cornel, *Cornus stolonifera* Michx., is common throughout the region and characterized by bright red branches; while usually a shrub, this species sometimes becomes a small tree.

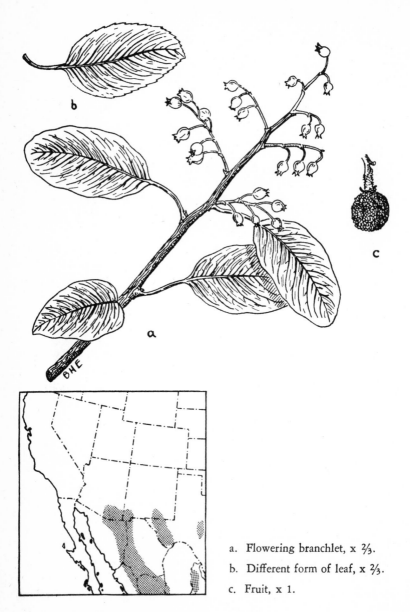

a. Flowering branchlet, x ⅔.
b. Different form of leaf, x ⅔.
c. Fruit, x 1.

ERICACEAE

TEXAS MADRONE

Arbutus texana Buckl.

HABIT. A shrub or small tree rarely 18–20 feet high and 8–10 inches in diameter; bole often crooked and branching.

LEAVES. Alternate; simple; oval, ovate, or lanceolate; 1–3 inches long and $\frac{2}{3}$–1$\frac{1}{2}$ inches wide; rounded or acute at apex; margins entire to serrate; thick and leathery; dark green and glabrous above; pale and usually slightly pubescent below; evergreen; petioles stout, pubescent, 1–1$\frac{1}{2}$ inches long.

FLOWERS. Regular; perfect; small ($\frac{1}{4}$ inch long) ; in terminal panicles; calyx 5-parted, persistent; corolla white, 5-toothed; stamens 10, shorter than corolla; ovary superior, pubescent, 4–5-celled; ovules numerous on central placenta.

FRUIT. Drupaceous, ripening into a granular-coated berry; $\frac{1}{3}$ inch in diameter; dark red; flesh dry and mealy; stone more or less completely formed. Seed: numerous in each of 5 cells, compressed, small, puberulous.

TWIGS. Stout; round; light red and pubescent at first, becoming dark red-brown and covered with small scales. Winter buds: scaly, $\frac{1}{8}$ inch long, rounded at apex, tomentose.

BARK. Furrowed and broken into dark, square plates at base of old trunks; elsewhere thin, tinged with red, separating into papery scales exposing light red inner bark.

WOOD. Heavy; hard; close-grained; diffuse-porous; heartwood brown, tinged with red; sapwood thick and lighter colored; sometimes used for handles of small tools.

SILVICAL CHARACTERS. Upper Sonoran zone of Texas and southeastern New Mexico; intolerant; on dry limestone hills and on low mountains; thick, hard roots.

* * *

ARIZONA MADRONE

Arbutus arizonica (A. Gray) Sarg.

In southern Arizona, southwestern New Mexico, and Mexico; similar to Texas madrone and differing from it in having a glabrous ovary and glabrous lower surface on the leaf; both formerly were considered as belonging to Mexican madrone, *Arbutus xalapensis* H.B.K. The distributions of both species are shown on the map.

[257]

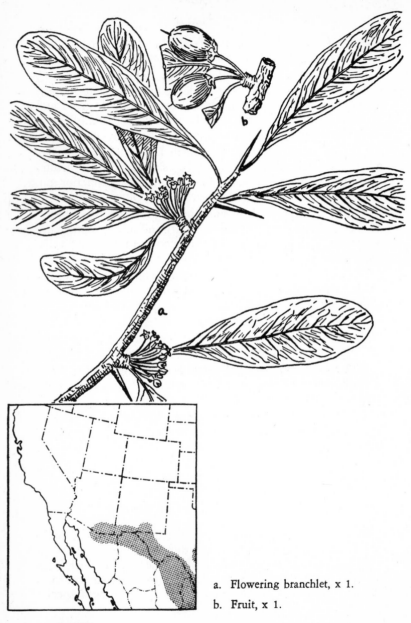

a. Flowering branchlet, x 1.
b. Fruit, x 1.

SAPOTACEAE

Gum Bumelia. Gum Elastic
Bumelia lanuginosa var. *rigida* A. Gray

HABIT. A shrub or small tree 40–50 feet high and 1–2 feet in diameter; narrow crown with short, spiny branches.

LEAVES. Alternate; simple; 1–3½ inches long; oblanceolate to obovate; rounded or apiculate at apex; margins entire; thin and firm; dark green above; soft, reflexed, rusty-brown hairs below; tardily deciduous in winter; stipules absent.

FLOWERS. Regular; perfect; minute (⅛ inch long); in 16–18-flowered, axillary clusters; on pubescent pedicels; calyx persistent, ovoid, 5-lobed, tomentose; corolla white, campanulate, 5-lobed; stamens 5, with 5 sterile, alternating filaments; ovary 5-celled; ovules solitary.

FRUIT. Drupe; oblong or slightly obovoid; ½ inch long; black; solitary or in 2–3-fruited clusters; thick flesh; usually 1-celled and 1-seeded; remnant of style at apex; on slender, drooping stalk. Seed: ¼ inch long, short-oblong, shiny.

TWIGS. Slender; rounded; somewhat zigzag; usually armed with stout spines; red-brown to ash-gray. Winter buds: scaly, small, obtuse, rusty-tomentose.

BARK. Thin (½ inch); dark gray-brown; divided into narrow ridges which are broken into thick scales.

WOOD. Heavy; rather soft; not strong; close-grained; ring-porous; heartwood light brown or yellow; sapwood thick and lighter colored; producing clear, viscid gum.

SILVICAL CHARACTERS. Upper Sonoran zone; intolerant; dry hills and cañons, or along streams; generally shrubby in Texas and forming high, dense thickets in Arizona.

* * *

The Texas Bumelia, *Bumelia texana* Buckl., a closely related form with glabrous, thick, deciduous leaves, forms a small tree in western Texas.

* * *

EBENACEAE

The Texas Persimmon, *Diospyros texana* Scheele, a shrub or tree entering west Texas is characterized by simple, alternate leaves; and a 3–8-seeded, black berry, ½–1 inch long.

[259]

OLEACEAE

The Ashes

Characteristics of the Genus *Fraxinus* L.

HABIT. Deciduous trees, or rarely shrubs; ornamental with handsome foliage; several species are important timber trees.

LEAVES. Opposite; odd-pinnately compound (rarely reduced to a single leaflet); without stipules; petiolate; leaflets serrate or entire, sessile or petiolulate.

FLOWERS. Regular; perfect; dioecious, or polygamous; small, but quite conspicuous in slender-branched panicles; appearing before or with the leaves; calyx 4-lobed or wanting; corolla usually 4-lobed or wanting; stamens usually 2 (rarely 3 or 4); single 2-celled ovary (rarely 3-celled); ovules suspended in pairs from inner angle of the cell.

FRUIT. Samara; 1-, rarely 2- or 3-seeded; with an elongated terminal wing. Seed: oblong, compressed, filling cavity in the fruit, chestnut-brown, albuminous.

TWIGS. Slender to stout; glabrous or pubescent; pith thick, rounded, homogeneous; leaf scars suborbicular to semi-circular, sometimes notched on the upper edge; bundle scars numerous. Winter buds: terminal larger than lateral, both with 1–3 pairs of scales, the inner accrescent.

BARK. Thick and furrowed or rarely thin and scaly.

WOOD. Ring-porous; late wood with rather few pores not in distinct radial lines and with tangential bands of parenchyma; tough; straight-grained; not structural timber but important for specialty purposes; sapwood not durable.

SILVICAL CHARACTERS. Rather intolerant trees; rapid growing; fibrous root system; reproducing well naturally and artificially; comparatively free from destructive attacks by insects and fungi.

GENERAL. This genus contains about 65 species of trees scattered through the Northern Hemisphere and extending into the tropical forests of Java and Cuba. In North America there are 18 recognized native species, 7 of which are found in the Rocky Mountain region.

[260]

KEY TO THE SPECIES FRAXINUS

I. Flowers with corolla, in terminal panicles; usually a shrub; Texas, New Mexico, Arizona, and Mexico......................
...............................1. *F. cuspidata,* p. 263.

II. Flowers without corolla, in axillary panicles; commonly reaching tree size in the United States.

  A. Leaves 10–12" long with 7–9 leaflets; fruit narrowly lanceolate, 1–2½" long; twigs round; widely distributed throughout region......................2. *F. pennsylvanica,* p. 265.

  B. Leaves 1½–7" long with 1–9 leaflets; fruit oblong to obovate; ½–1½" long; southern and central.

    1. Leaflets usually 1 (rarely 2–3); fruit not over ½" long, obovate; wing surrounding and shorter than compressed seed cavity; twigs 4-angled; southern and central........
...............................3. *F. anoma'a,* p. 263.

    2. Leaflets 3–9; fruit over ½" long, oblong-ovate; wing not surrounding seed cavity; southern.

      a. Leaves 1½–3" long; leaflets ½–¾" long with winged petioles, obscure veins and black dots on lower surface; fruit ½–⅔"long..........4. *F. greggii,* p. 269.

      b. Leaves 3–7" long; leaflets 1–4" long, with prominent veins and no black dots; fruit ¾–1½" long.

        (1) Twigs 4-angled; wing extending to base of much-compressed seed cavity; leaflets usually 5........
.......................5. *F. lowellii,* p. 269.

        (2) Twigs round; wing not extending to base of rounded seed cavity; leaflets 3–5.

          (a) Fruit ½–¾" long; leaves and twigs pubescent or glabrous; southwest...................
...................6. *F. velutina,* p. 267.

          (b) Fruit 1–1½" long; leaves and twigs glabrous; Texas......7. *F. berlandieriana* DC., p. 265.

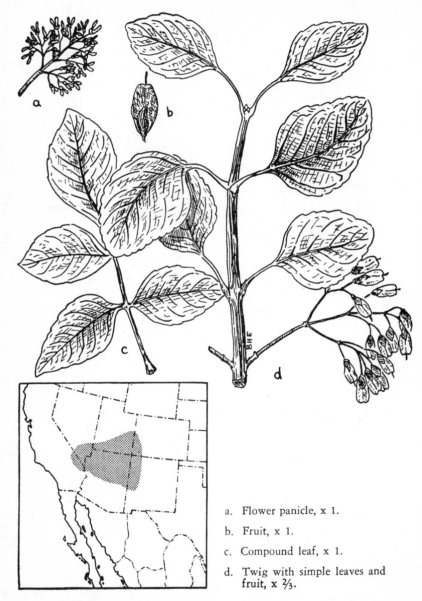

a. Flower panicle, x 1.

b. Fruit, x 1.

c. Compound leaf, x 1.

d. Twig with simple leaves and
   fruit, x 2/3.

OLEACEAE

SINGLELEAF ASH. DWARF ASH

Fraxinus anomala Torr.

HABIT. A shrub or small tree 18–20 feet high with a short trunk 6–7 inches in diameter; crown round-topped, with contorted branches; a distinct and interesting species.

LEAVES. Usually single but rarely with 2–5 leaflets; broadly ovate or suborbicular; 1–2 inches long and 1–2 inches wide (smaller if compound); apex rounded or acute; base cuneate or cordate; margins entire or sparingly crenate-serrate above middle; glabrous and dark green above, paler below and pubescent when young; thin but rather leathery; petiole ½–1½ inches long, rusty-pubescent when young.

FLOWERS. In short, compact, pubescent panicles; appearing when leaves about ⅔ grown; perfect or unisexual by abortion of stamens (both forms in same panicle); calyx cup-shaped, minutely 4-toothed; corolla absent; anthers orange-colored, on slender filaments nearly as long as stout, columnar style.

FRUIT. Obovate-oblong; ½ inch long; wing rounded or emarginate at apex, surrounding flattened seed cavity.

TWIGS. Quadrangular, slightly winged, puberulous, orange-colored and marked by pale lenticels and lunate leaf scars at first; later round and ash-gray. Winter buds: terminal broad ovoid, ⅛–¼ inch long, covered by orange tomentum.

BARK. Thin (½ inch); dark brown slightly tinged with red; divided by shallow furrows into narrow, scaly ridges.

WOOD. Heavy; hard; close-grained; heartwood light brown; sapwood lighter colored and thick; of no importance.

SILVICAL CHARACTERS. Lower and Upper Sonoran zones; intolerant; in the neighborhood of streams or on dry hillsides.

* * *

FRAGRANT ASH. FLOWERING ASH

Fraxinus cuspidata Torr.

A handsome shrub or low tree with showy white flowers and 1–5 small, entire leaflets; ranging from west Texas to northern Arizona and south into Mexico.

GREEN ASH

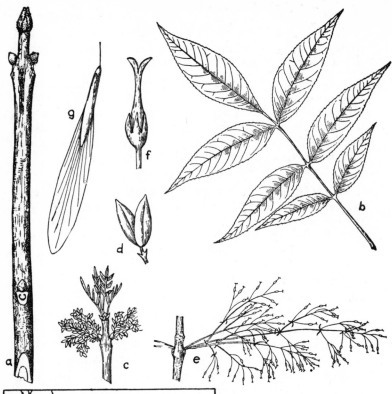

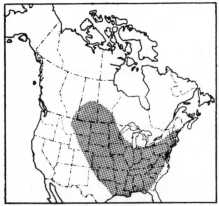

a. Winter twig, x 1.

b. Leaf, x ⅓.

c. Staminate flowering branchlet, x ½.

d. Staminate flower, enlarged.

e. Pistillate flowering branchlet, x ½.

f. Pistillate flower, enlarged.

g. Fruit, x 1.

OLEACEAE

Green Ash

Fraxinus pennsylvanica Marsh.
[*Fraxinus pennsylvanica* var. *lanceolata* (Borkh.) Sarg.]

HABIT. A tree rarely more than 60 feet high or 2 feet in diameter; irregular, compact, round-topped crown with spreading or upright branches.

LEAVES. 10–12 inches long; 7–9 leaflets, narrowly elliptical 4–6 inches long and 1–1½ inches wide, long-pointed, finely serrate to nearly entire, bright green on both surfaces, usually glabrous; terminal petiolule up to 1 inch long, lateral petiolules ⅛–¼ inch long.

FLOWERS. In compact panicles; appearing with leaves; dioecious; calyx-toothed and cup-shaped; corolla absent; anthers light green, linear-oblong; ovary nearly enclosed in calyx, narrowed into elongated style having 2 green stigmas.

FRUIT. Narrowly lanceolate; 1–2½ inches long, ¼–⅓ inch wide; wing thin, longer than and extending to the middle of the seed cavity; seed cavity terete, slender, many-rayed.

TWIGS. Rounded; stout; mostly glabrous; ash-gray and marked by pale lenticels and straight or only slightly notched leaf scars. Winter buds: the terminal about ⅛ inch long, ovoid, acute, with 3 pairs of rusty-pubescent scales.

BARK. Thin (½–⅔ inch); brown or dark gray; longitudinal, shallow furrows and scaly ridges.

WOOD. Heavy; hard; rather strong; brittle; coarse-grained; light brown heartwood; thick, lighter brown sapwood; second to white ash in commercial importance.

SILVICAL CHARACTERS. Upper Sonoran and Transition zones; intolerant; reproduction aggressive on moist sites; growth rapid; best on moist bottomlands, but exceedingly hardy to climatic extremes; shallow, wide-spreading root system.

GENERAL. Taxonomy of this species is confused. Check list does not recognize as distinct Red Ash (*F. pennsylvanica*) and Green Ash (*F. pennsylvanica* var. *lanceolata*).

* * *

F. berlandieriana A.DC., of Texas and Mexico, differs from Green Ash in having 3–5 leaflets, and fruit 1–1½ inches long.

[265]

VELVET ASH

a. Fruit, x 1.

b. One form of leaf, x ½.

c. Twig with leaves and fruit, x ½.

[266]

OLEACEAE

VELVET ASH

Fraxinus velutina Torr. (*Fraxinus standleyi* Rehd.)

HABIT. A small, slender tree 20–30 feet high (rarely 40–50 feet) and 12–18 inches in diameter; symmetrical, round-topped crown with stout, often spreading branches.

LEAVES. 4–5 inches long, with a broad, grooved, densely villous petiole; 3–5 leaflets; elliptic to ovate; 1–1½ inches long and ¾–1 inch wide; mostly acute at apex; finely crenate-serrulate above the middle; thick; pale green, glabrous above, tomentose below; tardily deciduous; terminal petiolule ½ inch long, lateral petiolules ⅙ inch or less.

FLOWERS. In elongated, pubescent panicles; from leafless, axillary buds; appearing with leaves; dioecious; calyx cup-shaped, densely pubescent; corolla absent; anthers oblong, apiculate; ovary nearly enclosed in calyx, shorter than nearly sessile lobes of stigma.

FRUIT. Oblong-obovate to elliptic; rarely more than ¾ inch long and ⅙ inch wide; wing shorter than and extending to below middle of terete seed cavity.

TWIGS. Rounded; slender; velvety pubescent first year; glabrous, ash-gray, and marked with large, obcordate, dark leaf scars in second year. Winter buds: the terminal ⅛ inch long, acute, with 3 pairs of tomentose scales.

BARK. Thin (⅓–½ inch); gray, slightly tinged with red; divided by furrows into broad, scaly ridges.

WOOD. Heavy; rather soft; not strong; close-grained; heartwood light brown; sapwood lighter colored and thick.

SILVICAL CHARACTERS. Lower Sonoran to Transition zones; intolerant; in mountain cañons up to 6,000 feet, and on banks of streams; hardy, growing well under arid conditions and in alkaline soils; extremely variable.

GENERAL. *F. velutina* passes into the following varieties: 1. *coriacea* (S. Wats.) Rehd., with thicker, leathery leaves. 2. *glabra* Rehd., with glabrous leaves and branches. 3. *toumeyi* (Britt.) Rehd., with lanceolate, acuminate leaflets, having petioles ⅛–½ inch long. A related form in southern New Mexico and southeast Arizona has been designated *F. papillosa* Lingelsh. The distribution on the map is for the entire species.

[267]

Leaves and fruit, x ½.

OLEACEAE

Lowell Ash
Fraxinus lowellii Sarg.
[*Fraxinus anomala* var. *lowellii* (Sarg.) Little]

HABIT. A small tree 20–25 feet high.

LEAVES. 3½–6 inches long, with a stout petiole; 5 (rarely 3–7) leaflets, ovate to elliptic-ovate, 2½–3 inches long, cuneate at base, remotely and slightly serrate, yellow-green, glabrous or slightly pubescent along midrib; on vigorous shoots leaves sometimes single and broadly ovate.

FLOWERS. Axillary; corolla absent.

FRUIT. In long glabrous panicles; oblong-obovate to oblong-elliptic; 1–1½ inches long and ¼–⅓ inch wide; wing broad or gradually narrowed, rounded or emarginate at apex, and extending to base of seed cavity; seed cavity thin, compressed, many-rayed, about ¾ the length of the fruit; ripening in July.

TWIGS. Quadrangular; often winged; stout; orange-brown.

BARK. Rather thick; dark; deeply furrowed.

SILVICAL CHARACTERS. Upper Sonoran zone; intolerant; on dry, rocky slopes and in cañons; check list treats this as a variety of *F. anomala*.

* * *

Gregg Ash. Littleleaf Ash
Fraxinus greggii A. Gray

This shrub or small tree, rarely 25 feet high, is characterized by 3–7 leaflets which are less than 1 inch long, usually entire, covered below with small, black dots, and obscurely veined; the twigs are slender and round, and the bark is thin and separates into papery scales; it has been reported from Santa Cruz County, Arizona, western Texas, and Mexico. A related newly described form from Santa Cruz County, Arizona, has been designated *F. gooddingii* Little.

* * *

Elbowbush
Forestiera pubescens Nutt.

Typically a shrub, but rarely a small tree of Texas and eastern New Mexico. Characterized by opposite, simple, pubescent, serrulate, obovate leaves, about 1 inch long; small dioecious flowers; and a small, blue-black, oblong, 1-celled, 1-seeded drupe.

[269]

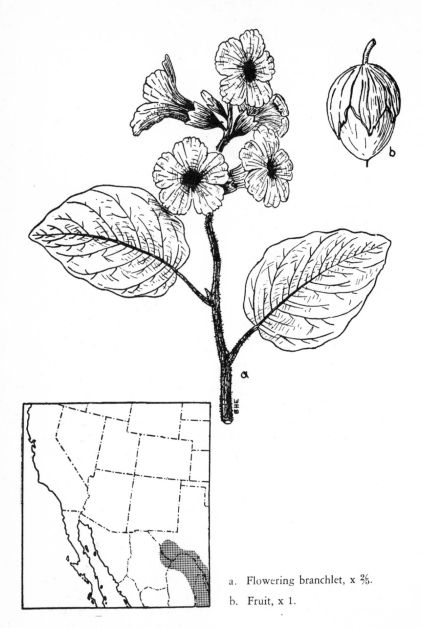

a. Flowering branchlet, x ⅖.

b. Fruit, x 1.

BORRAGINACEAE

ANACAHUITA

Cordia boissieri A. DC.

HABIT. An aromatic shrub or small tree 20–25 feet high and 6–8 inches in diameter; bole often crooked; crown round-topped.

LEAVES. Alternate; simple; oval to oblong-ovate; 4–5 inches long; acute or rounded at apex; entire or obscurely crenulate-serrate; thick and firm; dark green, wrinkled and more or less scabrous above, coated below with thick tomentum; pinnately veined; tardily deciduous at end of first year; petioles stout, tomentose, 1–1½ inches long; stipules absent.

FLOWERS. Regular; perfect; in terminal cymes; calyx tubular, 5-toothed, persistent; corolla funnel-form, 2 inches across, white with yellow spot in throat; stamens 5, on corolla tube; ovary single, with solitary ovule in each of 4 cells.

FRUIT. Drupaceous; ovoid; 1 inch long and ¾ inch broad; acute; lustrous, bright red-brown; enclosed entirely or partially by thin, fibrous, orange-brown, tomentose calyx; flesh thin, sweet, and pulpy; stone thick-walled, hard and bony, ovoid, light brown. Seed: 1–2 in each fruit; ¼ inch long; acute.

TWIGS. Stout, dark gray or brown, puberulous, marked by occasional large lenticels and by elevated obcordate leaf-scars.

BARK. Thin; gray, tinged with red; irregularly divided into broad, flat ridges; the surface with long thin scales.

WOOD. Light; rather soft; close-grained; diffuse-porous, dark brown heartwood; thick, light brown sapwood.

SILVICAL CHARACTERS. Lower Sonoran zone; intolerant; dry limestone ridges and depressions; planted as ornamental.

* * *

SOLANACEAE

TREE TOBACCO

Nicotiana glauca Graham

A South American shrub or small tree naturalized from southwestern Texas to southern California. Characterized by persistent, alternate, simple, entire, glaucous leaves, 2–7 inches long; white, regular, perfect flowers, 1½ inches long; and a 2-celled capsule about ½ inch long.

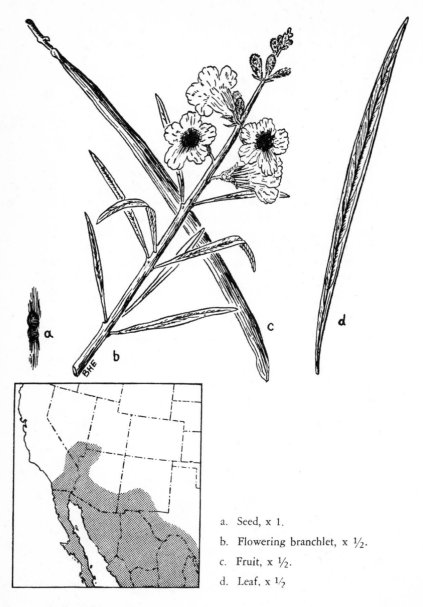

a. Seed, x 1.

b. Flowering branchlet, x ½.

c. Fruit, x ½.

d. Leaf, x ½

[272]

BIGNONIACEAE
Desertwillow

Chilopsis linearis (Cav.) Sweet. (*Chilopsis saligna* Don.)

HABIT. A shrub or small tree rarely 20–30 feet high; trunk usually reclining; crown narrow with slender, upright branches.

LEAVES. Opposite, alternate, or scattered; simple; linear or linear-lanceolate; 5–12 inches long and ¼–⅓ inch wide; acuminate; entire margins; 3-nerved; thin; light green; smooth or glutinous; deciduous during following winter; short-petioled or sessile; without stipules.

FLOWERS. Irregular; perfect; showy; in racemes or panicles 3–4 inches long; appearing in summer; calyx pale-pubescent, closed before anthesis; corolla white tinged with purple, yellow-spotted in throat, ¾–1½ inches long and ¾–1¼ inches wide, 2-lipped; stamens 4, inserted; ovary 2-celled, conic, glabrous; ovules inserted in many series on a central placenta.

FRUIT. Slender, elongated, thin-walled capsule, 7–12 inches long and ¼ inch thick; splitting into 2 concave valves; persistent into the winter. Seed: numerous; ⅓ inch long and ⅛ inch wide; compressed; oblong; seed coat thin, light brown, produced into broad, fringed, lateral wings.

TWIGS. Slender, glabrous or densely tomentose, light chestnut-brown becoming darker. Winter buds: terminal absent; lateral minute, compressed, scaly, rusty-pubescent.

BARK. Thin (⅛–¼ inch); dark brown; furrowed.

WOOD. Soft; not strong; close-grained; ring-porous; heartwood brown, streaked with yellow; sapwood very thin and light-colored; durable; used locally for fence posts.

SILVICAL CHARACTERS. Lower Sonoran zone; intolerant; short-lived; banks of desert and low mountain water courses; usually dry, well-drained sandy and gravelly soils; at elevations from sea level to 5,000 feet; a monotypic genus.

* * *

Northern Catalpa
Catalpa speciosa Engelm.

An eastern species but much planted in warmer portions of the region. A showy tree with handsome flowers; large, heart-shaped leaves (3–8 inches long); and fruit a cigar-like pod 6–15 inches long.

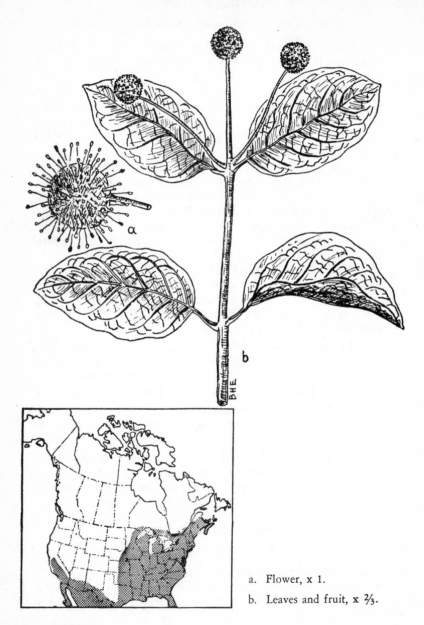

a. Flower, x 1.

b. Leaves and fruit, x ⅔.

RUBIACEAE

COMMON BUTTONBUSH

Cephalanthus occidentalis L.

HABIT. A shrub or rarely a small tree up to 50 feet high and 1–2 inches in diameter; open, spreading crown.

LEAVES. Opposite or whorled in 3's; simple; ovate, lanceolate, or elliptic; 2–7 inches long; acute or acuminate at apex; margins entire; thin; dark green and glabrous above; paler below, with yellow midrib; tardily deciduous during winter; petioles stout, grooved, glabrous, ½–¾ inch long.

FLOWERS. Regular; perfect; minute; in dense, globose heads 1–1½ inches in diameter; fragrant; calyx tube 4–5-lobed; corolla cream-white, salver-form, 4–5-lobed; stamens as many as and alternate with corolla lobes; ovary inferior, 2-celled, with protruding, threadlike style and capitate stigma.

FRUIT. Nutlike capsule; inversely pyramidal; splitting from base upwards into 2–4 closed, 1-seeded portions; in heads ⅝–¾ inch in diameter; green tinged with red, becoming dark red-brown. Seed: small, oblong, pendulous.

TWIGS. Stout; glabrous; thick pith; marked by large lenticels; opposite or in whorls of 3; light green at first, becoming red-brown. Winter buds: terminal absent; lateral minute, nearly immersed in the bark.

BARK. Thin; dark brown to nearly black; with broad, flat, superficially scaly ridges; contains tannin.

WOOD. Moderately heavy and hard; fine-grained; diffuse-porous; light red-brown; unimportant.

SILVICAL CHARACTERS. Lower Sonoran to Transition zones; rather tolerant; reproduction abundant; on moist sites or in dry stream beds; often forming dense thickets.

* * *

BIGNONIACEAE

TRUMPETFLOWER

Tecoma stans (L) H.B.K.

A shrub or small tree extending through Mexico into the southern parts of Texas, New Mexico, and Arizona. Characterized by showy, bright yellow flowers; opposite, pinnately compound leaves with 5–13 leaflets; and a linear capsule, 4–8 inches long.

[275]

a. Flower, x 5.

b. Fruit, x 2.

c. Flowering branchlet, x ⅔.

CAPRIFOLIACEAE
BLUEBERRY ELDER
Sambucus glauca Nutt. (*Sambucus cerulea* Raf.)

HABIT. A shrub or small tree 30–50 feet high and 12–18 inches in diameter; compact, round-topped crown.

LEAVES. Opposite; unequally pinnately compound; petiolate; deciduous; 5–7 inches long; leaflets 5–9, ovate or narrow oblong, acuminate at apex, coarsely serrate margin, 1–6 inches long and ⅓–1½ inches wide, green above, pale and glabrous to pubescent below, thin and rather firm, on slender petiolules.

FLOWERS. Regular; perfect; small (⅛ inch in diameter); in broad, terminal, long-branched corymbose cymes; calyx ovoid, red-brown, 5-lobed; corolla yellow-white, rotate, 5-lobed, as long as stamens; stamens 5, alternate to corolla lobes; ovary inferior, 3–5-celled, with solitary ovule in each cell.

FRUIT. Dense clusters of small, blue, berry-like drupes; each drupe subglobose, ¼ inch in diameter, with sweet, juicy flesh, used for jellies, pies, etc. Seed: 3–5 1-seeded nutlets in each drupe.

TWIGS. Stout; somewhat angled; pubescent first year; red-brown; nearly encircled by large, triangular leaf-scars marked by conspicuous bundle-scars; thick, soft, whitish pith. Winter buds: terminal absent; lateral scaly, greenish.

BARK. Thin; dark brown, tinged with red; irregularly furrowed and ridged.

WOOD. Light; soft; weak; coarse-grained; diffuse-porous; heartwood yellow tinged with brown, durable; sapwood thin and lighter colored; unimportant.

SILVICAL CHARACTERS. Upper Sonoran to Canadian zones; intolerant; short-lived; reproduction abundant, coppices freely; moist porous soils.

GENERAL. Three other shrubby species rarely reach tree size: *S. melanocarpa* A. Gray, ranging from Montana to New Mexico and west with flowers in a pyramidal cyme; *S. mexicana* Presl., with persistent leaves and a flat cyme and ranging from west Texas to central Arizona and California; *S. velutina* D. &. H., with hairy deciduous leaves and a flat cyme and found in the mountains of western Arizona.

[277]

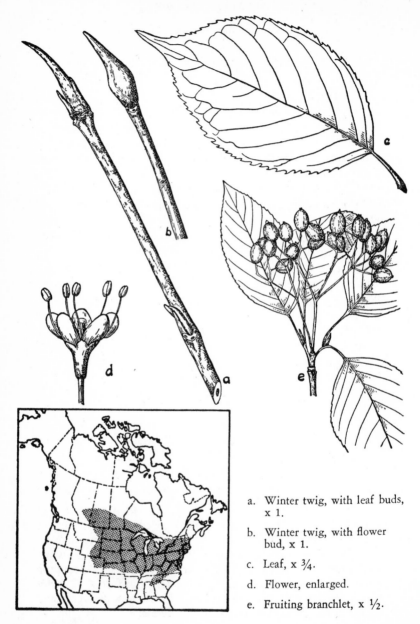

a. Winter twig, with leaf buds,
   x 1.

b. Winter twig, with flower
   bud, x 1.

c. Leaf, x ¾.

d. Flower, enlarged.

e. Fruiting branchlet, x ½.

CAPRIFOLIACEAE

NANNYBERRY

Viburnum lentago L.

HABIT. A shrub or small tree 15–30 feet high and 6–10 inches in diameter; bushy, compact, rounded crown with slender, tortuous, rather pendulous branches.

LEAVES. Opposite; simple; ovate; 2–4 inches long and 1–2 inches wide; acuminate or sometimes rounded at apex; sharply serrate; thick and firm; lustrous and bright green above; yellow-green and marked with minute, black dots below; deciduous; petioles broad, grooved, more or less winged, about 1 inch long; turning orange and red in autumn.

FLOWERS. Regular; perfect; small ($\frac{1}{4}$ inch in diameter); fragrant; in stout-branched, scurfy, terminal cymes 3–5 inches across; calyx tubular, 5-lobed; corolla tubular, 5-lobed, cream-colored to white; stamens 5, with yellow anthers, inserted on tube of corolla and alternate to its lobes; ovary inferior, 1-celled, with short, thick style and broad stigma; ovule solitary, suspended from apex of cell.

FRUIT. Few-fruited, red-stemmed clusters of small, juicy, blue-black, berry-like drupes; each drupe oval or ovoid, flattened, and covered with glaucous bloom. Seed: solitary within oval, rough, flattened nutlet.

TWIGS. Slender; tough and flexible; light green and rusty-pubescent at first, becoming dark red-brown. Winter buds: large, scurfy-pubescent, enclosed by one pair of valvate scales; flower buds $\frac{3}{4}$ inch long, grayish, swollen at base and long-pointed; terminal leaf bud 1 inch long, light red, narrow, and long-pointed; lateral leaf buds much smaller.

BARK. Red-brown; irregularly broken into small, thick plates which are superficially scaly.

WOOD. Heavy; hard; close-grained; diffuse-porous; ill-scented; heartwood dark orange-brown; sapwood thin and whitish.

SILVICAL CHARACTERS. Transition zone; very hardy; prefers rich, moist soils bordering forests, rivers, or marshes, but is found on rocky hillsides; an attractive small ornamental tree; coppices freely; endures city smoke.

[279]

SAGE BRUSH

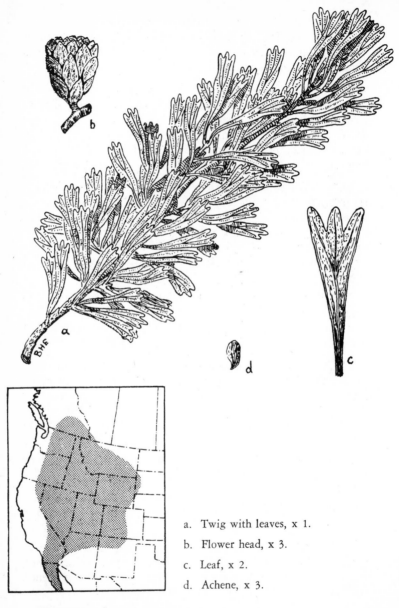

a. Twig with leaves, x 1.

b. Flower head, x 3.

c. Leaf, x 2.

d. Achene, x 3.

COMPOSITAE

SAGE BRUSH. BLACK SAGE

Artemisia tridentata Nutt.

HABIT. Usually a shrub, but on moist sites occasionally becoming a small tree 8–20 feet high and 4–12 inches in diameter; trunk sinuous and malformed; branches erect or ascending.

LEAVES. Alternate; simple; ½–1¼ inches long; wedge-shaped; 3-toothed at broad apex, or upper leaves not toothed; narrowed to nearly sessile base; margins entire; gray with appressed hairs on both surfaces; persistent; stipules absent; odor characteristic; taste bitter.

FLOWERS. Regular; perfect; minute; in 5–8-flowered heads, about ⅛ inch long; in large, dense panicles at end of branches; involucral bracts nearly or quite as long as flowers; ray flowers absent; calyx wanting; corolla tubular, yellow or geeenish; stamens 4–5, with anthers united laterally; ovary inferior, oblong or linear, 1-celled, 1-ovuled, narrowed above into slender style which branches into 2 stigmas.

FRUIT. Obovoid or oblong achene; rounded at apex; without crown of bristles (pappus).

TWIGS. Slender; round; at first gray-green and covered with closely matted hairs, soon becoming roughened. Winter buds: minute, hairy.

BARK. Thin; gray; rough; shreddy.

WOOD. Moderately soft and light; tending to fall apart at growth rings; ill-scented; fine-grained; ring-porous; heartwood dark brown; sapwood lighter colored; unimportant.

SILVICAL CHARACTERS. Upper Sonoran and Transition zone; intolerant; the most abundant shrub of the western arid and semi-arid plains; reported reaching tree size from southern Colorado and New Mexico; root system two-storied, shallow-fibrous and deep-spreading; indicator of deep soils largely free from alkali.

GENERAL. About 200 species are recognized in this genus, most of them being herbaceous; plants of this group are known as wormwood, and some are grown for drug products.

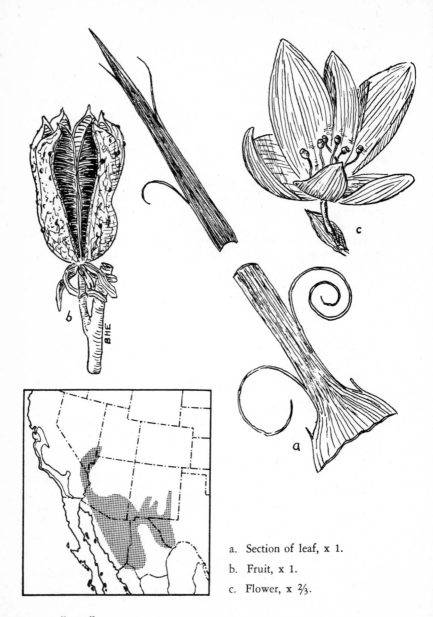

a. Section of leaf, x 1.

b. Fruit, x 1.

c. Flower, x ⅔.

LILIACEAE
SOAPTREE YUCCA. SPANISH-BAYONET
Yucca elata Engelm.

HABIT. A tree often 15–20 feet high and 7–8 inches in diameter with a deep, branched, underground stem; simple or branched at top; covered with pendent, persistent dead leaves.

LEAVES. Alternate; simple; 20–30 inches long and ¼–½ inch wide; thin and flat above, rounded below; glabrous; yellow-green; entire pale margins soon splitting into slender filaments; parallel-veined; persistent; stipules absent.

FLOWERS. Regular; perfect; in compound, terminal panicles, 4–6 feet high; perianth cup-shaped, white 3½–4 inches across; stamens 6; ovary 6-sided, 3-celled; ovules numerous.

FRUIT. Erect, oblong capsule, 1½–2 inches long; 3-valved; light brown, thin and woody outside; light yellow inside; edible. Seed: numerous, black, ⅓ inch wide.

BARK. Dark brown; with thin plates; ¼ inch thick.

WOOD. Light; soft; spongy; pale brown or yellow; in concentric layers.

SILVICAL CHARACTERS. Lower Sonoran zone; intolerant; on high, desert plateaus; large roots used as substitute for soap.

* * *

Seven species of Yucca reach tree size in the Southwest:
1. Fruit erect, dehiscent; flower clusters long-stalked; leaves filamentose, thin pale yellow-green...................1. *Y. elata.*
1. Fruit pendent, indehiscent; flower clusters sessile or short-stalked; leaves concave above the middle.
   2. Fruit with thin, dry flesh; leaves blue-green, serrate; southwestern Utah to California...............................
   ....2. *Y. brevifolia* Engelm., Joshua Tree.
   2. Fruit with succulent flesh; leaves with no, or minute teeth.
      3. Panicle hoary-tomentose; leaves flexible. 2½–3 feet long; margins not filamentous; southern Arizona...........
      ....*Y. schottii* Engelm., Schotts Yucca
      3. Panicle glabrous or puberulous; margins filamentous.
         4. Leaves 2½–4 feet long, dark green; Texas.
            5. Leaves concave; perianth nearly free ....
            ....*Y. treculeana* Carr.; Trecul Yucca
            5. Leaves flat, perianth united into tube..........
            ....*Y. faxoniana* Sarg.; *Faxon Yucca*
         4. Leaves 1½–2 feet long, light yellow-green.
            6. Style elongated; western Texas to eastern Arizona............*Y. torreyi* Shaf.; Torrey Yucca
            6. Style short; southeastern Nevada, northwestern Arizona....*Y. mohavensis* Sarg.; Mohave Yucca

a. Leaf petiole, x ⅓.

b. Leaf, x 1/9.

c. Part of fruit cluster, x ⅔.

PALMAE

ARIZONA WASHINGTONIA. FANLEAF PALM

Washingtonia filifera H. Wendl.

(*Washingtonia arizonica* Cook) (*Washingtonia robusta* Wendl.)

HABIT. An evergreen tree 30–50 feet high and 1–2 feet in diameter; crown broad, consisting of large leaves; columnar trunk clothed with thatchlike mass of pendent dead leaves and remains of sheaths and petioles, becoming smooth with age.

LEAVES. Clustered at top of stem; 3–6 feet long; fan-shaped; nearly circular; with 40–70 ribbon-like folds deeply slashed ½–⅔ of distance to base; the margins of the divisions separating into numerous threadlike filaments; petioles 3–5 feet long, 1–3 inches wide, armed along margins with stout, hooked spines.

FLOWERS. Regular; perfect; minute; in compound clusters 8–10 feet long; appearing from axils of upper leaves; calyx tubular; corolla white, tubular; stamens 6; ovary 3-lobed and 3-celled with a single ovule in each cell.

FRUIT. Drupelike berry; ⅜ inch long; black when ripe in September; ellipsoidal; with a thin, dry, sweet pulp; produced in large quantities. Seed: ¼ inch long, ⅛ inch wide, pale chestnut-brown.

BARK. Stem with thick barklike rind; narrowly furrowed; pale cinnamon to dull red-brown.

WOOD. Light; soft; spongy and fibrous; yellowish, with numerous, conspicuous, dark orange-colored, fibro-vascular bundles; unimportant.

SILVICAL CHARACTERS. Lower Sonoran zone; moderately tolerant when young, becoming intolerant; reproduction plentiful; long, deep roots; alkaline soils; dry, warm mountain cañons.

GENERAL. This palm is reported from Yuma County, southwestern Arizona, often occurring there in large numbers. Considerable confusion exists as to the nomenclature and classification of the forms of *Washingtonia*. According to some authors there are three southwestern species, *W. robusta* Wendl. (*W. sonorae* S. Wat.), native to Mexico, *W. filifera* H. Wendl., native to California, and *W. arizonica* Cook, native to Arizona. The characters of the leaf margins, petiole spines, and trunk size, which separates these forms, vary so greatly that they are of doubtful value as species criteria.

GLOSSARY

Abortive. Imperfectly or not developed; barren.

Accrescent. Increasing in size with age.

Achene. A dry indehiscent, 1-celled and 1-seeded fruit or carpel.

Acuminate. Gradually tapering to the apex; long-pointed.

Acute. Sharply pointed, but not drawr. out.

Adnate. Descriptive of unlike organs or parts fused together.

Alternate. Scattered singly along axis; not opposite.

Ament. A scaly, bracted spike of usually unisexual flowers, frequently deciduous in one piece.

Anther. The pollen-bearing part of the stamen.

Anthesis. The time when fertilization takes place.

Apetalous. Without petals.

Apiculate. Ending in a minute, short, pointed tip.

Apophysis. That part of a cone scale which is exposed when the cone is closed.

Appressed. Lying close and flat against.

Arborescent. Attaining the size or character of a tree.

Aril. An appendage growing out from the hilum and covering the seed partly or wholly.

Attenuate. Slenderly tapering; acuminate.

Awl-shaped. Tapering from the base to a slender and stiff point.

Axil. The upper angle formed by a leaf or branch with the stem.

Axillary. Situated in an axil.

Berry. A fleshy or pulpy fruit with immersed seeds.

Blade. The expanded portion of a leaf.

Bloom. A powdery or waxy substance easily rubbed off.

Bole. The stem of a tree.

Boss. A raised projection, usually pointed.

Bract. A modified leaf subtending a flower o- belonging to an inflorescence.

Bractlet. The bract of a pedicel or ultimate flower stalk; a secondary bract.

Bud. The undeveloped state of a branch or flower cluster, with
or without scales.

Bud scales. Modified leaves covering a bud.

Bundle (leaf). Strand of fibro-vascular tissue found in cross
section of leaf.

Caducous. Falling off very early.

Calyx. The flower-cup or exterior part of a perianth.

Campanulate. Bell-shaped.

Canescent. Gray-pubescent and hoary.

Capsule. A dry fruit of more than one carpel which splits at
maturity to release its seeds.

Carpel. A simple pistil or an element of a compound pistil.

Catkin. The same as an ament.

Caudate. Furnished with a tail or with a slender tip.

Cell. The unit of structure of living things; a cavity of an
ovary or anther.

Chambered. Said of pith which is interrupted by hollow spaces.

Ciliate. Fringed with hairs on the margin.

Cone. A fruit with woody, overlapping scales.

Coniferous. Pertains to cone-bearing; or the order Coniferales

Coppice. Growth arising from sprouts at the stump.

Cordate. Heart-shaped.

Coriaceous. Of the texture of leather.

Corolla. Inner part of the perianth, composed of petals.

Corymb. A flat-topped flower cluster, the flowers opening from
the outside inward.

Crenate. Dentate with the teeth much rounded.

Crenulate. Diminutive of crenate, finely crenate.

Crown. The upper part of a tree, including the living branches
with their foliage.

Cuneate. Wedge-shaped, or triangular with an acute angle
downward.

Cuspidate. Tipped with a sharp, rigid point.

Cylindric. Shaped like a cylinder.

Cyme. A flat-topped flower cluster, the flowers opening from
the center outward.

Deciduous. Not persistent; falling away as the leaves of a tree
in autumn.

Decurrent. Running down, as of the blades of leaves extending down their petioles.

Decussate. In pairs alternately crossing at right angles.

Dehiscent. The opening of an anther or capsule by slits or valves.

Deltoid. Delta-shaped, triangular.

Dentate. Toothed, with the teeth directed outward.

Denticulate. Minutely toothed.

Diadelphous. Stamens formed into two groups through the union of their filaments.

Dimorphous. Occurring in two forms.

Dioecious. Unisexual, the staminate and pistillate flowers on different individuals.

Disk. A development of the receptacle at or around the base of the pistil.

Dissemination. The spreading abroad of ripe seeds from the parent plant.

Divergent. Spreading apart; pointing away.

Dorsal. Relating to the back or outer surface of an organ; the lower surface of a leaf.

Downy. Clothed with a coat of soft, fine hairs.

Drupaceous. Resembling or relating to a drupe.

Drupe. A stone fruit, such as a plum.

E. A Latin prefix denoting that parts are missing, as eglandular, without glands.

Ellipsoidal. Of the shape of an elliptical solid.

Elliptic. Of the form of an elipse.

Emarginate. Notched at the apex.

Entire. Leaf margin without divisions, lobes or teeth.

Erose. Descriptive of an irregularly toothed or eroded margin.

Excrescences. Warty outgrowths or protuberances.

Exfoliate. To cleave or peel off in thin layers.

Exserted. Prolonged beyond the surrounding organs, as stamens from the corolla.

Falcate. Scythe- or sickle-shaped.

Fascicle. Dense cluster or bundle.

Fibro-vascular. Consisting of woody fibers and ducts.

Filament. The stalk of an anther.

Fluted. Regularly marked by alternating ridges and groovelike depressions.

Foliaceous. Leaflike in texture or appearance.

Fugacious. Falling or withering away very early.
Fulvous. Tawny; dull yellow with gray.
Furrowed. With longitudinal channels or grooves.

Gibbous. Swollen on one side.
Glabrous. Smooth, not pubescent or hairy.
Gland. Secreting surface or structure; a protuberance having
    appearance of such an organ.
Glandular. Furnished with glands.
Glaucous. Covered or whitened with a bloom.
Globose. Spherical in form or nearly so.

Habit. The general appearance of a plant; best seen from a
    distance.
Habitat. The place where a plant naturally grows.
Halberd-like. Like an arrowhead, but with the basal lobes
    pointing outward nearly at right angles.
Hilum. The scar or place of attachment of a seed.
Hirsute. Covered with rather coarse or stiff, long hairs.
Hoary. Covered with a close, whitish or gray-white pubescence.
Hybrid. A cross between two nearly related species.

Imbricate. Overlapping, like shingles on a roof.
Indehiscent. Not splitting open; remaining closed.
Inferior ovary. Appearing to grow below the adnate calyx.
Inserted. Attached to or growing out of.
Intolerant. Not capable of doing well under dense forest cover.
Involucre. A circle of bracts surrounding a flower cluster.
Irregular flower. Not symmetrical, similar parts of different
    shapes or sizes.

Keeled. With a central ridge like the keel of a boat.

Laciniate. Cut into narrow, pointed lobes.
Lanceolate. Lance-shaped.
Lateral. Situated on the side; not at apex.
Leaflet. One of the small blades of a compound leaf.
Leaf scar. Scar left on twig by the falling of a leaf.
Legume. Fruit of the pea family; podlike and splitting open
    by both sutures.
Lenticel. Corky growth on young bark which admits air to
    the interior of a twig or branch.

Linear. Long and narrow, with parallel edges.
Lobe. A somewhat rounded division of an organ.
Lobulate. Divided into small lobes.
Lustrous. Glossy, shining.

Membranaceous. Thin and somewhat translucent.
Midrib. The central vein of a leaf or leaflet.
Monoecious. The stamens and pistils in separate flowers but borne on the same individual.
Mucro. A small and abrupt tip to a leaf.
Mucronate. Furnished with a mucro.

Naked buds. Buds without scales.
Nut. A hard and indehiscent, 1-seeded pericarp produced from a compound ovary.
Nutlet. A diminutive nut or stone.

Ob. Latin prefix signifying inversion.
Obconic. Inverted cone-shaped.
Oblanceolate. Lanceolate, with the broadest part toward the apex.
Oblong. About three times longer than broad with nearly parallel sides.
Oblique. Slanting or with unequal sides.
Obcordate. Inverted heart shape.
Obovate. Ovate with the broader end toward the apex.
Obovoid. An ovate solid with the broadest part toward the apex.
Obtuse. Blunt or rounded at apex.
Odd-pinnate leaf. Pinnate with a terminal leaflet.
Orbicular. A flat body circular in outline.
Oval. Broad elliptic, rounded at ends and about $1\frac{1}{2}$ times as long as broad.
Ovary. The part of a pistil that contains the ovules.
Ovate. Shaped like the longitudinal section of an egg, with the broad end basal.
Ovoid. Solid ovate or solid oval.
Ovule. The part of the flower which after fertilization becomes the seed.

Palmate. Radiately lobed or divided, **veins** arising from one **point.**

Panicle. A loose, compound flower cluster.

Papilionaceous. Butterfly-like; typical flower shape of legumes.

Pedicel. Stalk of a single flower in a compound inflorescence.

Pedicellate. Borne on a pedicel.

Peduncle. A general flower stalk supporting either a cluster of flowers or a solitary flower.

Peltate. Shield-shaped and attached by its lower surface to the central stalk.

Pendent. Hanging downward.

Pendulous. More or less hanging or declined.

Perfect. Flower with both stamens and pistil.

Perianth. The calyx and corolla of a flower considered as a whole.

Persistent. Remaining attached, not falling off.

Petiolate. Having a petiole.

Petiole. The footstalk of a leaf.

Petiolule. Footstalk of a leaflet.

Pilose. Hairy, with soft and distinct hairs.

Pinnate. A compound leaf with leaflets arranged along each side of a common petiole.

Pistil. Female organ of a flower, consisting of ovary, style, and stigma.

Pistillate. Female flowers without fertile stamens.

Pith. The central, softer part of a stem.

Pollen. The fecundating grains borne in the anther.

Polygamo-dioecious. Flowers sometimes perfect, sometimes unisexual and dioecious.

Polygamo-monoecious. Flowers sometimes perfect and sometimes unisexual, the 2 forms borne on the same individual.

Polygamous. Flowers sometimes perfect and sometimes unisexual.

Pome. An inferior fruit of 2 or several carpels inclosed in thick flesh; an apple.

Prickle. A small spine growing from the bark.

Prostrate. Lying flat on the ground.

Puberulous. Minutely pubescent.

Pubescent. Clothed with soft, short hairs.

Pungent. Terminating in a rigid, sharp point; acrid.

Pyramidal. Shaped like a pyramid.

Raceme. A simple inflorescence of stalked flowers on a more or less elongated rachis.

Racemose. In racemes; resembling racemes.

Rachis. An axis bearing flowers or leaflets.

Receptacle. The more or less expanded portion of an axis which bears the organs of a flower or the collected flowers of a head.

Recurved. Curving downward or backward.

Reflexed. Abruptly turned downward.

Remotely. Scattered, not close together.

Reniform. Kidney-shaped.

Repand. With a slightly sinuate margin.

Reticulate. Netted.

Retrorsely. Directed backward or downward.

Revolute. Rolled backward, margin rolled toward the lower side.

Rhombic. Having the shape of a rhombus.

Rufous. Red-brown.

Rugose. Wrinkled.

Samara. An indehiscent, winged fruit.

Scabrous. Rough to the touch.

Scarious. Thin, dry, membranaceous, not green.

Scorpioid. A form of unilateral inflorescence circinately coiled in the bud.

Scurfy. Covered with small branlike scales.

Serrate. Toothed, the teeth pointing upward or forward.

Sessile. Without a stalk.

Sheath. A tubular envelope, or enrolled part or organ.

Shrub. A woody, bushy plant, branched at or near the base and usually less than 15 feet in height.

Sinuate. With a strong, wavy margin.

Sinus. The cleft or space between two lobes.

Spike. A simple inflorescence of sessile flowers arranged on a common, elongated axis.

Spine. A sharp, woody outgrowth from a stem.

Spinose. Furnished with spines.

Stamen. The pollen-bearing organ of the male flower.

Staminate. Male flowers provided with stamens but without pistils.

Stellate. Star-shaped.

Sterigmata. Short, persistent leaf bases found on spruces and hemlocks.

Stigma. The part or surface of a pistil which receives pollen for the fecundation of the ovules.

Stipule. An appendage at the base of the petiole, usually one on each side.

Stoma An orifice in the epidermis of a leaf used to connect internal cavities with air.

Stomata. Plural of stoma.

Stomatiferous. Furnished with stomata.

Strobile. A cone.

Style. The attenuated portion of a pistil between the ovary and the stigma.

Sub. A Latin prefix denoting somewhat or slightly.

Subtend. To lie under or opposite to.

Subulate. Awl-shaped.

Succulent. Juicy; fleshy.

Superior ovary. Free from and inserted above calyx; hypogynous.

Superposed. Placed above, as one bud above another at a node.

Suture. A junction or line of dehiscence.

Syncarp. A multiple fleshy fruit.

Taproot. The primary descending root, which may be either very large or absent at the maturity of the tree.

Terete. Circular in transverse section.

Terminal. Situated at the end of a branch.

Ternate. In groups of three.

Tolerant. Capable of enduring shade.

Tomentose. Densely pubescent with matted wool or tomentum.

Tomentulose. Slightly pubescent with matted wool.

Torulose. Cylindric, with swollen partitions at intervals.

Tree. A plant with a woody stem, unbranched at or near base, and at least 8 feet in height and 2 inches in diameter.

Truncate. Ending abruptly, as if cut off at the end.

Tubercle. A small tuber or excrescence.

Turbinate. Top-shaped.

Umbel. A simple inflorescence of flowers with pedicels all arising from the same point.

Umbo. A boss or protuberance.

Undulate. With wavy surface or margin.

Unisexual. Of one sex, either staminate or pistillate.

Valvate. Leaf buds meeting at the edges, not overlapping.

Valve. One of the pieces into which a capsule splits.

Veins. Threads of fibro-vascular tissue in a leaf or other flat organ.

Ventral. Belonging to the anterior or inner face of an organ; the upper surface of a leaf.

Vernal. Appearing in the spring.

Vesicle. A little bladder or cavity.

Villose. Hairy with long and soft hairs.

Whorled. Three or more organs arranged in a circle round an axis.

Wing. A membranous or thin and dry expansion or appendage of an organ.

Woolly. Covered with long and matted or tangled hairs.

SELECTED BIBLIOGRAPHY

The following references, used by the author in preparing the descriptions and distribution maps, are recommended for students desiring to make a thorough study of the trees of this region:

Barkley, F. A. *A Monographic Study of Rhus and Its Immediate Allies in North and Central America.* Annals of the Missouri Botanical Garden, 1937, Vol. 24, pp. 265-498.

Benson, L. and Darrow, R. A. *A Manual of Southwestern Desert Trees and Shrubs.* Univ. of Ariz., Tucson, Biol. Bul. No. 6, April, 1944.

Britton, N. L. *North American Trees.* New York, Henry Holt and Company, 1908.

Cory, V. L. *Catalogue of the Flora of Texas,* Texas Agri. Exp. Sta., Bul. No. 55, July, 1937.

Coulter, J. M. *Botany of Western Texas.* U. S. Natl. Herbarium, 1891–99, Vol. 2, Nos. 1–3.

————, and A. Nelson. *A New Manual of Botany of the Central Rocky Mountains.* American Book Company, 1909.

Dayton, W. A. *Important Western Browse Plants.* U.S.D.A., Misc. Pub. No. 101, July, 1931.

————, and Others. *Range Plant Handbook.* U.S.D.A., March, 1937.

Gibson, H. H. *American Forest Trees.* Chicago, Hardwood Record, 1913.

Harlow, W. M., and E. S. Harrar. *Textbook of Dendrology.* New York, McGraw Hill Book Co., Inc., 1941.

Kearney, T. H. and Peebles, R. H. *Flowering Plants and Ferns of Arizona.* U.S.D.A., Misc. Pub. No. 423, May, 1942.

Kirkwood, J. E. *Northern Rocky Mountain Trees and Shrubs.* Stanford University Press, 1930.

Little, E. L. *Check List of the Native and Naturalized Trees of the United States Including Alaska.* U.S.D.A., 1953.

Longyear, B. O. *Trees and Shrubs of the Rocky Mountain Region.* New York, G. P. Putnam's Sons, 1927.

Merriam, C. H. and others. *North America Fauna.* U. S. Biol.
  Survey, 1890–1917.
     No. 3. *Biological Survey of Arizona,* 1890.
     No. 33. *Biological Survey of Colorado,* 1911.
     No. 5. *Biological Survey of South-Central Idaho,* 1891.
     No. 35. *Biological Survey of New Mexico,* 1913.
     Bul. 10. *Life Zones and Crop Zones of the United
     States,* 1898.
     No. 42. *Life Zone Investigations in Wyoming,* 1917.
Rehder, A. *Manual of Cultivated Trees and Shrubs.* New
  York, Macmillan Company, 1927.
Rydberg, P. A. *Flora of Colorado.* Experiment Station, Fort
  Collins, Colorado, 1906.
————. *Flora of Prairies and Plains of Central North America,*
  New York Botanical Garden, 1932.
————. *Flora of Rocky Mountains and Adjacent Plains.* New
  York Botanical Garden, 1922.
Sargent, C. S. *Manual of the Trees of North America.* Boston,
  Houghton Mifflin Company, 1933. (Dover reprint)
Shaw, G. R. *The Genus Pinus.* Publications of the Arnold
  Arboretum, 1914, No. 5.
Standley, P. C. *Trees and Shrubs of Mexico.* U. S. Natl. Her-
  barium, 1920–26, Vol. 23, parts 1–5.
Sudworth, G. B. *Check List of the Forest Trees of the United
  States.* U.S.D.A., Misc. Cir. 92, 1927.
————. *Trees of the Rocky Mountain Region,* U.S.D.A. Bul-
  letins, Nos. 207, 327, 420, 460, 680, 1915-34.
————. *Forest Trees of the Pacific Slope.* U.S.D.A., Forest
  Service, 1908. (Dover reprint)
Tidestrom, I. *Flora of Utah and Nevada.* U. S. Natl. Herba-
  rium, 1925, Vol. 25.
Trelease, Wm. *The American Oaks.* National Academy of
  Sciences, Memoirs XX, 1924.
Van Dersal, Wm. R. *Native Woody Plants of the United
  States.* U.S.D.A., Misc. Pub. 303, 1938.
Wooton, E. O., and P. C. Standley. *Flora of New Mexico,* U.S.
  Natl. Herbarium, 1915, Vol. 19.

INDEX

*An X preceding a species name signifies that it is a hybrid.

A CATALOGUE OF SELECTED DOVER BOOKS
IN ALL FIELDS OF INTEREST

A CATALOGUE OF SELECTED DOVER BOOKS
IN ALL FIELDS OF INTEREST

AMERICA'S OLD MASTERS, James T. Flexner. Four men emerged unexpectedly from provincial 18th century America to leadership in European art: Benjamin West, J. S. Copley, C. R. Peale, Gilbert Stuart. Brilliant coverage of lives and contributions. Revised, 1967 edition. 69 plates. 365pp. of text.

21806-6 Paperbound $2.75

FIRST FLOWERS OF OUR WILDERNESS: AMERICAN PAINTING, THE COLONIAL PERIOD, James T. Flexner. Painters, and regional painting traditions from earliest Colonial times up to the emergence of Copley, West and Peale Sr., Foster, Gustavus Hesselius, Feke, John Smibert and many anonymous painters in the primitive manner. Engaging presentation, with 162 illustrations. xxii + 368pp.

22180-6 Paperbound $3.50

THE LIGHT OF DISTANT SKIES: AMERICAN PAINTING, 1760-1835, James T. Flexner. The great generation of early American painters goes to Europe to learn and to teach: West, Copley, Gilbert Stuart and others. Allston, Trumbull, Morse; also contemporary American painters—primitives, derivatives, academics—who remained in America. 102 illustrations. xiii + 306pp. 22179-2 Paperbound $3.00

A HISTORY OF THE RISE AND PROGRESS OF THE ARTS OF DESIGN IN THE UNITED STATES, William Dunlap. Much the richest mine of information on early American painters, sculptors, architects, engravers, miniaturists, etc. The only source of information for scores of artists, the major primary source for many others. Unabridged reprint of rare original 1834 edition, with new introduction by James T. Flexner, and 394 new illustrations. Edited by Rita Weiss. 6⅝ x 9⅝.

21695-0, 21696-9, 21697-7 Three volumes, Paperbound $13.50

EPOCHS OF CHINESE AND JAPANESE ART, Ernest F. Fenollosa. From primitive Chinese art to the 20th century, thorough history, explanation of every important art period and form, including Japanese woodcuts; main stress on China and Japan, but Tibet, Korea also included. Still unexcelled for its detailed, rich coverage of cultural background, aesthetic elements, diffusion studies, particularly of the historical period. 2nd, 1913 edition. 242 illustrations. lii + 439pp. of text.

20364-6, 20365-4 Two volumes, Paperbound $5.00

THE GENTLE ART OF MAKING ENEMIES, James A. M. Whistler. Greatest wit of his day deflates Oscar Wilde, Ruskin, Swinburne; strikes back at inane critics, exhibitions, art journalism; aesthetics of impressionist revolution in most striking form. Highly readable classic by great painter. Reproduction of edition designed by Whistler. Introduction by Alfred Werner. xxxvi + 334pp.

21875-9 Paperbound $2.25

ALPHABETS AND ORNAMENTS, Ernst Lehner. Well-known pictorial source for decorative alphabets, script examples, cartouches, frames, decorative title pages, calligraphic initials, borders, similar material. 14th to 19th century, mostly European. Useful in almost any graphic arts designing, varied styles. 750 illustrations. 256pp. 7 x 10. 21905-4 Paperbound $3.50

PAINTING: A CREATIVE APPROACH, Norman Colquhoun. For the beginner simple guide provides an instructive approach to painting: major stumbling blocks for beginner; overcoming them, technical points; paints and pigments; oil painting; watercolor and other media and color. New section on "plastic" paints. Glossary. Formerly *Paint Your Own Pictures*. 221pp. 22000-1 Paperbound $1.75

THE ENJOYMENT AND USE OF COLOR, Walter Sargent. Explanation of the relations between colors themselves and between colors in nature and art, including hundreds of little-known facts about color values, intensities, effects of high and low illumination, complementary colors. Many practical hints for painters, references to great masters. 7 color plates, 29 illustrations. x + 274pp.
20944-X Paperbound $2.50

THE NOTEBOOKS OF LEONARDO DA VINCI, compiled and edited by Jean Paul Richter. 1566 extracts from original manuscripts reveal the full range of Leonardo's versatile genius: all his writings on painting, sculpture, architecture, anatomy, astronomy, geography, topography, physiology, mining, music, etc., in both Italian and English, with 186 plates of manuscript pages and more than 500 additional drawings. Includes studies for the Last Supper, the lost Sforza monument, and other works. Total of xlvii + 866pp. 7⅞ x 10¾. 22572-0, 22573-9 Two volumes, Paperbound $10.00

MONTGOMERY WARD CATALOGUE OF 1895. Tea gowns, yards of flannel and pillow-case lace, stereoscopes, books of gospel hymns, the New Improved Singer Sewing Machine, side saddles, milk skimmers, straight-edged razors, high-button shoes, spittoons, and on and on . . . listing some 25,000 items, practically all illustrated. Essential to the shoppers of the 1890's, it is our truest record of the spirit of the period. Unaltered reprint of Issue No. 57, Spring and Summer 1895. Introduction by Boris Emmet. Innumerable illustrations. xiii + 624pp. 8½ x 11⅝.
22377-9 Paperbound $6.95

THE CRYSTAL PALACE EXHIBITION ILLUSTRATED CATALOGUE (LONDON, 1851). One of the wonders of the modern world—the Crystal Palace Exhibition in which all the nations of the civilized world exhibited their achievements in the arts and sciences—presented in an equally important illustrated catalogue. More than 1700 items pictured with accompanying text—ceramics, textiles, cast-iron work, carpets, pianos, sleds, razors, wall-papers, billiard tables, beehives, silverware and hundreds of other artifacts—represent the focal point of Victorian culture in the Western World. Probably the largest collection of Victorian decorative art ever assembled—indispensable for antiquarians and designers. Unabridged republication of the Art-Journal Catalogue of the Great Exhibition of 1851, with all terminal essays. New introduction by John Gloag, F.S.A. xxxiv + 426pp. 9 x 12.
22503-8 Paperbound $4.50

THE ARCHITECTURE OF COUNTRY HOUSES, Andrew J. Downing. Together with Vaux's *Villas and Cottages* this is the basic book for Hudson River Gothic architecture of the middle Victorian period. Full, sound discussions of general aspects of housing, architecture, style, decoration, furnishing, together with scores of detailed house plans, illustrations of specific buildings, accompanied by full text. Perhaps the most influential single American architectural book. 1850 edition. Introduction by J. Stewart Johnson. 321 figures, 34 architectural designs. xvi + 560pp.
22003-6 Paperbound $4.00

LOST EXAMPLES OF COLONIAL ARCHITECTURE, John Mead Howells. Full-page photographs of buildings that have disappeared or been so altered as to be denatured, including many designed by major early American architects. 245 plates. xvii + 248pp. 7⅞ x 10¾. 21143-6 Paperbound $3.00

DOMESTIC ARCHITECTURE OF THE AMERICAN COLONIES AND OF THE EARLY REPUBLIC, Fiske Kimball. Foremost architect and restorer of Williamsburg and Monticello covers nearly 200 homes between 1620-1825. Architectural details, construction, style features, special fixtures, floor plans, etc. Generally considered finest work in its area. 219 illustrations of houses, doorways, windows, capital mantels. xx + 314pp. 7⅞ x 10¾. 21743-4 Paperbound $3.50

EARLY AMERICAN ROOMS: 1650-1858, edited by Russell Hawes Kettell. Tour of 12 rooms, each representative of a different era in American history and each furnished, decorated, designed and occupied in the style of the era. 72 plans and elevations, 8-page color section, etc., show fabrics, wall papers, arrangements, etc. Full descriptive text. xvii + 200pp. of text. 8⅜ x 11¼.
21633-0 Paperbound $5.00

THE FITZWILLIAM VIRGINAL BOOK, edited by J. Fuller Maitland and W. B. Squire. Full modern printing of famous early 17th-century ms. volume of 300 works by Morley, Byrd, Bull, Gibbons, etc. For piano or other modern keyboard instrument; easy to read format. xxxvi + 938pp. 8⅜ x 11.
21068-5, 21069-3 Two volumes, Paperbound $8.00

HARPSICHORD MUSIC, Johann Sebastian Bach. Bach Gesellschaft edition. A rich selection of Bach's masterpieces for the harpsichord: the six English Suites, six French Suites, the six Partitas (Clavierübung part I), the Goldberg Variations (Clavierübung part IV), the fifteen Two-Part Inventions and the fifteen Three-Part Sinfonias. Clearly reproduced on large sheets with ample margins; eminently playable. vi + 312pp. 8⅛ x 11. 22360-4 Paperbound $5.00

THE MUSIC OF BACH: AN INTRODUCTION, Charles Sanford Terry. A fine, non-technical introduction to Bach's music, both instrumental and vocal. Covers organ music, chamber music, passion music, other types. Analyzes themes, developments, innovations. x + 114pp. 21075-8 Paperbound $1.25

BEETHOVEN AND HIS NINE SYMPHONIES, Sir George Grove. Noted British musicologist provides best history, analysis, commentary on symphonies. Very thorough, rigorously accurate; necessary to both advanced student and amateur music lover. 436 musical passages. vii + 407 pp. 20334-4 Paperbound $2.25

JOHANN SEBASTIAN BACH, Philipp Spitta. One of the great classics of musicology, this definitive analysis of Bach's music (and life) has never been surpassed. Lucid, nontechnical analyses of hundreds of pieces (30 pages devoted to St. Matthew Passion, 26 to B Minor Mass). Also includes major analysis of 18th-century music. 450 musical examples. 40-page musical supplement. Total of xx + 1799pp.
(EUK) 22278-0, 22279-9 Two volumes, Clothbound $15.00

MOZART AND HIS PIANO CONCERTOS, Cuthbert Girdlestone. The only full-length study of an important area of Mozart's creativity. Provides detailed analyses of all 23 concertos, traces inspirational sources. 417 musical examples. Second edition. 509pp. (USO) 21271-8 Paperbound $3.50

THE PERFECT WAGNERITE: A COMMENTARY ON THE NIBLUNG'S RING, George Bernard Shaw. Brilliant and still relevant criticism in remarkable essays on Wagner's Ring cycle, Shaw's ideas on political and social ideology behind the plots, role of Leitmotifs, vocal requisites, etc. Prefaces. xxi + 136pp.
21707-8 Paperbound $1.50

DON GIOVANNI, W. A. Mozart. Complete libretto, modern English translation; biographies of composer and librettist; accounts of early performances and critical reaction. Lavishly illustrated. All the material you need to understand and appreciate this great work. Dover Opera Guide and Libretto Series; translated and introduced by Ellen Bleiler. 92 illustrations. 209pp.
21134-7 Paperbound $1.50

HIGH FIDELITY SYSTEMS: A LAYMAN'S GUIDE, Roy F. Allison. All the basic information you need for setting up your own audio system: high fidelity and stereo record players, tape records, F.M. Connections, adjusting tone arm, cartridge, checking needle alignment, positioning speakers, phasing speakers, adjusting hums, trouble-shooting, maintenance, and similar topics. Enlarged 1965 edition. More than 50 charts, diagrams, photos. iv + 91pp. 21514-8 Paperbound $1.25

REPRODUCTION OF SOUND, Edgar Villchur. Thorough coverage for laymen of high fidelity systems, reproducing systems in general, needles, amplifiers, preamps, loudspeakers, feedback, explaining physical background. "A rare talent for making technicalities vividly comprehensible," R. Darrell, *High Fidelity*. 69 figures. iv + 92pp. 21515-6 Paperbound $1.00

HEAR ME TALKIN' TO YA: THE STORY OF JAZZ AS TOLD BY THE MEN WHO MADE IT, Nat Shapiro and Nat Hentoff. Louis Armstrong, Fats Waller, Jo Jones, Clarence Williams, Billy Holiday, Duke Ellington, Jelly Roll Morton and dozens of other jazz greats tell how it was in Chicago's South Side, New Orleans, depression Harlem and the modern West Coast as jazz was born and grew. xvi + 429pp.
21726-4 Paperbound $2.50

FABLES OF AESOP, translated by Sir Roger L'Estrange. A reproduction of the very rare 1931 Paris edition; a selection of the most interesting fables, together with 50 imaginative drawings by Alexander Calder. v + 128pp. 6½x9¼.
21780-9 Paperbound $1.25

POEMS OF ANNE BRADSTREET, edited with an introduction by Robert Hutchinson. A new selection of poems by America's first poet and perhaps the first significant woman poet in the English language. 48 poems display her development in works of considerable variety—love poems, domestic poems, religious meditations, formal elegies, "quaternions," etc. Notes, bibliography. viii + 222pp.

22160-1 Paperbound $2.00

THREE GOTHIC NOVELS: THE CASTLE OF OTRANTO BY HORACE WALPOLE; VATHEK BY WILLIAM BECKFORD; THE VAMPYRE BY JOHN POLIDORI, WITH FRAGMENT OF A NOVEL BY LORD BYRON, edited by E. F. Bleiler. The first Gothic novel, by Walpole; the finest Oriental tale in English, by Beckford; powerful Romantic supernatural story in versions by Polidori and Byron. All extremely important in history of literature; all still exciting, packed with supernatural thrills, ghosts, haunted castles, magic, etc. xl + 291pp.

21232-7 Paperbound $2.00

THE BEST TALES OF HOFFMANN, E. T. A. Hoffmann. 10 of Hoffmann's most important stories, in modern re-editings of standard translations: Nutcracker and the King of Mice, Signor Formica, Automata, The Sandman, Rath Krespel, The Golden Flowerpot, Master Martin the Cooper, The Mines of Falun, The King's Betrothed, A New Year's Eve Adventure. 7 illustrations by Hoffmann. Edited by E. F. Bleiler. xxxix + 419pp.

21793-0 Paperbound $2.50

GHOST AND HORROR STORIES OF AMBROSE BIERCE, Ambrose Bierce. 23 strikingly modern stories of the horrors latent in the human mind: The Eyes of the Panther, The Damned Thing, An Occurrence at Owl Creek Bridge, An Inhabitant of Carcosa, etc., plus the dream-essay, Visions of the Night. Edited by E. F. Bleiler. xxii + 199pp.

20767-6 Paperbound $1.50

BEST GHOST STORIES OF J. S. LEFANU, J. Sheridan LeFanu. Finest stories by Victorian master often considered greatest supernatural writer of all. Carmilla, Green Tea, The Haunted Baronet, The Familiar, and 12 others. Most never before available in the U. S. A. Edited by E. F. Bleiler. 8 illustrations from Victorian publications. xvii + 467pp.

20415-4 Paperbound $2.50

THE TIME STREAM, THE GREATEST ADVENTURE, AND THE PURPLE SAPPHIRE— THREE SCIENCE FICTION NOVELS, John Taine (Eric Temple Bell). Great American mathematician was also foremost science fiction novelist of the 1920's. *The Time Stream,* one of all-time classics, uses concepts of circular time; *The Greatest Adventure,* incredibly ancient biological experiments from Antarctica threaten to escape; The *Purple Sapphire,* superscience, lost races in Central Tibet, survivors of the Great Race. 4 illustrations by Frank R. Paul. v + 532pp.

21180-0 Paperbound $3.00

SEVEN SCIENCE FICTION NOVELS, H. G. Wells. The standard collection of the great novels. Complete, unabridged. *First Men in the Moon, Island of Dr. Moreau, War of the Worlds, Food of the Gods, Invisible Man, Time Machine, In the Days of the Comet.* Not only science fiction fans, but every educated person owes it to himself to read these novels. 1015pp.

20264-X Clothbound $5.00

LAST AND FIRST MEN AND STAR MAKER, TWO SCIENCE FICTION NOVELS, Olaf Stapledon. Greatest future histories in science fiction. In the first, human intelligence is the "hero," through strange paths of evolution, interplanetary invasions, incredible technologies, near extinctions and reemergences. Star Maker describes the quest of a band of star rovers for intelligence itself, through time and space: weird inhuman civilizations, crustacean minds, symbiotic worlds, etc. Complete, unabridged. v + 438pp. 21962-3 Paperbound $2.00

THREE PROPHETIC NOVELS, H. G. WELLS. Stages of a consistently planned future for mankind. *When the Sleeper Wakes*, and *A Story of the Days to Come*, anticipate *Brave New World* and *1984*, in the 21st Century; *The Time Machine*, only complete version in print, shows farther future and the end of mankind. All show Wells's greatest gifts as storyteller and novelist. Edited by E. F. Bleiler. x + 335pp. (USO) 20605-X Paperbound $2.00

THE DEVIL'S DICTIONARY, Ambrose Bierce. America's own Oscar Wilde—Ambrose Bierce—offers his barbed iconoclastic wisdom in over 1,000 definitions hailed by H. L. Mencken as "some of the most gorgeous witticisms in the English language." 145pp. 20487-1 Paperbound $1.25

MAX AND MORITZ, Wilhelm Busch. Great children's classic, father of comic strip, of two bad boys, Max and Moritz. Also Ker and Plunk (Plisch und Plumm), Cat and Mouse, Deceitful Henry, Ice-Peter, The Boy and the Pipe, and five other pieces. Original German, with English translation. Edited by H. Arthur Klein; translations by various hands and H. Arthur Klein. vi + 216pp. 20181-3 Paperbound $1.50

PIGS IS PIGS AND OTHER FAVORITES, Ellis Parker Butler. The title story is one of the best humor short stories, as Mike Flannery obfuscates biology and English. Also included, That Pup of Murchison's, The Great American Pie Company, and Perkins of Portland. 14 illustrations. v + 109pp. 21532-6 Paperbound $1.00

THE PETERKIN PAPERS, Lucretia P. Hale. It takes genius to be as stupidly mad as the Peterkins, as they decide to become wise, celebrate the "Fourth," keep a cow, and otherwise strain the resources of the Lady from Philadelphia. Basic book of American humor. 153 illustrations. 219pp. 20794-3 Paperbound $1.25

PERRAULT'S FAIRY TALES, translated by A. E. Johnson and S. R. Littlewood, with 34 full-page illustrations by Gustave Doré. All the original Perrault stories—Cinderella, Sleeping Beauty, Bluebeard, Little Red Riding Hood, Puss in Boots, Tom Thumb, etc.—with their witty verse morals and the magnificent illustrations of Doré. One of the five or six great books of European fairy tales. viii + 117pp. 8⅛ x 11. 22311-6 Paperbound $2.00

OLD HUNGARIAN FAIRY TALES, Baroness Orczy. Favorites translated and adapted by author of the *Scarlet Pimpernel*. Eight fairy tales include "The Suitors of Princess Fire-Fly," "The Twin Hunchbacks," "Mr. Cuttlefish's Love Story," and "The Enchanted Cat." This little volume of magic and adventure will captivate children as it has for generations. 90 drawings by Montagu Barstow. 96pp. (USO) 22293-4 Paperbound $1.95

"ESSENTIAL GRAMMAR" SERIES

All you really need to know about modern, colloquial grammar. Many educational shortcuts help you learn faster, understand better. Detailed cognate lists teach you to recognize similarities between English and foreign words and roots—make learning vocabulary easy and interesting. Excellent for independent study or as a supplement to record courses.

ESSENTIAL FRENCH GRAMMAR, Seymour Resnick. 2500-item cognate list. 159pp.
(EBE) 20419-7 Paperbound $1.25

ESSENTIAL GERMAN GRAMMAR, Guy Stern and Everett F. Bleiler. Unusual shortcuts on noun declension, word order, compound verbs. 124pp.
(EBE) 20422-7 Paperbound $1.25

ESSENTIAL ITALIAN GRAMMAR, Olga Ragusa. 111pp.
(EBE) 20779-X Paperbound $1.25

ESSENTIAL JAPANESE GRAMMAR, Everett F. Bleiler. In Romaji transcription; no characters needed. Japanese grammar is regular and simple. 156pp.
21027-8 Paperbound $1.25

ESSENTIAL PORTUGUESE GRAMMAR, Alexander da R. Prista. vi + 114pp.
21650-0 Paperbound $1.25

ESSENTIAL SPANISH GRAMMAR, Seymour Resnick. 2500 word cognate list. 115pp.
(EBE) 20780-3 Paperbound $1.25

ESSENTIAL ENGLISH GRAMMAR, Philip Gucker. Combines best features of modern, functional and traditional approaches. For refresher, class use, home study. x + 177pp.
21649-7 Paperbound $1.25

A PHRASE AND SENTENCE DICTIONARY OF SPOKEN SPANISH. Prepared for U. S. War Department by U. S. linguists. As above, unit is idiom, phrase or sentence rather than word. English-Spanish and Spanish-English sections contain modern equivalents of over 18,000 sentences. Introduction and appendix as above. iv + 513pp.
20495-2 Paperbound $2.00

A PHRASE AND SENTENCE DICTIONARY OF SPOKEN RUSSIAN. Dictionary prepared for U. S. War Department by U. S. linguists. Basic unit is not the word, but the idiom, phrase or sentence. English-Russian and Russian-English sections contain modern equivalents for over 30,000 phrases. Grammatical introduction covers phonetics, writing, syntax. Appendix of word lists for food, numbers, geographical names, etc. vi + 573 pp. 6⅛ x 9¼.
20496-0 Paperbound $3.00

CONVERSATIONAL CHINESE FOR BEGINNERS, Morris Swadesh. Phonetic system, beginner's course in Pai Hua Mandarin Chinese covering most important, most useful speech patterns. Emphasis on modern colloquial usage. Formerly *Chinese in Your Pocket.* xvi + 158pp.
21123-1 Paperbound $1.50

PLANETS, STARS AND GALAXIES: DESCRIPTIVE ASTRONOMY FOR BEGINNERS, A. E. Fanning. Comprehensive introductory survey of astronomy: the sun, solar system, stars, galaxies, universe, cosmology; up-to-date, including quasars, radio stars, etc. Preface by Prof. Donald Menzel. 24pp. of photographs. 189pp. 5¼ x 8¼.
21680-2 Paperbound $1.50

TEACH YOURSELF CALCULUS, P. Abbott. With a good background in algebra and trig, you can teach yourself calculus with this book. Simple, straightforward introduction to functions of all kinds, integration, differentiation, series, etc. "Students who are beginning to study calculus method will derive great help from this book." Faraday House Journal. 308pp.
20683-1 Clothbound $2.00

TEACH YOURSELF TRIGONOMETRY, P. Abbott. Geometrical foundations, indices and logarithms, ratios, angles, circular measure, etc. are presented in this sound, easy-to-use text. Excellent for the beginner or as a brush up, this text carries the student through the solution of triangles. 204pp.
20682-3 Clothbound $2.00

TEACH YOURSELF ANATOMY, David LeVay. Accurate, inclusive, profusely illustrated account of structure, skeleton, abdomen, muscles, nervous system, glands, brain, reproductive organs, evolution. "Quite the best and most readable account,' Medical Officer. 12 color plates. 164 figures. 311pp. 4¾ x 7.
21651-9 Clothbound $2.50

TEACH YOURSELF PHYSIOLOGY, David LeVay. Anatomical, biochemical bases; digestive, nervous, endocrine systems; metabolism; respiration; muscle; excretion; temperature control; reproduction. "Good elementary exposition," The Lancet. 6 color plates. 44 illustrations. 208pp. 4¼ x 7. 21658-6 Clothbound $2.50

THE FRIENDLY STARS, Martha Evans Martin. Classic has taught naked-eye observation of stars, planets to hundreds of thousands, still not surpassed for charm, lucidity, adequacy. Completely updated by Professor Donald H. Menzel, Harvard Observatory. 25 illustrations. 16 x 30 chart. x + 147pp. 21099-5 Paperbound $1.25

MUSIC OF THE SPHERES: THE MATERIAL UNIVERSE FROM ATOM TO QUASAR, SIMPLY EXPLAINED, Guy Murchie. Extremely broad, brilliantly written popular account begins with the solar system and reaches to dividing line between matter and nonmatter; latest understandings presented with exceptional clarity. Volume One: Planets, stars, galaxies, cosmology, geology, celestial mechanics, latest astronomical discoveries; Volume Two: Matter, atoms, waves, radiation, relativity, chemical action, heat, nuclear energy, quantum theory, music, light, color, probability, antimatter, antigravity, and similar topics. 319 figures. 1967 (second) edition. Total of xx + 644pp. 21809-0, 21810-4 Two volumes, Paperbound $4.00

OLD-TIME SCHOOLS AND SCHOOL BOOKS, Clifton Johnson. Illustrations and rhymes from early primers, abundant quotations from early textbooks, many anecdotes of school life enliven this study of elementary schools from Puritans to middle 19th century. Introduction by Carl Withers. 234 illustrations. xxxiii + 381pp.
21031-6 Paperbound $2.50

CATALOGUE OF DOVER BOOKS

The Philosophy of the Upanishads, Paul Deussen. Clear, detailed statement of upanishadic system of thought, generally considered among best available. History of these works, full exposition of system emergent from them, parallel concepts in the West. Translated by A. S. Geden. xiv + 429pp.
21616-0 Paperbound $3.00

Language, Truth and Logic, Alfred J. Ayer. Famous, remarkably clear introduction to the Vienna and Cambridge schools of Logical Positivism; function of philosophy, elimination of metaphysical thought, nature of analysis, similar topics. "Wish I had written it myself," Bertrand Russell. 2nd, 1946 edition. 160pp.
20010-8 Paperbound $1.35

The Guide for the Perplexed, Moses Maimonides. Great classic of medieval Judaism, major attempt to reconcile revealed religion (Pentateuch, commentaries) and Aristotelian philosophy. Enormously important in all Western thought. Unabridged Friedländer translation. 50-page introduction. lix + 414pp.
(USO) 20351-4 Paperbound $2.50

Occult and Supernatural Phenomena, D. H. Rawcliffe. Full, serious study of the most persistent delusions of mankind: crystal gazing, mediumistic trance, stigmata, lycanthropy, fire walking, dowsing, telepathy, ghosts, ESP, etc., and their relation to common forms of abnormal psychology. Formerly *Illusions and Delusions of the Supernatural and the Occult.* iii + 551pp. 20503-7 Paperbound $3.50

The Egyptian Book of the Dead: The Papyrus of Ani, E. A. Wallis Budge. Full hieroglyphic text, interlinear transliteration of sounds, word for word translation, then smooth, connected translation; Theban recension. Basic work in Ancient Egyptian civilization; now even more significant than ever for historical importance, dilation of consciousness, etc. clvi + 377pp. 6½ x 9¼.
21866-X Paperbound $3.75

Psychology of Music, Carl E. Seashore. Basic, thorough survey of everything known about psychology of music up to 1940's; essential reading for psychologists, musicologists. Physical acoustics; auditory apparatus; relationship of physical sound to perceived sound; role of the mind in sorting, altering, suppressing, creating sound sensations; musical learning, testing for ability, absolute pitch, other topics. Records of Caruso, Menuhin analyzed. 88 figures. xix + 408pp.
21851-1 Paperbound $2.75

The I Ching (The Book of Changes), translated by James Legge. Complete translated text plus appendices by Confucius, of perhaps the most penetrating divination book ever compiled. Indispensable to all study of early Oriental civilizations. 3 plates. xxiii + 448pp. 21062-6 Paperbound $2.75

The Upanishads, translated by Max Müller. Twelve classical upanishads: Chandogya, Kena, Aitareya, Kaushitaki, Isa, Katha, Mundaka, Taittiriyaka, Brhadaranyaka, Svetasvatara, Prasna, Maitriyana. 160-page introduction, analysis by Prof. Müller. Total of 826pp. 20398-0, 20399-9 Two volumes, Paperbound $5.00

JIM WHITEWOLF: THE LIFE OF A KIOWA APACHE INDIAN, Charles S. Brant, editor. Spans transition between native life and acculturation period, 1880 on. Kiowa culture, personal life pattern, religion and the supernatural, the Ghost Dance, breakdown in the White Man's world, similar material. 1 map. xii + 144pp.
22015-X Paperbound $1.75

THE NATIVE TRIBES OF CENTRAL AUSTRALIA, Baldwin Spencer and F. J. Gillen. Basic book in anthropology, devoted to full coverage of the Arunta and Warramunga tribes; the source for knowledge about kinship systems, material and social culture, religion, etc. Still unsurpassed. 121 photographs, 89 drawings. xviii + 669pp.
21775-2 Paperbound $5.00

MALAY MAGIC, Walter W. Skeat. Classic (1900); still the definitive work on the folklore and popular religion of the Malay peninsula. Describes marriage rites, birth spirits and ceremonies, medicine, dances, games, war and weapons, etc. Extensive quotes from original sources, many magic charms translated into English. 35 illustrations. Preface by Charles Otto Blagden. xxiv + 685pp.
21760-4 Paperbound $3.50

HEAVENS ON EARTH: UTOPIAN COMMUNITIES IN AMERICA, 1680-1880, Mark Holloway. The finest nontechnical account of American utopias, from the early Woman in the Wilderness, Ephrata, Rappites to the enormous mid 19th-century efflorescence; Shakers, New Harmony, Equity Stores, Fourier's Phalanxes, Oneida, Amana, Fruitlands, etc. "Entertaining and very instructive." *Times Literary Supplement*. 15 illustrations. 246pp.
21593-8 Paperbound $2.00

LONDON LABOUR AND THE LONDON POOR, Henry Mayhew. Earliest (c. 1850) sociological study in English, describing myriad subcultures of London poor. Particularly remarkable for the thousands of pages of direct testimony taken from the lips of London prostitutes, thieves, beggars, street sellers, chimney-sweepers, street-musicians, "mudlarks," "pure-finders," rag-gatherers, "running-patterers," dock laborers, cab-men, and hundreds of others, quoted directly in this massive work. An extraordinarily vital picture of London emerges. 110 illustrations. Total of lxxvi + 1951pp. 6⅝ x 10.
21934-8, 21935-6, 21936-4, 21937-2 Four volumes, Paperbound $14.00

HISTORY OF THE LATER ROMAN EMPIRE, J. B. Bury. Eloquent, detailed reconstruction of Western and Byzantine Roman Empire by a major historian, from the death of Theodosius I (395 A.D.) to the death of Justinian (565). Extensive quotations from contemporary sources; full coverage of important Roman and foreign figures of the time. xxxiv + 965pp. 21829-5 Record, book, album. Monaural. $2.75

AN INTELLECTUAL AND CULTURAL HISTORY OF THE WESTERN WORLD, Harry Elmer Barnes. Monumental study, tracing the development of the accomplishments that make up human culture. Every aspect of man's achievement surveyed from its origins in the Paleolithic to the present day (1964); social structures, ideas, economic systems, art, literature, technology, mathematics, the sciences, medicine, religion, jurisprudence, etc. Evaluations of the contributions of scores of great men. 1964 edition, revised and edited by scholars in the many fields represented. Total of xxix + 1381pp. 21275-0, 21276-9, 21277-7 Three volumes, Paperbound $7.75

CATALOGUE OF DOVER BOOKS

ADVENTURES OF AN AFRICAN SLAVER, Theodore Canot. Edited by Brantz Mayer. A detailed portrayal of slavery and the slave trade, 1820-1840. Canot, an established trader along the African coast, describes the slave economy of the African kingdoms, the treatment of captured negroes, the extensive journeys in the interior to gather slaves, slave revolts and their suppression, harems, bribes, and much more. Full and unabridged republication of 1854 edition. Introduction by Malcom Cowley. 16 illustrations. xvii + 448pp. 22456-2 Paperbound $3.50

MY BONDAGE AND MY FREEDOM, Frederick Douglass. Born and brought up in slavery, Douglass witnessed its horrors and experienced its cruelties, but went on to become one of the most outspoken forces in the American anti-slavery movement. Considered the best of his autobiographies, this book graphically describes the inhuman treatment of slaves, its effects on slave owners and slave families, and how Douglass's determination led him to a new life. Unaltered reprint of 1st (1855) edition. xxxii + 464pp. 22457-0 Paperbound $2.50

THE INDIANS' BOOK, recorded and edited by Natalie Curtis. Lore, music, narratives, dozens of drawings by Indians themselves from an authoritative and important survey of native culture among Plains, Southwestern, Lake and Pueblo Indians. Standard work in popular ethnomusicology. 149 songs in full notation. 23 drawings, 23 photos. xxxi + 584pp. 6⅝ x 9⅜. 21939-9 Paperbound $4.00

DICTIONARY OF AMERICAN PORTRAITS, edited by Hayward and Blanche Cirker. 4024 portraits of 4000 most important Americans, colonial days to 1905 (with a few important categories, like Presidents, to present). Pioneers, explorers, colonial figures, U. S. officials, politicians, writers, military and naval men, scientists, inventors, manufacturers, jurists, actors, historians, educators, notorious figures, Indian chiefs, etc. All authentic contemporary likenesses. The only work of its kind in existence; supplements all biographical sources for libraries. Indispensable to anyone working with American history. 8,000-item classified index, finding lists, other aids. xiv + 756pp. 9¼ x 12¾. 21823-6 Clothbound $30.00

TRITTON'S GUIDE TO BETTER WINE AND BEER MAKING FOR BEGINNERS, S. M. Tritton. All you need to know to make family-sized quantities of over 100 types of grape, fruit, herb and vegetable wines; as well as beers, mead, cider, etc. Complete recipes, advice as to equipment, procedures such as fermenting, bottling, and storing wines. Recipes given in British, U. S., and metric measures. Accompanying booklet lists sources in U. S. A. where ingredients may be bought, and additional information. 11 illustrations. 157pp. 5⅝ x 8⅛. (USO) 22090-7 Clothbound $3.50

GARDENING WITH HERBS FOR FLAVOR AND FRAGRANCE, Helen M. Fox. How to grow herbs in your own garden, how to use them in your cooking (over 55 recipes included), legends and myths associated with each species, uses in medicine, perfumes, etc.—these are elements of one of the few books written especially for American herb fanciers. Guides you step-by-step from soil preparation to harvesting and storage for each type of herb. 12 drawings by Louise Mansfield. xiv + 334pp. 22540-2 Paperbound $2.50

INCIDENTS OF TRAVEL IN YUCATAN, John L. Stephens. Classic (1843) exploration of jungles of Yucatan, looking for evidences of Maya civilization. Stephens found many ruins; comments on travel adventures, Mexican and Indian culture. 127 striking illustrations by F. Catherwood. Total of 669 pp.

20926-1, 20927-X Two volumes, Paperbound $5.00

INCIDENTS OF TRAVEL IN CENTRAL AMERICA, CHIAPAS, AND YUCATAN, John L. Stephens. An exciting travel journal and an important classic of archeology. Narrative relates his almost single-handed discovery of the Mayan culture, and exploration of the ruined cities of Copan, Palenque, Utatlan and others; the monuments they dug from the earth, the temples buried in the jungle, the customs of poverty-stricken Indians living a stone's throw from the ruined palaces. 115 drawings by F. Catherwood. Portrait of Stephens. xii + 812pp.

22404-X, 22405-8 Two volumes, Paperbound $6.00

A NEW VOYAGE ROUND THE WORLD, William Dampier. Late 17-century naturalist joined the pirates of the Spanish Main to gather information; remarkably vivid account of buccaneers, pirates; detailed, accurate account of botany, zoology, ethnography of lands visited. Probably the most important early English voyage, enormous implications for British exploration, trade, colonial policy. Also most interesting reading. Argonaut edition, introduction by Sir Albert Gray. New introduction by Percy Adams. 6 plates, 7 illustrations. xlvii + 376pp. 6½ x 9¼.

21900-3 Paperbound $3.00

INTERNATIONAL AIRLINE PHRASE BOOK IN SIX LANGUAGES, Joseph W. Bátor. Important phrases and sentences in English paralleled with French, German, Portuguese, Italian, Spanish equivalents, covering all possible airport-travel situations; created for airline personnel as well as tourist by Language Chief, Pan American Airlines. xiv + 204pp.

22017-6 Paperbound $2.00

STAGE COACH AND TAVERN DAYS, Alice Morse Earle. Detailed, lively account of the early days of taverns; their uses and importance in the social, political and military life; furnishings and decorations; locations; food and drink; tavern signs, etc. Second half covers every aspect of early travel; the roads, coaches, drivers, etc. Nostalgic, charming, packed with fascinating material. 157 illustrations, mostly photographs. xiv + 449pp.

22518-6 Paperbound $4.00

NORSE DISCOVERIES AND EXPLORATIONS IN NORTH AMERICA, Hjalmar R. Holand. The perplexing Kensington Stone, found in Minnesota at the end of the 19th century. Is it a record of a Scandinavian expedition to North America in the 14th century? Or is it one of the most successful hoaxes in history. A scientific detective investigation. Formerly *Westward from Vinland*. 31 photographs, 17 figures. x + 354pp.

22014-1 Paperbound $2.75

A BOOK OF OLD MAPS, compiled and edited by Emerson D. Fite and Archibald Freeman. 74 old maps offer an unusual survey of the discovery, settlement and growth of America down to the close of the Revolutionary war: maps showing Norse settlements in Greenland, the explorations of Columbus, Verrazano, Cabot, Champlain, Joliet, Drake, Hudson, etc., campaigns of Revolutionary war battles, and much more. Each map is accompanied by a brief historical essay. xvi + 299pp. 11 x 13¾.

22084-2 Paperbound $6.00

MATHEMATICAL PUZZLES FOR BEGINNERS AND ENTHUSIASTS, Geoffrey Mott-Smith. 189 puzzles from easy to difficult—involving arithmetic, logic, algebra, properties of digits, probability, etc.—for enjoyment and mental stimulus. Explanation of mathematical principles behind the puzzles. 135 illustrations. viii + 248pp.

20198-8 Paperbound $1.25

PAPER FOLDING FOR BEGINNERS, William D. Murray and Francis J. Rigney. Easiest book on the market, clearest instructions on making interesting, beautiful origami. Sail boats, cups, roosters, frogs that move legs, bonbon boxes, standing birds, etc. 40 projects; more than 275 diagrams and photographs. 94pp.

20713-7 Paperbound $1.00

TRICKS AND GAMES ON THE POOL TABLE, Fred Herrmann. 79 tricks and games— some solitaires, some for two or more players, some competitive games—to entertain you between formal games. Mystifying shots and throws, unusual caroms, tricks involving such props as cork, coins, a hat, etc. Formerly *Fun on the Pool Table.* 77 figures. 95pp.

21814-7 Paperbound $1.00

HAND SHADOWS TO BE THROWN UPON THE WALL: A SERIES OF NOVEL AND AMUSING FIGURES FORMED BY THE HAND, Henry Bursill. Delightful picturebook from great-grandfather's day shows how to make 18 different hand shadows: a bird that flies, duck that quacks, dog that wags his tail, camel, goose, deer, boy, turtle, etc. Only book of its sort. vi + 33pp. 6½ x 9¼. 21779-5 Paperbound $1.00

WHITTLING AND WOODCARVING, E. J. Tangerman. 18th printing of best book on market. "If you can cut a potato you can carve" toys and puzzles, chains, chessmen, caricatures, masks, frames, woodcut blocks, surface patterns, much more. Information on tools, woods, techniques. Also goes into serious wood sculpture from Middle Ages to present, East and West. 464 photos, figures. x + 293pp.

20965-2 Paperbound $2.00

HISTORY OF PHILOSOPHY, Julián Marias. Possibly the clearest, most easily followed, best planned, most useful one-volume history of philosophy on the market; neither skimpy nor overfull. Full details on system of every major philosopher and dozens of less important thinkers from pre-Socratics up to Existentialism and later. Strong on many European figures usually omitted. Has gone through dozens of editions in Europe. 1966 edition, translated by Stanley Appelbaum and Clarence Strowbridge. xviii + 505pp.

21739-6 Paperbound $2.75

YOGA: A SCIENTIFIC EVALUATION, Kovoor T. Behanan. Scientific but non-technical study of physiological results of yoga exercises; done under auspices of Yale U. Relations to Indian thought, to psychoanalysis, etc. 16 photos. xxiii + 270pp.

20505-3 Paperbound $2.50

Prices subject to change without notice.
Available at your book dealer or write for free catalogue to Dept. GI, Dover Publications, Inc., 180 Varick St., N. Y., N. Y. 10014. Dover publishes more than 150 books each year on science, elementary and advanced mathematics, biology, music, art, literary history, social sciences and other areas.